McKEACHIE'S
TEACHING TIPS

Strategies, Research, and Theory for College and University Teachers

· ·

TENTH EDITION

Wilbert J. McKeachie

University of Michigan

with chapters by

Graham Gibbs, The Open University

Diana Laurillard, The Open University

Nancy Van Note Chism, Ohio State University

Robert Menges, Late of Northwestern University

Marilla Svinicki, University of Texas at Austin

Claire Ellen Weinstein, University of Texas at Austin

HOUGHTON MIFFLIN COMPANY   Boston   New York

Senior Sponsoring Editor: Loretta Wolozin
Editorial Assistant: Jean Zielinski DeMayo
Associate Editor: Lisa Mafrici
Senior Project Editor: Christina M. Horn
Senior Production/Design Coordinator: Jennifer Waddell
Manufacturing Manager: Florence Cadran
Marketing Manager: Pamela Laskey

Cover designed by Rebecca Fagan.

Printed in the U.S.A.

Library of Congress Catalog Card Number: 98-72060

ISBN: 0-395-90345-9

4 5 6 7 8 9-FFG-02 01 00 99

In memory of Bob Menges
good scholar
good human being
good friend

CONTENTS

6 Lecturing   66

PART 3

Adding to Your Repertoire of Skills and Strategies for Facilitating Student Learning   131

10 Teaching Students to Learn Through Writing: Papers, Journals, and Reports   132

11 Teaching Students How to Learn More from Textbooks and Other Reading   143

15 Project Methods, Independent Study, and One-on-One Teaching

16 Problem-based Learning: Teaching with Cases, Simulations, and Games

17 Using Communication and Information Technologies Effectively

By Diana Laurillard, THE OPEN UNIVERSITY

27 Teaching Thinking 326

28 Teaching Values: Should We? Can We? 332

TEACHING TIPS was written to answer the questions posed by new college teachers, to place them at ease in their jobs, and to get them started effectively in the classroom. It has proven useful as well to experienced college instructors, who often find the research on teaching it provides to be an entirely new domain.

The organization of the book moves from those issues and techniques most relevant to beginning teachers (Parts 1 and 2) to methods that will increase the teacher's repertoire of skills and strategies for dealing with different types of classes (Part 3). But effective teaching demands more than the acquisition of skills. To adapt to the educational needs of a particular class at a particular time, the teacher needs to understand the underlying theory of learning and teaching so that each teacher can develop his or her own methods. Thus the "teaching tips" are supported by discussion of relevant research and theory. To start to contextualize this information, the effective teacher also needs to understand students (Part 4), to commit to lifelong learning (Part 5), and to consider higher-order objectives (Part 6). But skill in teaching is not something to be learned and simply repeated; what makes it exciting is that there is always room to grow. *Teaching Tips* concludes with discussion of the long-range goals of education and how to achieve them.

This streamlined and updated tenth edition of *Teaching Tips* reads more like a handbook than earlier editions did: It is full of study aids and more user-friendly. As with any revision, this one reflects the changes that have occurred outside its pages. Issues that have become more salient since the last edition came out in 1994 are discussed in both theoretical and practical terms. Cooperative learning, low-stakes writing, and cognitive learning strategies and skills are examined and illustrated for the neophyte and veteran instructor alike. Entirely new to this edition is Chapter 17, "Using Communication and Information Technologies Effectively." Its emphasis is on the rationale, use, and support of information and communication technologies. Diana Laurillard, an expert in this field, contributed this chapter—she offers a significant perspective in this increasingly technological information age. Chapters on planning, diversity, learning, and ethics are also updated by specialists. Contributing authors to the tenth edition are listed in the table of contents. Chapter 3, "Planning Your Students' Learning Activities," sustains and enlarges the book's focus on active learning. This chapter shows you how to maximize student effort outside class to complement what goes on inside the classroom.

Teaching Tips has stressed learner-centered teaching since the very first edition, in which I emphasized the importance of active learning. In the second edition I introduced a longer section on learner-centered teaching and the role of the teacher as a facilitator of learning. It is gratifying that in the last few years authors have begun to write about the shift from teacher-centered to learner-centered education and the shift of the teacher's role from that of dispenser of information to facilitator of learning. Whether *Teaching Tips* has contributed to that shift, I do not know, but I hope that "learning-centered" does not become one of the buzz words that come and go—like the fifties' "master teachers" (who were to be televised and teach large numbers of students), or the sixties' "programmed learning" (which would teach more efficiently), or the seventies' "technological revolution." All were believed to be panaceas (and all contained worthwhile elements), but after a period of ascendancy, all faded before the next great enthusiasm. What counts in education is not so much what the teacher does as what goes on in the students' minds, and this will be true even if the term "learner-centered" falls into disuse.

"Learner-centered" may appear to diminish the importance of the teacher. Not so! Your unique qualities as a person, your integrity, your commitment to your students' development—these are even more important than they were when the teacher's role was simply that of a talking textbook. Your role is now expanded to include that of mediator between your content specialization and your students' understanding of it, on multiple, and increasingly high, levels. There is no one best way of teaching. What I offer are ideas and suggestions that you must shape to fit your own styles and purposes. What is best for you may be quite different from what is best for me.

I am pleased that so many copies of previous editions of this guide have been used outside the United States. My increased interaction with colleagues in other countries who are concerned about improving teaching makes me aware of the cultural bias of much of my writing. I trust that *Teaching Tips* will nevertheless have value for everyone concerned with teaching and student learning.

The first edition of this book was prepared in collaboration with Gregory Kimble. His wit and wisdom are still evident at many points in the tenth edition. My thanks go to Jean Zielinski DeMayo, my editor at Houghton Mifflin, who made many helpful suggestions, and to Barbara Hofer, Diane Halpern, and all the reviewers, who will see evidence of the impact of their comments:

Shirley M. Adams, *University of Scranton*
Charles S. Claxton, *Appalachian State University*
Robert M. Diamond, *Syracuse University*
Maureen McHale, *Faculty Development Programs, Houghton Mifflin Company*
Rainer Nyberg, *Abo Akademi University, Finland*
Charles F. Roth, Jr., *Kutztown University*
Delivee L. Wright, *University of Nebraska, Lincoln*
Donald H. Wulff, *University of Washington*
Melissa Zantello, *Faculty Development Programs, Houghton Mifflin Company.*

WILBERT J. MCKEACHIE

FOR TEACHING ASSISTANTS AND GRADUATE STUDENT INSTRUCTORS

TEACHING TIPS was originally written for my own teaching assistants. I am pleased that more experienced teachers have also found it to be helpful, but I still think of my primary audience as being beginning teachers. I began teaching as a teaching assistant (TA) and have worked with teaching assistants ever since. I try to involve my TAs in course planning both before and during the term. We grade tests in a group the evening after a test is given, bringing in sandwiches and brownies to maintain our energy and good spirits during sessions that may last until midnight. In short, I try to develop the spirit of a collaborative team.

However, I recognize that TAs are in the difficult position of being in the middle between the students and me. As TAs you want to be liked and respected by your students as well as by your professor; yet there are times when you don't agree with the professor's point of view or even with some of the course policies. You will be tempted to blame the professor or the system when students complain, but overusing this strategy only leads to students perceiving you as weak and powerless. On the other hand, this doesn't mean that you have to defend everything your professor says. Students, particularly first-year students, need to learn that absolute truth is hard to come by and that it is possible to have well-reasoned differences.

Yet one must be aware of student anxiety when TA and lecturer seem always to be at odds with one another. Support your lecturer when you can, disagree when you must, but recognize that sometimes your students' learning will be best served by your silence. Often your role is that of a coach helping students develop skills in learning and thinking, using the knowledge provided by the lecturer and textbook.

Many of you will find it hard to believe that the students will accept your authority and expertise, and you will be ambivalent about whether to dazzle them with your brilliance or to play the role of being just one of the group. Relax! The power of role expectations always amazes me. If you are the teacher, students will accept your authority and expertise. You don't need to be dictatorial, but you do need to be clear about your expectations of the students. Think of yourself as a more experienced scholar who can be a valuable coach. You may not know everything, but you have enough subject-matter expertise to be helpful. I hope this book will add to your helpfulness.

W. J. M.

Getting Started

CHAPTER

Introduction

The first few months and years of teaching are all-important. Experiences during this period can blight a promising teaching career or start one on a path of continued growth and development.

Most of us go into our first classes as teachers with a good deal of fear and trembling. We don't want to appear to be fools; so we have prepared well, but we dread the embarrassment of not being able to answer students' questions. We want to be liked and respected by our students; yet we know that we have to achieve liking and respect in a new role which carries expectations, such as evaluation, that make our relationship with students edgy and uneasy. We want to get through the first class with éclat, but we don't know how much material we can cover in a class period.

In most cases anxiety passes as one finds that students do respond positively, that one does have some expertise in the subject, and that class periods can be exciting. But for some teachers the first days are not happy experiences. Classes get off on the wrong foot. Sullen hostility sets in. The teacher asserts authority and the students resist. The teacher knows that things are not going well but doesn't know what to do about it.

2

One likely response of the teacher is retreat—retreat to reading lectures with as little eye contact with students as possible, retreat to threats of low grades as a motivating device, retreat to research and other aspects of the professional role.

What makes the difference in these first few days?

It's probably not the subject matter. More often than not, the key to a good start is not the choice of interesting content (important as that may be) but rather the ability to manage the activities of the class effectively. Simple teaching techniques get the students involved so that they can get to work and learn.

The new teacher who has techniques for breaking the ice, for encouraging class participation, and for getting the course organized is more likely to get off to a good start. Once you find that teaching can be fun, you enjoy devoting time to it, you will think about it, and you will develop into a competent teacher.

When you are just starting, discussions of philosophy of education and theories of learning and teaching can be helpful, but they are probably not as important as learning enough techniques and simple skills to get through the first few weeks without great stress and with some satisfaction. Once some comfort has been achieved, you can think more deeply about the larger issues.

THE COLLEGE OR UNIVERSITY CULTURE

A course cannot be divorced from the total college or university culture.

First of all, the institution makes certain requirements of instructors. In most you must submit grades for the students' work. You probably must give a final course examination. A classroom is assigned for the class, and the class meets in this assigned place. The class meets at certain regularly scheduled periods.

There are, in addition, areas not covered by the formal rules of the college, in which instructors must tread lightly. For example, in most college cultures instructors who become intimately involved with their students are overstepping the bounds of propriety. Certain limits on class discussion of religion, sex, or politics may exist. Instructors must learn not only to operate within the fences of college regulations but also to skirt the pitfalls of the college mores.

But instructors who consider only college mores in plans for their courses are ignoring a far more important limitation on teaching, for the college or university culture has not only placed limitations on instructors but also pretty much hobbled the students. To stay in college, students must show evidence of achievement. Admission to good careers depends on evidence of outstanding achievement.

In many institutions, students have had experience in previous classes with instructors who, in a more or less fatherly way, gave information and rewarded those students who could best give it back. Not only has the role of the teacher been similar in these classes, but teaching procedures were probably much the same. Depending on the college or university, the method used may have been lecture, question and answer, discussion, or something else. The sort of tests, frequency of tests, and methods of grading also have conformed closely to certain norms. As a result, instructors who attempt to revolutionize teaching with new methods or techniques may find that they are only frustrating the needs and expectations their students have developed in the culture of the college. So, if you are trying something new, be sure that students understand why the new method is likely to be valuable.

Each reader will need to adapt my suggestions to the college culture of which he or she is a part. When you begin a new teaching position, talk to other faculty members about how they teach and perceive others as teaching. Ask for examples of syllabi, tests, and other course materials.

RESEARCH VERSUS TEACHING?

One aspect of the local culture critical for new teachers is the definition of the proper role of a faculty member. In many universities, for example, formal definitions of the criteria for promotion give research and teaching equal weight, but it is not uncommon to find that research is "more equal."

Studies demonstrated that research and teaching are not necessarily in conflict. Many faculty members are excellent researchers and excellent teachers as well. Some excellent researchers are poor teachers; some excellent teachers do not publish research.

Teaching as Scholarship

In 1990, Ernest Boyer's book *Scholarship Reconsidered* stimulated discussion throughout higher education about the nature of scholarship. In most American universities scholarship has been evaluated in terms of published research. Boyer suggested that teachers who keep up with current developments, who devise better ways to help students learn, or who do research on methods of teaching are also scholars. As a result of the debates about Boyer's proposal, there is increasing acceptance of the idea that good teaching involves much scholarly activity.

Find out what the local norms are, and if you feel a conflict, choose the balance that suits your own talents and interests with an informed awareness of the likelihood of support for that self-definition. Although time is not infinitely elastic, most faculty members find that a 50- to 60-hour work week is satisfying because they enjoy both teaching and research.

Whatever your choice, it is likely that teaching will be a part of your role. *Teaching skillfully may be less time consuming than teaching badly.* Teaching well is more fun than teaching poorly. Moreover, you will be better able to focus on your research if you are not worrying about teaching. Thus some investment of time and attention to developing skill in teaching is likely to have substantial payoff in self-satisfaction and effectiveness in your career.

A FEW WORDS ABOUT THE ORGANIZATION OF *TEACHING TIPS*

As the Table of Contents and Preface indicate, *Teaching Tips* begins with the practical information needed to prepare for and teach your first course. Part II provides suggestions about questioning, lecturing, leading discussions, testing, and the basic skills needed in most courses. Part III deals with a broader array of skills, strategies, and methods. Parts I through III all are directed to ways of facilitating learning. By developing a repertoire of skills and strategies, you should be better able to reach all sorts of learners. Part IV focuses specifically on learners and how to deal with differences among them. Part V shifts the focus to you, the teacher, and your development. Finally, in Part VI we come to a more explicit consideration of the goals that have implicitly guided our activities from the beginning.

IN CONCLUSION

Because the suggestions I make are based on my own philosophy of teaching, you should be forewarned of six of my biases or hypotheses.

1. What is important is learning, not teaching. Teaching effectiveness depends not on what the teacher does, but rather on what the student does. Teaching involves listening as much as talking. It's important that both teacher and students are actively thinking, but most important is what goes on in the students' minds. Those minds are not blank slates. They hold expectations, experiences, and conceptions that will shape their interpretation of the knowledge you present. Your task is to help them develop mental representations of your subject matter that will provide a basis for further learning, thinking, and use.

2. Instructors can occasionally be wrong. If they are wrong too often, they should not be teaching. If they are never wrong, they belong in heaven, not a college classroom.

3. Classes are unpredictable. This can be frustrating, but it also makes teaching continually fascinating. Don't be discouraged if some students don't appreciate your teaching. You can interest all of your students some of the time; you can interest some of your students all of the time; but you can't interest all of your students all of the time.

4. There are many important goals of college and university teaching. Not the least of these is that of increasing the student's motivation and ability to *continue* learning after leaving college.

5. Most student learning occurs outside the classroom. This is a both humbling and reassuring thought for the beginning teacher. It means that the students' education will neither succeed nor fail simply because of what you do or don't do in the classroom. At the same time it reminds one to direct attention to stimulating and guiding student learning outside class even more than to preparing to give a dazzling classroom performance.

6. One key to improvement is reflection—thinking about what you want to accomplish, and what you and the students need to do to achieve these goals. What is contained in this book will not make you a Great Teacher. It may be that Great Teachers are born and not made, but anyone with ability enough to get a job as a college teacher can be a *good* teacher. This book will give you some tips for avoiding common problems and some concepts to think with, but eventually it comes down to you, your personality, and your values. My hope is that this book will help you feel enough at ease that you can reveal the best that is in you.

Supplementary Reading

When the first edition of *Teaching Tips* was published, it was almost the only book offering guidance to college teachers. Now there are a great many, as well as journals and newsletters published in the United States and other countries. Almost every discipline has a journal concerned with teaching that discipline. Check out the holdings of your institution's library. If your institution has a faculty/instructional developmental center, it will have lots of material and a helpful staff.

I am reluctant to list only a few of the many good books on college teaching because I see them all as meeting a need and complementing one another as well as *Teaching Tips*. I will limit myself to seven.

S. D. Brookfield, *The Skillful Teacher* (San Francisco: Jossey-Bass, 1995).

B. G. Davis, *Tools for Teaching* (San Francisco: Jossey-Bass, 1993).

B. L. Erickson and D. W. Strommer, *Teaching College Freshmen* (San Francisco: Jossey-Bass, 1991).

A. E. Grasha, *Teaching with Style* (Pittsburgh, PA: Alliance Publishers, 1996).

F. Marton, D. Hounsell, and N. Entwistle, *The Experience of Learning: Implications for Teaching and Studying in Higher Education*, 2nd ed. (Edinburgh: Scottish Academic Press, 1997).

P. Ramsden, *Learning to Teach in Higher Education* (London: Routledge, 1992).

And especially for science faculty members: Committee on Undergraduate Science Education, *Science Teaching Reconsidered: A Handbook* (Washington, DC: National Academy Press, 1997).

Many university faculty development centers publish newsletters for their own faculties. In addition there are two national publications on college teaching: *The National Teaching and Learning Forum* and *The Teaching Professor*. Both have helpful articles.

Countdown for Course Preparation

For teachers, courses do not start on the first day of classes. Rather, a course begins well before you meet your students.

TIME: THREE MONTHS BEFORE THE FIRST CLASS*

Write Objectives, Goals, or Outcomes

The first step in preparing for a course is working out course objectives, because the choice of text, the selection of the type and order of assignments, the choice of teaching techniques, and all the decisions involved in course planning should derive from your objectives. At this point your list of goals or objectives should be taken only as a rough reminder to be revised as you develop other aspects of the course plan and to be further revised in interaction with students. Writing out your goals helps clarify your thinking.

Some of you have heard of behavioral or performance objectives and may wish to phrase your objectives in behavioral terms.

---

* I have borrowed the idea of three months, two months, and so on from P. G. Zimbardo and J. W. Newton, *Instructor's Resource Book to Accompany Psychology and Life* (Glenview, IL: Scott, Foresman, 1975).

If so, do so. The advantage of stating what you expect students to be able to do is that it guides both you and the students toward outcome assessment. One of the most common weaknesses in teaching is that our evaluation methods are often pale reflections of the goals we proclaimed (and may or may not have achieved!). But don't omit important objectives simply because you can't think of good ways to convert them to behavioral language. The purpose of phrasing objectives behaviorally is to encourage you to be specific, but usually the performance specified in a behavioral objective is an indicator of a more general objective you want to achieve.* Your objectives have the great advantage of pointing clearly to what you can look for as evidence that the objective has been achieved. Your students see your methods of assessing or testing achievement of the objectives as the most important operational definition of your goals; hence goals and testing are inseparable teaching tasks. This does not mean that all of your goals should be assessed and count toward a grade. Some of your goals will involve motivational, attitudinal, and value outcomes, as discussed in Chapters 25, 26, and 28. Course grades are typically based only on cognitive and skill outcomes.

What Goals?

The answer obviously depends on the course and discipline, but it is important to note that the overall course objectives involve *educating students*; the objective of a course is not to cover a certain set of topics, but rather *to facilitate student learning and thinking*. Ordinarily we are not concerned simply with the learning of a set of facts, but rather with learning that can be applied and used in situations outside course examinations. In fact, *in most courses we are concerned about helping our students in a lifelong learning process*; that is, *we want to develop interest in further*

---

* Duchastel and Merrill (1973) have reviewed empirical studies of the effects of behavioral objectives. Amidst the plethora of nonsignificant results are some studies indicating that sharing behavioral objectives with students may help focus their attention or assist them in organizing material. So, if you've worked out objectives, let your students know what they are, and if possible give them a chance to help revise them. (This study and others mentioned in the text are found in the References at the back of the book.)

learning and provide a base of concepts and skills that will facilitate further learning and thinking. Thus, in framing your goals, think about what will be meaningful to your students. Will these goals really be relevant to them now and in the future?

Your personal values inevitably enter into your choice of goals. Although many of us were taught to be strictly objective, I have through the years come to believe that this is impossible. Our teaching is always influenced by our values, and students have a fairer chance to evaluate our biases or to accept our model if we are explicit about them. Hiding behind the cloak of objectivity simply prevents honest discussion of vital issues.

In thinking about your goals, remember that each course contributes to other general goals of a university education that transcend specific subject matter, such as critical thinking, being willing to explore ideas contrary to one's own beliefs, and knowing when information or data are relevant to an issue and how to find that information.

In addition to this general perspective, you need to keep in mind characteristics of the setting in which you teach. What is the role of this course in the curriculum? Are other instructors depending on this course to provide specific kinds of background knowledge or skill? What are your students like? What are their current concerns? Self-discovery? Social action? Getting a job? Talk to some of your colleagues.

A committee of college and university examiners developed two books, which are now classics, to assist faculty members in thinking about their objectives: *Taxonomy of Educational Objectives, Handbook I: Cognitive Domain* (Bloom, 1956) and *Handbook II: Affective Domain* (Krathwohl et al., 1964). Krathwohl and others are now working on a new edition which may be published by the time you read this.

Having said all this about the importance of starting with clear goals, I would nonetheless not want to make you feel guilty if you started on your syllabus with only vague notions about goals. Although it seems logical to start with goals, content, teaching methods, and the nature of the students, all of these interact in dynamic ways. So, if you find it easier to start by outlining the content of the course, do so. Ideally you would then tie the content to goals, but many effective teachers never state their goals very explicitly, yet their students achieve the kinds of motivational and cognitive outcomes that we all desire. College teachers are individualists. There are lots of different ways to do a good job. Goals emerge as you teach.

Order Textbooks or Other Resources Students May Need

Should You Use a Text?   With paperback books, reprint series, photocopiers, and the World Wide Web, young instructors are immediately beguiled by the thought that they can do a much better job of compiling a set of required readings than any previous author or editor.

There is much to be said for such a procedure. It provides flexibility, a variety of points of view, and an opportunity to maintain maximum interest. Moreover, since no single text covers every topic equally well, the use of a variety of sources enables the teacher to provide more uniformly excellent materials, ranging from theoretical papers and research reports to case studies.

The disadvantages of not using a textbook are apparent. Without a text the task of integration may be so overwhelming that great pressure is placed on instructors to provide integration. This may limit your freedom to use the class period for problem solving, applications, or other purposes. With a well-chosen textbook, you may rely on the students to obtain the basic content and structure of the subject matter through reading and thus be freer to vary procedures in the classroom. Moreover, the managerial task of determining appropriate readings and arranging to have them available for students is not to be taken lightly. If students are expected to use certain sources in the library, consult a librarian to be sure enough copies are available. Access to course resources is particularly important in distance learning.

A final consideration is the extent to which you want to use required versus free reading, as in my use of a journal (see Chapter 10). I use a text as a base to provide structure and then require students to write journal entries on readings they choose. To assign diverse required readings and additional free reading

---

* Check the copyright laws before making multiple copies.

seems to me to require too much integration even for well-prepared, bright students.

Choosing a Text or Reading Materials*

In choosing reading materials the most important thing is that they fit your objectives. One of the most annoying and confusing practices for students is instructor disagreement with the text-book. It is doubtful that any book will satisfy you completely, but if you use a text, choose one that is as much in line with your view as possible.

Students prefer going through a book as it was written. If the author also wrote the book in a systematic way, building one concept on another, there may be good pedagogical reasons for following the author's order. Since I know of no text that completely suits many teachers, however, I can only recommend that you keep skipping around to a minimum.

There is no substitute for detailed review of the competing texts for the course you are teaching. As texts multiply, it becomes increasingly tempting to throw up your hands in frustration over the time required for a conscientious review and to choose the book primarily on the basis of appearance, the personality of the sales representative, or the inclusion of your name as author of one of the studies cited. Yet research on teaching suggests that the major influence on what students learn is not the teaching method but the textbook. What should you do?

1. Winnow the possibilities down to two to five.** You may be able to do some winnowing on the basis of the table of contents and preface, by checking with colleagues who have taught the course, or by reading reviews.

---

* Some of these ideas were stimulated by Russell Dewey's article, "Finding the right introductory psychology textbook, *APS Observer*, March 1995, 32–35.

** In my introductory psychology course, my teaching assistants and I choose three or four textbooks and then allow each student to choose the book he or she prefers. All the texts cover the essential material, but having a choice helps student motivation. Before students make their choice, they discuss in small groups what characteristics of textbooks help their learning. Each student compares at least two books, reporting back to the class for further discussion and the final decision.

2. Read a couple of chapters. It is tempting to simply leaf through each book, reading snatches here and there. But reading a couple of complete chapters will give you a better idea of the difficulty and interest level of each book. Try picking one chapter on a topic you know well and one that is not in your area of expertise.

3. Pick three or four key concepts. See how each text explains them. Will the explanations be clear to students? Interesting?

TIME: TWO MONTHS BEFORE THE FIRST CLASS

Work Out a Tentative Set of Assignments for the Students

The next point at which course objectives influence preparation for the course is in terms of the kind, length, and content of assignments.

To summarize the argument so far in this chapter, the following schedule suggests the way in which a course may be planned in a preliminary way.

1. Decide what you want the students to gain from the course.

2. Choose one or more texts or other sources that make the points you want made.

3. Plan the course for the term in such a way as to allot appropriate amounts of time to various topics.

It is on this third point that elaboration appears to be necessary. In making plans for the term you need to consult (in addition to textbooks and your conscience) the college catalogue or bulletin in order to anticipate some or all of the following circumstances:

1. For a given term you are allowed a certain number of class periods (about 40 to 45 for a three-hour course in a typical semester). Your wisdom must therefore be compressed into a period of somewhat less than two clock days. You will want to decide ahead of time approximately the number of sessions to be allotted to each of the topics you want to cover.

2. My estimate of 40 to 45 days includes
   a. one day for orientation (which I recommend).
   b. one day for a final summing up (which the students will probably insist on).
   c. one or more class periods devoted to examinations.

   This, of course, reduces the students' time at your disposal to 35 to 40 hours.

3. Students (unlike the faculty) get holidays. One must consider them in planning a course in order, insofar as is possible, to avoid
   a. tests or important class sessions just before or just after holidays or major college events, such as homecoming.
   b. having closely related materials presented partly before and partly after a recess.

4. Midterm or other preliminary grades may be required for some students. Such estimates of student achievement should be based on at least one, and preferably more, examinations or other evidence of achievement.

5. Allow some time to talk about the goals of the course—not just at the beginning, but regularly relating topics and methods to the goals.

Choose Appropriate Teaching Methods

A final point at which your preparation for a course is determined by your objectives is in the type of instruction you will use. For some goals and for some materials, an orthodox lecture presentation is as good as or better than any other. For others, discussion may be preferable. For the accomplishment of still other ends, cooperative learning or role-playing techniques described later in the book may be useful. Probably most successful teachers vary their methods to suit their objectives. Thus you may wish one day to present some new material in a lecture. You may then follow this with a class discussion on implications of this material or with a laboratory or field exercise. Since your choice in the matter is determined as much by your own personality as by your course objectives, I shall not dwell on it here. From the description of these techniques in later sections of the book, you may be able to decide which techniques are suited to your philosophy of teaching, your abilities, the class you are teaching, and the particular goals you are emphasizing at a particular time.

Generally speaking, it will be wise to find out how the course has been taught in the past and to avoid *major* modifications unless there is some departmental dissatisfaction with the course.

Begin Drafting a Syllabus for the Course

When we think about teaching, we usually think about what goes on in the classroom, but most student learning occurs outside the classroom. Planning assignments and out-of-class activities is even more important than planning for class meetings. A syllabus typically contains such a plan, with assignments correlated with topics to be discussed in class. If you are teaching a distance learning course, a syllabus is indispensable. Like a contract, a syllabus should help students understand both their responsibilities and yours.

Constructing your syllabus will force you to begin thinking about the practicalities of what you must give up in order to achieve the most important objectives within the limitations of time, place, students, and resources.

What Should Be in the Syllabus?   If you have followed my recommendations up to this point, you now have a list of goals, have chosen a textbook, and have a general schedule of when you will cover each topic. The core of your syllabus will be that schedule. In introducing the schedule, explain the purpose for the organization you have chosen.

Under the topic headings, you can schedule assignments and the dates when they are due. This relieves you of the task of making assignments every few days and of repeating the assignments for students who have been absent when each assignment was announced.

As you lay out your schedule, consider alternate ways students might achieve the goals of a particular day or week of class. You will seldom have perfect attendance at every class. Why not build in periodic alternatives to your lecture or class discussion? Be sure also to consider the diversity of your students. Alternative assignments can help. Students who have options and a sense of personal control are likely to be more highly motivated for learning.

Other items that are appropriate to include in such a schedule are the dates when examinations, quizzes, or laboratory exercises are scheduled; announcements of films to be shown in connection with various topics; and the particular libraries in which collateral reading materials have been placed on reserve if the library facilities in your university are decentralized. You may also include other items that will be helpful for student learning, such as sites on the World Wide Web, interesting readings to supplement textbook assignments, strategies for maximizing learning, and what to do when having difficulty.

Finally, you may include any special rules you want to emphasize, such as a statement to the effect that assignments for the course are to be completed by the dates indicated in the course outline.

But isn't a syllabus that is printed or on a web site a cue that the course is really instructor centered and that student needs are not going to be considered? Not necessarily so. Research by Mann et al. (1970) suggests that students may take a nondirective approach to indicate that the teacher is not interested in the class. The syllabus helps students discover at the outset what is expected of them and gives them the security of knowing where they are going. At the same time, your wording of assignment topics can convey excitement and stimulate curiosity.

Check Resources Needing Advance Work

Order films and make arrangements for field work, guest lecturers, slides, demonstrations, and other resources needing advance work.

Begin Preparing Lectures (If You Plan to Lecture)

(See Chapter 6.)

TIME: TWO WEEKS BEFORE THE FIRST CLASS

Preparation and planning are not done when you've firmed up the syllabus. Now look back over the syllabus to see what resources are required. Presumably your check with a colleague has turned up any gross problems—such as assuming an unlimited budget for films. What are the library policies relevant to putting on reserve any books you may want? Can you assume unlimited photocopying of exams and course materials to give to students? What do you do if you want to show a film? Go on a field trip? Visit the classroom you've been assigned. Will the seating be conducive to discussion? Can it be darkened for films? If the room is unsuitable, ask for another.

Don't assume that assignments are unchangeable. You probably can't change the time schedule the first time you are assigned it, since a certain time may already be in print with student schedules built around it. But with a term's head start you may be able to shift time of day, length of class period, and other scheduling details.

TIME: ONE WEEK BEFORE THE FIRST CLASS

At this point you're ready to prepare for the first class. For ideas about what to do and how to handle this meeting, read Chapters 3 and 4.

SUPPLEMENTARY READING

A good brief source on defining objectives is J. E. Stice, a first step toward improved teaching, *Engineering Education* 1976, *66*, 394–398.

Chapter 7 of Robert Diamond's *Designing and Improving Courses and Curricula in Higher Education* (San Francisco: Jossey-Bass, 1989), is a practical guide for linking objectives to assessment.

Barbara Davis's good book *Tools for Teaching* (San Francisco: Jossey-Bass, 1993) has a fine chapter on the syllabus (pp. 14–28).

Chapter 6, The natural history of the classroom, in *The College Classroom* by Richard Mann, S. M. Arnold, J. Bender, S. Cytrynbaum, B. M.

Newman, B. Ringwald, J. Ringwald, and R. Rosenwein (New York: Wiley, 1970), is still the best material on the changing needs of classes over the course of a semester.

Teaching Within the Rhythms of the Semester by Donna K. Duffy and Janet W. Jones (San Francisco: Jossey-Bass, 1995) is also a perceptive and readable guide to thinking about the flow of the course over the term.

An excellent aid for preparing your syllabus is M. A. Lowther, J. S. Stark, and G. G. Martens, *Preparing Course Syllabi for Improved Communication* (Ann Arbor: NCRIPTAL, University of Michigan, 1989).

3 Planning Your Students' Learning Activities

A good deal of your students' learning will take place outside your classes. Your students will read their textbooks, review their notes, tackle your writing assignments, problems, or term papers, and prepare themselves for your classes and tests. This will involve them in a wide variety of learning activities— activities through which they learn. You can improve the effectiveness of your course by paying special attention to these out-of-class learning activities. This chapter is concerned with planning these learning activities so that students know what is expected of them, spend sufficient time on your course, and use this time purposefully and effectively. It will give examples of ways to plan courses that put student learning activity, rather than the teaching, at the center. Chapter 10 deals with using journals, reports, and papers to focus out-of-class activity, and Chapter 15 deals with course designs that emphasize independent study. This chapter emphasizes planning regular weekly student effort *out of class* to complement what goes on *in class*.

This chapter was written by Graham Gibbs of the Open University.

FOCUSING ON LEARNING

It is easy for teachers to imagine that what happens in class is overwhelmingly important to students' learning and that they and their classes are at the center of students' learning universe. It is the component of student learning that teachers see—the rest is often invisible. When they do their planning, most teachers give their attention to covering content in class rather than to what happens out of class (Stark & Lattuca, 1997). However, in studies of what students believe most influenced change during the college years, and of what students believe were their most important experiences at college, ideas presented by instructors in courses, and instructors themselves, rank far behind a range of other influences (Feldman & Newcomb, 1969). In many courses students spend as much time studying out of class as they do in class, and for advanced courses they may spend several hours out of class for each hour in class. What happens out of class can be as important, or more important, than what happens in class. And it is what students do, not what teachers do, that determines learning outcomes. Teachers cannot learn for students—students have to do it for themselves and usually by themselves. There has been a paradigm shift, in both cognitive research and educational advice, away from seeing students as passive recipients of teaching toward seeing them as actively processing knowledge and constructing their own understanding (Barr & Tagg, 1995). Despite this shift many teachers have little or no idea what their students do out of class: how many hours they dedicate to course work or what they do with those hours. It could be argued that what students do is up to them and is not the responsibility of the teacher. However, you may more easily be able to improve student performance in your course by changing what students do than by changing what you do in class.

How Much Class Contact Do You Need?

There is no clear evidence that lots of class contact is good for students or even necessary. An hour spent on a range of independent study activities has been found to be as effective as an hour in a lecture for the purpose of memorizing information, and more effective for understanding and problem solving (Bligh, 1971). The comparative effects of in-class and out-of-class activity are summarized in Chapter 15. In Holland students have been found to work on their studies for about 42 hours a week, including both in- and out-of-class activities, regardless of how many hours they spend in class (Vos, 1991). If class hours are lowered, then these students simply spend more time studying out of class to bring the total up to a reasonably hard-working week. In this context increasing class contact simply reduces out-of-class studying. One of the main reasons students take a surface approach to their learning (attempting only to memorize) rather than a deep approach (attempting to understand) is overload—in which students simply do not have enough time to do the study necessary to understand the course material (Ramsden & Entwistle, 1981). Much of the worldwide revolution in medical education in recent years has involved dramatic reductions in class contact and especially in the number of lectures, to allow more time for students to learn and to apply what they have learned to tackling medical problems. "Time on task" is one of the most important learning principles (Chickering & Gamson, 1987). If students don't spend enough time on it they simply won't learn it. Planning a course so that students spend enough time tackling the necessary learning activities is one of the most important things teachers can do. As you plan each week of your course, you should be thinking about these learning activities as much as about your classes.

I teach at the Open University in the United Kingdom, which has open admission and about 200,000 undergraduate and postgraduate students in distance learning programs. These students spend an average of less than 10 percent of their total learning time in contact with their instructors and still achieve standards and pass rates comparable to those at conventional universities. The Open University is among the top ten universities in England in the government's assessment of teaching quality, despite some of its courses involving no face-to-face contact at all. Face-to-face teaching cannot be argued to be either necessary or sufficient for effective learning. The course design task at the Open University is to plan how our students will engage in learning activities, not to plan classes. It can be helpful to conceive of conventional course planning in the same way. If it is to be effective, this planning of out-of-class activity needs to be just as careful and thorough as the planning of a lecture.

How Much Student Time Does Your Course Involve?

It is easy to imagine that your course is the only one your students are taking. After all, it is the only one you see. However, your students may be taking three, four, or five other courses in parallel. Given a realistic studying week of about 40 hours, you therefore have between about 6 and 10 hours a week of your students' time available to allocate to learning on your course, including in-class time. If your students spend 3 hours a week in class with you, then you have between 3 and 6 hours a week of out-of-class learning activity to plan. You should expect to use all of this time, and you should be quite explicit with your students about what you expect them to do with it. Exactly how many hours you have and are taking up is rather important. Students experience wide variations in demands among courses because teachers often do not estimate or plan this time carefully. The most common problems are caused by, at one extreme, specifying nothing, and leaving students to their own devices. At the other extreme, teachers overload students with inappropriate and unproductive activities which actually limit their learning. For example, science teachers often fill their students' time with writing up lab reports, leaving them no time to read. It can be helpful to calculate the total number of study hours available to your course and to plan what all of those hours would ideally be used for, estimating the time demands of each activity. In reality students will vary. Some will work harder or slower than others, and some will spend more of their time on some learning activities, and on some of their courses, than on others. But being explicit will help you to make realistic demands and will help students to see what is expected of them.

How Do Your Students Spend Their Time out of Class?

What students actually do with their time out of class is a crucial evaluation issue—at least as important as student feedback on what teachers do in class. Assumptions made about the demands of learning activities when planning a course need to be checked out in practice. In the United States, although instructors may expect students to study for more than 2 hours out of class for each hour in class (Gardiner, 1997), they actually spend only between 0.3 and 1.0 hours (Boyer, 1990; Brittingham, 1988; Hutchings et al., 1991; Moffat, 1989). This is clearly only an average, but it is a lower average than is usually reported in Europe. For example, students at Leeds Metropolitan University work between 1.4 and 3.0 hours out of class for each hour in class (Innis, 1996). There is unlikely to be anything very different about European students. It is probable that teacher expectations are different and out-of-class activities are more explicit and demanding.

In some institutions the size of courses is defined in terms of teacher hours. In Chapter 2 a "3-hour" one-semester course is described as 40 to 45 classes. From the evidence cited above you might be able to expect as little as 12 hours of total student effort out of class for such a course. In other institutions courses are defined in terms of student hours. The example shown in the box on page 25 comes from Oxford Brookes University, where students are expected to study for 1,200 hours a year and normally take ten 120-hour courses a year: but these are learning hours, not teaching hours. This course has been planned specifying all student learning activity, in and out of class. Note that here students spend about 4 hours out of class for each hour in class; 95 out-of-class learning hours are generated using only 25 hours of class time. Note also that the course description focuses on process, on learning activity, rather than on content to be covered. You may not have the freedom to change your class contact hours, but you can still think about how to generate learning activity outside of your classes. Planning your course should include a rough estimate of how your students will spend their time.

Course: Geography and the Contemporary World

This course is designed on the assumption that students will spend their 120 hours in the following ways:

4 hours in formal lectures

3 hours in workshops on library skills

6 hours in seminars to discuss project ideas

56 hours in independent fieldwork investigation (details in the fieldwork guide)

10 hours in workshops to present and discuss the outcomes of the fieldwork investigations

2 hours in tutorials

18 hours preparing a project notebook for assessment (6 hours reading, 12 hours writing)

21 hours preparing reports: 6 hours on a resource paper and 15 hours per student preparing a group project report (6 hours reading, 6 hours writing, and 3 hours in group meetings).

Total: 120 hours (25 hours contact, 95 hours study)

Based on Gibbs (1992).

PLANNING LEARNING ACTIVITIES

What Should Learning Activities Consist Of?

The first requirement for constructing a learning activity is that it involve the use of the skill or competence you are trying to develop. If you want students to learn how to solve problems, then their learning activity should involve solving problems. If you want them to be able to be critical of texts, then they should spend their time critiquing texts. If you want them to learn how to design experiments, then there is no sensible alternative but to require them to design experiments. Many traditional study activities actually involve rather little of the competence supposedly being taught. Undertaking experiments a teacher has designed may teach little about experimental design. Asking students to design experiments and then getting them to critique each other's designs just might, and these activities can be carried out outside the laboratory on students' own time.

In Table 3.1, the first six weeks of a Western civilization course have been designed in terms of 12 student exercises which are linked to twice-weekly classes. Each exercise involves the use of skills the course is attempting to develop (Walvoord & Breihan, 1997) Only half of the 12 exercises are listed here. The course this had replaced described what went on solely in terms of topics the teacher covered in class:

- Renaissance/Reformation
- Seventeenth-century crisis
- Absolutism

Exercise	Skills
1. Summarize book chapter	Perceiving authorship; accurate reporting
2. Paragraph narrating eight scrambled events	Accurate reporting of chronology; narration
5. Analysis of primary source accounts	Perceiving authorship and theses; using sources of evidence
6. Analysis of secondary source accounts	Perceiving authorship; using sources of evidence
7. Worksheet for classroom debate—Summary of evidence for assigned position	Perceiving theses; using sources as evidence; Stating and defending a thesis
11. Data worksheet: Was Burke or Paine more correct about the French Revolution?	Using sources of evidence; stating and defending theses; defending against counterarguments

TABLE 3.1   A Skill-oriented Western Civilization Course

- Age of Reason
- French Revolution
- Burke and Paine

The shift of emphasis is almost total: from teacher-presented content in class to student activity out of class, involving skills.

Simply asking a student to "learn" or "read" or even "spend time on" something is unlikely to generate focused and productive learning activity unless your students are quite sophisticated as learners. I have trouble reading a book unless I have a job to be done with which the content of the book can help me. Chapters 10 and 11 are concerned with how to help your students to become more sophisticated learners through writing and reading. You can help students directly in their reading in a variety of ways. Many textbooks today have study guides with questions and exercises that make it easier for students to read actively. You can devise such activities and questions yourself and even design your whole course in terms of learning activities related to a textbook instead of around your classes (Kember, 1991).

Many students find poorly specified and focused "homework" not to be very active, and they quickly lose concentration and interest. Even if they manage to put the time in, it may not be very productive time. Good teachers are good at devising productive learning activities. Reading books or notes may be a valuable adjunct to such activities but are seldom ends in themselves. To give an example of this difference, a passive task might involve asking students to read a chapter about experimental design and then read a journal article that contained an exemplary experimental design. In contrast, an active task might involve asking students to design an alternative to the experimental design in the article, using principles in the chapter for guidance. Here the activity gives purpose to study. Learning is often best seen as an incidental by-product of being engaged in a task rather than a deliberate and primary focus. Students find learning activities more engaging when they are novel and when they relate to their interests (Covington & Wiedenhaupt, 1997). The second requirement is therefore to devise tasks that are inherently engaging; that capture students' time and generate productive learning activity.

How Should Learning Activities Relate to Class Contact?

Learning activities are often planned to take place after a class: revising lecture notes or doing followup reading. Some subjects traditionally use class time to "model" such activity. For example, math students are often expected to tackle more math problems of the kind modeled in class by the teacher. The assumption is that the real learning will happen later when students try it for themselves. In effect the teacher is saying, "Now do some more like the ones I showed you—that's how you'll learn." Law teachers take legal cases apart in class to model how legal principles and precedents are used. They then assign students cases to read and analyze in a similar way. The class time is used not so much to present new material as to show what to *do* with new material. The same principle can apply to other text-based subjects. Class time can be used to say, "Here is how I use this theory [or technique] with material of this kind. I'd like you to do the same kind of job on the following material before the next class." It then makes sense to give students the chance to try using this theory or technique in a brief task, in class, in order to model it effectively, and clear up students' problems, before they go off on their own. The example in the box below involves tasks being presented on an overhead projector transparency during very large lecture classes in geography, to show students how to approach difficult theoretical reading material for homework. This is an account of the last third of a lecture to about 80 students in the context of a first-year undergraduate human geography course. After presenting new material in summary form, the class becomes more active as the focus shifts to preparing students for the study that will follow the lecture.

A Geography Lecture

Students are assigned a task involving interpreting changes over time in the location of towns, on four simplified maps shown on the overhead projector. The task is to explain the changes using

(cont.)

central place theory, presented earlier in the lecture. Students work in pairs. (6 minutes)

The lecturer completes the analysis of the maps and moves on, in a short lecture, to apply the concepts to various other situations. (3 minutes)

The class is given an open-ended question that involves applying the theory to a completely new context. Students will need to complete this after the lecture. (3 minutes)

The lecturer goes over material in a handout which has not been discussed so far. The handout will structure how students study after the lecture. (6 minutes)

Based on Gibbs and Jenkins (1984).

Learning activities can also be planned to take place *before* classes.

- At the University of Wolverhampton, math students are expected to tackle problems individually and then meet in groups of eight to discuss these problems, immediately *before* a class in which the teacher deals with difficulties and elaborations. Having already discovered that none of their friends can do the problems either, students are much more willing to ask questions and join in even quite large classes after such out-of-class preparation.

- In science, students can be expected to pass a short quiz before going into a laboratory session, to ensure that they put time into reading about and understanding the theory and methodology *before* they tackle the experiment, instead of afterwards. Requiring students to hand in a completed lab report as they leave the lab has a similar impact on student preparation, as it is impossible to write such a report during the lab class. Students quickly find that they have to prepare the theory and methodology sections, data recording sheets, graphs ready for plotting, and so on *beforehand*.

- The "Harvard case method" succeeds in getting students to read and analyze management case studies in detail *before* large classes, because students could be asked challenging questions in public during the class.

- At Strathclyde University, engineering students are required to bring their attempts at tackling a problem sheet handed out at a previous class, which is marked by other students then and there, during a large lecture class, using marking sheets as guidance. This has a dramatic effect on overall student performance because it results in their doing the problems properly to avoid the social embarrassment of their peers' seeing shoddy work (Forbes & Spence, 1991).

Whether or not such socially manipulative methods are desirable, the intention in each case is sound: to generate focused learning activity outside and before classes so that precious class time is as productive as possible. What happens in class is designed with a primary focus on its impact on out-of-class learning activity. When planning your classes you, too, should have this focus: What impact will it have on how my students prepare and on how they will study afterwards?

How Should Learning Activities Relate to Assessment?

Whether we like it or not, what is assessed drives student learning activity out of class to a very considerable extent. Students may even progressively abandon what they were initially interested in studying and orient themselves almost completely to the assessment system. Students in their senior year have been found to spend only 5 percent of their total study time on nonassessed work but 60 percent of their time on assessed tasks (Innis, 1996) and may become highly strategic, as illustrated by this student from MIT: "I just don't bother doing the homework now. I approach the courses so I can get an A in the easiest manner, and it's amazing how little work you can do if you really don't like the course. This just isn't the right way to approach education, particularly when you are a senior." (Snyder, 1970, p. 50) It is therefore crucial that assessment have an appropriate impact on what students do with their time. How to construct tests and examinations is dealt with in Chapter 7. Here we are concerned with the by-products of tests and examinations: with how they affect student learning activity out of class.

The choice between, for example, short papers and multiple-choice tests is as much a choice about appropriate learning activity as it is about validity or reliability of testing. Asking students to write a short paper, whether or not it is marked, is more likely to result in their "reading around" a topic than is asking them to prepare for a quiz. Even where final examinations are used, the form of these examinations can have a dramatic effect on student learning activity. In the case study given in the box below, a change in the demands of the examination transformed what students did in order to learn.

Case Study

Before

A philosophy of education examination used to ask essay-type questions, such as "Compare and contrast the philosophies of X and Y." The effect this had on students was to encourage memorization of facts about the philosophers covered in the lectures, in the hope that they would be able to use these facts in the examination. Student time out of class was spent on activities such as repeatedly rewriting lists of facts from their most recent lecture notes or from notes taken while reading philosophy.

After

The conventional examination was replaced with a videotape recording of a school teacher confronting difficult classroom problems with a philosophical dimension to them, such as issues of power and equality. The students were told that in the examination they would be shown a video extract, which they had never seen before, of a teacher in a classroom. There would be just one question: "Comment on what is going on in this classroom, from a philosophical point of view. Advise the teacher on her future teaching, from a philosophical point of view." The same question was used every year, but the video extract changed, focusing on different classroom phenomena into which philosophy offered potential insights.

(cont.)

The only way to prepare for such an exam is to practice analyzing what goes on in classrooms, using ideas from philosophy. Students stopped memorizing notes and instead sought opportunities to view videos of classrooms and even to sit in classrooms. They read before but especially after such observations, seeking philosophical ideas that helped them to interpret what they had seen. They asked questions in class about the relevance of the lecture content to incidents they had witnessed.

Philosophy teachers usually regard discussion as central to learning philosophy—but it seldom happens outside of class. Here students spontaneously discussed their analyses with other students, because it was difficult to do on their own. Students read more, and more actively, and spent far more time out of class studying than previously. Most importantly, they learned to apply philosophy to teaching. The lectures and the reading list remained as before. All that changed was the examination question.

IN CONCLUSION

When planning courses it is common for teachers to decide what to teach, then think up a way to assess it, and finally to hope that students use their time out of class wisely in preparing for this assessment. This can result in dull and lifeless out-of-class learning activity. Instead, teachers can start by devising an engaging assessment and then think about how they could best prepare students for it with engaging learning activities. Class contact can then be designed which prepares students best for such activities or which debriefs students after having engaged in such activities. Teaching, assessment, and studying are intimately linked together and need to be perceived and planned as an organic whole. To influence out-of-class activity you have to recognize these interrelationships from the students' point of view.

Supplementary Reading

R. B. Barr and J. Tagg, From teaching to learning—A new paradigm for undergraduate education, *Change*, 1995, 27, (6) 12–25. A powerful argument for focusing on learning rather than teaching.

B. E. Walvoord and J. R. Breihan, Helping faculty design assignment-centered courses. In D. DeZure (ed.), *To Improve the Academy*, Vol. 16 (Stillwater: New Forum Press and the Professional and Organisational Development Network in Higher Education, 1997), pp. 349–372.

D. Kember, *Writing Study Guides* (Bristol: Technical and Educational Services, 1991). A practical guide about how to design learning activities around textbooks.

Meeting a Class for the First Time

The first class meeting, like any other situation in which you are meeting a group of strangers who will affect your well-being, is at the same time exciting and anxiety-producing for both students and teacher. Some teachers handle their anxiety by postponing it, simply handing out the syllabus and leaving. This does not convey the idea that class time is valuable, nor does it capitalize on the fact that first-day excitement can be constructive. If you have prepared as suggested in Chapter 2, you're in good shape; the students will be pleased that the instruction is under control, and focusing on meeting the students' concerns cannot only help you quell your own anxiety but also make the first class interesting and challenging.

Other things being equal, anxiety is less disruptive in situations where stimulus events are clear and unambiguous. When the students know what to expect they can direct their energy more productively. An important function of the first day's meeting in any class is to provide this structure; that is, to present the classroom situation clearly, so that the students will know from the date of this meeting what you are like and what you expect. They come to the first class wanting to know what the course is all about and what kind of person the teacher is. To this end, the following concrete suggestions are offered.

One point to keep in mind both the first day and throughout the term is that yours is not the students' only class. They come to you from classes in chemistry, music, English, or physical education, or rushing from their dormitory beds or from parking lots. The first few minutes need to help this varied group shift their thoughts and feelings to you and your subject.

You can ease them into the course gradually, or you can grab their attention with something dramatically different, but in either case you need to think consciously about how you set the stage to facilitate achieving the course objectives. Even before the class period begins you can communicate nonverbally with such actions as arranging the seats in a circle, putting your name on the board, and chatting with early arrivals about what class they have come from or anything else that would indicate your interest in them. While students are coming in, suggest that they spend the time before class starts by getting acquainted with the students sitting near them.

BREAKING THE ICE

You will probably want to use the first period for getting acquainted and establishing goals. You might begin by informally asking first-year students to raise their hands, then sophomores, juniors, seniors, or out-of-staters. This gives you some idea of the composition of the class and gets students started participating.

In my relatively large lecture classes I have then asked the students to take a minute or two to write down words and phrases that describe their feelings on the first day of class. I then ask them, "What have you written?" and list their responses on the blackboard.

Next I ask them, "How do you think your teacher feels on the first day of class?" This takes them aback, but they begin writing. We now list these responses in a second column, and they see some parallels. I comment briefly on my own feelings. (I remember with special affection the senior who came up to me after class and said, "I've been at this university almost four years, and this is the first time it ever occurred to me that professors have feelings.")

In a small class you might then ask all class members (including yourself) to introduce themselves, tell where they're from, mention their field of concentration, and answer any questions the group has. Or you can ask each student to get acquainted with the persons sitting on each side and then go around the class with each student introducing the next or each repeating the names of all those who have been introduced—a good device for developing rapport and for helping you learn the names, too. A more demanding, but surprisingly effective device is to have each person introduce everyone who was introduced before, ending with the teacher repeating everyone's names. (Try it! You'll be surprised at how well you do.)

Learning names is a start, but students are probably even more interested in you than in their classmates; so give them a chance to ask questions of you. Sometimes I have asked for one or two students to act as interviewers for the class, asking questions they think the other students would like to ask.

Even if you remembered all of the students' names in the "Name Game," you may not recall them later; so it is helpful to supplement the memory in your head with an external memory. I pass out file cards and ask students to write their names, phone numbers, e-mail addresses, and other information on the card. The "other information" might include previous experience relevant to the course, interests, distinctive characteristics that will help me remember them, possible major field, and so on.

Having established some freedom of communication, you can then go on to assess student expectations and goals, and let them know what yours are. One technique for doing this is problem posting.

PROBLEM POSTING*

The technique of posting problems is not only a useful first-day icebreaker, but also of value whenever your goal is to stimulate

---

* This technique is one I learned from Norman R. F. Maier and is described in his book *Problem-Solving Discussions and Conferences: Leadership Methods and Skills* (New York: McGraw-Hill, 1963). It is useful in either small or large classes.

interest and assist students in communicating their problems to one another. This may be the case not only at the beginning of the course, but also after a lecture or other classroom method has aroused anxiety or defensiveness. The technique may also be useful to you when you wish to avoid answering questions immediately yourself. This might be because you don't wish to establish an atmosphere in which you dominate, because you wish to lay more groundwork, or because you don't wish to reinforce or to engage in a colloquy with a particular questioner whose concerns are not likely to contribute to the goals of the class as a whole.

Do these potentialities intrigue you? All you need do is to say something like, "Let's see if we can get all the questions out so that we can see what they are and how to handle them."

For this first class meeting, you might say, "Let's see what problems you'd like to tackle during the course. What sorts of concerns do you think we might deal with?" or "What kinds of things have you heard about this course?" "What are your goals?"

Your task then becomes that of understanding and recording student responses on the chalkboard or overhead. This means that you must be ready to accept all contributions whether or not you yourself feel they are important. To test your understanding of the problem it may be useful to restate the problem in different words. Restatement may also be useful in removing emotional loading or in bringing out implicit feelings. When you feel that a question is ambiguous or too general, it is helpful to ask for an illustration or to ask other group members to help you understand.

If possible, the posting should not be ended before there has been a good pause, since some of the most deeply felt problems will not come out until the students have seen that the teacher is really accepting and noncritical. This is a point at which sensitivity is particularly important, for one can often see the visible signs of conflict about whether or not to raise an emotion-laden problem.

It is important in problem posting to maintain an accepting, nonevaluative atmosphere. Thus, if other members of the group argue that someone's contribution is not really a problem or that the real problem is different from that stated, the teacher needs to make it clear that, even though not everyone agrees about a given problem, anything that is a problem for any member of the group is entitled to be listed. Disagreement should be used to get additional problems out rather than to persuade a group member to withdraw a contribution.

Inevitably some discussion will come out about solutions. Although this should not be abruptly censored, if it becomes involved or lengthy the teacher may point out that the task of dealing with the problems comes later.

By the end of the problem posting the class normally has become better acquainted, has become used to active participation, has taken the first step toward developing an attitude of attempting to understand rather than competing with one another, has reduced the attitude that everything must come from the teacher, has learned that the teacher can listen as well as talk (and is not going to reject ideas different from his or her own), and, I hope, has begun to feel some responsibility for solving its own problems rather than waiting for them to be answered by the instructor.

INTRODUCING THE SYLLABUS

Your syllabus will provide some of the answers to the concerns raised in the problem posting. In presenting the syllabus outline and mechanics you give the students some notion of the kind of person you are. In a sense, the syllabus is a contract between you and your students. But a contract cannot be one-sided. Thus it is important to give students time to read and discuss it. Give them a chance to make inputs and to be sure that they understand what you expect. Help the students understand the reasons for the plan you have presented, but if they have good reasons for changes, accept them. The students are, of course, interested in course requirements, but they are at least as much interested in what kind of person you are. One important issue is fairness.

Promoting the notion that you are objective or fair can best be handled in connection with marks and the assignment of grades (see Chapters 7 and 9). A large part of the students' motivation in the classroom situation is (perhaps unfortunately) directed toward the grades they hope to get from the course. The very least that students can expect of you is that their marks will be arrived at on some impartial basis. Thus give some time to discussing this section of your syllabus.

The simplest way to show students that you are objective and fair is to let them know that you are willing to meet and advise them. Indicate your office hours. In addition, students appreciate it if you are willing (and have the time) to spend a few minutes in the classroom after each class, answering specific questions. Such queries most often concern questions of fact which can be answered briefly and would hardly warrant a trip to your office at a later time. If time permits, adjournment to a convenient snack bar or lounge may give students with special interests a chance to pursue them and get to know you better. If you teach an evening class, schedule some evening time to see students.

The first class is not the time to make sure students understand your inadequacies and limitations. Frankly admitting that you don't know something is fine after the course is under way, but apologies in advance for lack of experience or expertise simply increase student insecurity.

INTRODUCING THE TEXTBOOK

To continue with the discussion of the first meeting of the class, we turn now to the presentation of the textbook. Explain the features that led you to choose it. Describe how students can learn from it most effectively. In case disagreement between the teacher and the text is inevitable, the students have a right to know what they are supposed to do about such discrepancies on examinations. By facing the situation squarely, you cannot only escape from the horns of this dilemma but also turn it to your advantage. Explain that rival interpretations stand or fall on the basis of pertinent evidence and plan to give your reasons for disagreeing with the textbook. This procedure will accomplish two things: (1) it will give the student the notion that your opinions are based on evidence, and (2) it will frequently point out current problems in theory which often have great appeal for the serious student.

ASSESSING PRIOR KNOWLEDGE

The most important characteristic determining student learning is prior knowledge. Thus you need to get some sense of the diversity of your class's background. You might simply ask questions like, "How many have had more than X previous courses in this subject?" or you might give a short, noncredit test of relevant knowledge sometime during the first few class sessions. For students who lack sufficient background, you might advise that they transfer to the needed courses, or if this isn't feasible, you can at least suggest materials for their own self-study which would help them keep up with the other students. For those with very high scores, you might suggest that they skip your course and go on to a more advanced course, or at least suggest supplementary materials that would be enriching and challenging.

QUESTIONS

Even in a large lecture it seems wise to interrupt these first descriptions of the course for student questions. Some of the questions will be designed as much to test you as to get information. Often the underlying questions are such:

- "Are you rigid?"
- "Will you really try to help students?"
- "Are you easily rattled?"
- "Are you a person as well as a teacher?"
- "Can you handle criticism?"

Ask students to take two minutes at the end of class to write their reactions to the first day (anonymously). This accomplishes two things: (1) it indicates your interest in learning from them and starts building a learning climate in which they are responsible for thinking about their learning and influencing your teaching; and (2) it gives you feedback, often revealing doubts or questions students were afraid to verbalize orally.

WHAT ABOUT SUBJECT MATTER?

Many instructors simply pass out the syllabus, mention the assignment for the next class, and dismiss class early on the first day. As the preceding sections indicate, I think the first day is important even though the students have had no prepared assignment. I like to give at least some time to subject matter. Typically I give at least a brief overview of the course, indicate some of the questions we'll try to answer, and perhaps introduce a few key concepts. Either on the first day or during the second class period, I ask students to fill in concepts on a concept map (a diagram of key concepts and their relationships).

But there is a limit to what you can do. The balance between content and other activities is one that different teachers will decide in different ways. My only admonition is to use the time. The first day is important, and by using it fully you communicate that you take class periods seriously.

IN CONCLUSION

By the end of the first day, students will have

1. A sense of where they're going and how they'll get there.
2. A feeling that the other members of the class are not strangers, that you and they are forming a group in which it's safe to participate.
3. An awareness that you care about their learning.
4. An expectation that the class will be both valuable and fun.

Supplementary Reading

The first day of class: Advice and ideas, *The Teaching Professor,* August/September 1989, 3 (7), 1–2.

Barbara Gross Davis, *Tools for Teaching* (San Francisco: Jossey-Bass, 1993), Ch. 3.

Basic Skills for Facilitating Student Learning

Facilitating Discussion: Posing Problems, Listening, Questioning

Active learning is the buzz word (or phrase) in contemporary higher education. The prototypic teaching method for active learning is discussion. Discussion methods are among the most valuable tools in the teacher's repertoire. Often teachers in large classes feel that they must lecture because discussion is impossible. In fact, discussion techniques can be used in classes of all sizes. Generally, smaller classes *are* more effective, but large classes should not be allowed to inhibit the teacher's ability to stimulate active learning—learning experiences in which the students are *thinking* about the subject matter.

Discussion techniques seem particularly appropriate when the instructor wants to do the following:

1. Help students learn to think in terms of the subject matter by giving them practice in thinking.

2. Help students learn to evaluate the logic of and evidence for their own and others' positions.

3. Give students opportunities to formulate applications of principles.

4. Help students become aware of and formulate problems using information gained from readings or lectures.

5. Develop motivation for further learning.

6. Get prompt feedback on student understanding or misunderstanding.

Why should discussion be the method of choice for achieving such objectives? The first justification is a very simple extrapolation of the old adage "Practice makes perfect." If instructors expect students to learn how to integrate, apply, and think, it seems reasonable that students should have an opportunity to practice these skills. Most importantly, learning should be facilitated if this practice is accompanied by feedback so that the students can identify their errors and successes.

Learning is most effective if there is sufficient guidance to ensure some successes. Research reveals that guidance is most helpful in the early stages of learning, suggesting that the instructor should play a more directive role at the beginning of a course than at its end.

A LITTLE BIT OF THEORY

Research in cognitive psychology has found that memory is affected by how deeply we process new knowledge (see Chapter 26). Simply listening to or repeating something is likely to store it in such a way that we have difficulty finding it when we want to remember it. If we elaborate our learning by thinking about its relationship to other things we know or by talking about it— explaining, summarizing, or questioning —we are more likely to remember it when we need to use it later.

Because many students are accustomed to listening passively to lectures, in introducing discussion you need to explain why and how discussion will help them construct knowledge they can find and apply when needed.

PROBLEMS IN TEACHING BY DISCUSSION

In discussion groups the instructor is faced with several problems:

1. Getting participation in the discussion.
2. Making progress (or making the student aware of the progress) toward course objectives.
3. Handling emotional reactions of students.

The type of discussion method used will determine the extent to which particular roles are dominant. Student-centered discussions tend to be more effective than teacher-centered methods, but first I will describe a middle-of-the-road discussion method particularly useful in a problem-solving discussion. For such a discussion to work, students must have a sense that a problem exists and that it would be interesting to try to work on that problem.

DEVELOPMENTAL DISCUSSION

The term *developmental discussion* was coined by Professor Norman R. F. Maier (1952) to describe a problem-solving discussion technique in which the teacher breaks problems into parts so that all group members are working on the same part of the problem at the same time. One of the reasons discussion often seems ineffective and disorganized is that different members of the group are working on different aspects of the problem and are thus often frustrated by what they perceive as irrelevant comments by other students.

Stages of Developmental Discussion

In developmental discussion the teacher tries to keep the students aware of the stage of discussion that is the current focus. Typical stages might be

1. Formulating the problem.
2. Suggesting hypotheses.
3. Getting relevant data.
4. Evaluating alternative solutions.

Often an appropriate problem for discussion is the application or implications of principles or findings presented in the assignment or lecture. When starting a discussion with a question or problem, take time after stating the problem to write it on the chalkboard or overhead. This gives students time to think, and it decreases the possibility that the discussion will wander away from the topic. You might ask the students to use the time in listing concepts that seem relevant.

Breaking a Problem into Subproblems

One of Maier's important contributions to effective group problem solving, as well as to teaching, is to point out that groups are likely to be more effective if they tackle one aspect of a problem at a time rather than skipping from formulation of the problem, to solutions, to evidence, to "what-have-you," as different members of the group toss in their own ideas. In developmental discussion the group tackles one thing at a time.

One of the first tasks is likely to be a *clarification of the problem.* Often groups are ineffective because different participants have different ideas of what the problem is, and group members may feel frustrated at the end of the discussion because "the group never got to the real problem."

A second task is likely to be: What do we know? or *What data are relevant?*

A third task may be: *What are the characteristics of an acceptable solution?*—for example: What is needed?

A fourth step could be: *What are possible solutions?* and a fifth step may be to *evaluate these solutions* against the criteria for a solution determined in the previous step.

The developmental discussion technique can be used even in large groups, since there are a limited number of points to be made at each step regardless of the number of participants. Maier and Maier (1957) have shown that developmental discussion techniques improve the quality of decisions compared with freer, more nondirective discussion methods.

SKILLS IN LEADING DISCUSSION

In a developmental discussion the teacher attempts to guide a discussion along a certain line, but not to push it beyond the group's interest and acceptance. Obviously this requires skill in initiating discussion, getting student participation, appraising group progress, asking questions, and overcoming resistance.

Starting Discussion

After a class has been meeting and discussing problems success-fully, there is little problem in initiating discussion, for it will develop almost spontaneously from problems encountered in reading, from experiences, or from unresolved problems from the previous meeting. But during the first meetings of new groups, the instructor may need to assume the initiative in beginning the discussion.

Starting Discussion with a Common Experience   One of the best ways of starting a discussion is to provide a concrete, common experience through presentation of a demonstration, film, role play, short skit, or brief reading. Following such a presentation it's easy to ask, "Why did ———————?"

Such an opening has a number of advantages. Because every-one in the group has seen it, everyone knows something about the topic under discussion. In addition, by focusing the discus-sion on the presentation, the instructor takes some of the pressure off anxious or threatened students who are afraid to reveal their own opinions or feelings.

However, you will not always be able to find the presentation you need to introduce each discussion, and you may be forced to turn to other techniques of initiating discussion. One such tech-nique is problem posting, which was discussed in Chapter 4.

Starting Discussion with a Controversy   A second technique of stimulating discussion is through disagreement. Experimental evidence is accumulating to indicate that a certain degree of sur-prise or uncertainty arouses curiosity, a basic motive for learning (Berlyne, 1960). Some teachers effectively play the role of devil's advocate; others are effective in pointing out differences in point of view.

I have some concerns about the devil's advocate role. I believe that it can be an effective device in getting students to think actively rather than accept passively the instructor's every sentence as "Truth." Yet it has its risks, the most important of which is that it may create lack of trust in the instructor. Of course, instructors want students to challenge their ideas, but few want their students to feel they are untrustworthy, lying about their own beliefs.

Two other dangers lurk in the devil's advocate role. One is that it will be perceived as manipulative. Students may feel (with justification) that the instructor "is just playing games with us—trying to show how smart he is and how easily he can fool us." It can also be seen as a screen to prevent students from ever successfully challenging the instructor.

Not only are all of these possible problems infuriating for the student, but they maintain a superior-subordinate relationship antithetical to the sort of learning environment that this book is plugging for.

Yet the devil's advocate role can be effective. Its success depends a good deal on the spirit with which it is played. My own compromise solution is to make it clear when I'm taking such a role by saying, "Suppose I take the position that ————" or "Let me play the role of devil's advocate for a bit."

In any case the instructor should realize that disagreement is not a sign of failure but may be used constructively. When rigid dogmatism interferes with constructive problem solving following a disagreement, the instructor may ask the disagreeing students to switch sides and argue the opposing point of view. Such a technique seems to be effective in developing awareness of the strengths of other positions.

As Maier has shown in his studies of group leadership, one barrier to effective problem solving is presenting an issue in such a way that participants take sides arguing the apparent solution rather than attempting to solve the problem by considering data and devising alternative solutions. Maier suggests the following principles for group problem solving*:

1. Success in problem solving requires that effort be directed toward overcoming surmountable obstacles.

* N. R. F. Maier, *Problem-Solving Discussions and Conferences* (New York: McGraw-Hill, 1963).

2. Available facts should be used even when they are inadequate.
3. The starting point of the problem is richest in solution possibilities.
4. Problem-mindedness should be increased while solution-mindedness should be delayed.
5. The "idea-getting" process should be separated from the "idea evaluation" process because the latter inhibits the former.

Questioning

The most common discussion opener is the question, and the most common error in questioning is not allowing students time enough to think. You should not expect an immediate response to every question. If your question is intended to stimulate thinking, give the students time to think. Five seconds of silence may seem an eternity, but a pause for 5–30 seconds will result in better discussion. In some cases you may plan for such a thoughtful silence by asking the students to think about the question for a few seconds and then write down one element that might help answer the question. Such a technique increases the chance that the shyer or slower students will participate, since they now know what they want to say when the discussion begins. In fact, you may even draw one in by saying, "You were writing vigorously, Ronnie. What's your suggestion?"

Factual Questions   There are times when it is appropriate to check student background knowledge with a series of brief factual questions, but more frequently you want to stimulate problem solving. One common error in phrasing questions for this purpose is to ask a question in a form conveying to students the message, "I know something you don't know and you'll look stupid if you don't guess right."

Application and Interpretation Questions Rather than dealing with factual questions, discussions need to be formulated so as to get at relationships, applications, or analyses of facts and materials. Solomon, Rosenberg, and Bezdek (1964) found that teachers who used interpretation questions produced gains in student comprehension. A question of the type: How does the idea that————————apply to————————? is much more likely to stimulate discussion than the question: What is the definition of ————————? The secret is not to avoid questions or to lecture in statements, but rather to listen and to reflect on what is heard. Dillon (1982), a leading researcher on questioning, advises that once you have defined the issue for discussion, keep quiet unless you are perplexed or didn't hear a comment. Questions are tools for teaching, but as Dillon demonstrated, they sometimes interfere with, as well as facilitate, achievement of teaching goals. What happens depends on the question and its use.

Problem Questions   A question may arise from a case, or it may be a hypothetical problem. It may be a problem whose solution the instructor knows; it may be a problem which the instructor has not solved. In any case it should be a problem that is meaningful to the students, and for the sake of morale, it should be a problem they can make some progress on. And even if the teacher knows an answer or has a preferred solution, the students should have a chance to come up with new solutions. The teacher's job is not to sell students on a particular solution, but rather to listen and to teach them how to solve problems themselves.

A common error in question phrasing is to frame the question at a level of abstraction inappropriate for the class. Students are most likely to participate in discussion when they feel that they have an experience or idea that will contribute to the discussion. This means that discussion questions need to be phrased as problems that are meaningful to the students as well as to the instructor. Such questions can be devised more easily if you know something of the students' background. An experiment by Sturgis (1959) showed that a teacher's knowledge of student background makes a significant difference in students' learning.

Another error in raising questions is to ask your question before finding out about the students' problems. Often a good question fails to elicit responses because students are hung up on some prior problem.

Suppose you ask a question and no one answers, or the student simply says, "I don't know." Discouraging as this may be, it should not necessarily be the end of the interaction. Usually the student can respond if the question is rephrased. Perhaps you need to give an example of the problem first; perhaps you need to suggest some alternative answer; perhaps you need to reformulate a prior question. More often than not, you can help the students discover that they are more competent than they thought.

Other Types of Questions   *Connective and causal effect questions* involve attempts to link material or concepts that otherwise might not seem related. One might, for example, cut across disciplines to link literature, music, and historical events or one might ask, "What are the possible causes of this phenomenon?"

Comparative questions, as the name suggests, ask for comparisons between one theory and another, one author and another, one research study and another. Such questions help students determine important dimensions of comparison.

Evaluative questions ask not only for comparisons but for a judgment of the relative value of the points being compared; for example, "Which of two theories better accounts for the data? Which of two essays better contributes to an understanding of the issue?"

Critical questions examine the validity of an author's arguments or discussion. Being so critical that students feel that their reading has been a waste of time is not helpful, but presenting an alternative argument or conclusion may start students analyzing their reading more carefully, and eventually you want students to become critical readers who themselves challenge assumptions and conclusions.

Socratic Discussion

The "classic" (and I do mean *classic*) discussion technique is the Socratic method. In television, novels, and anecdotes about the first year of law school it is usually portrayed as a sadistic, anxiety-producing method of eliciting student stupidity, and even when I place myself in the role of slave boy taught by Socrates in the *Meno,* I feel more like a pawn than an active learner.

Perhaps this is why I've never been very good at Socratic teaching; nonetheless I believe that it can be used as an effective method of stimulating student thinking, and it can have the quality of an interesting game rather than of an inquisition. The leading modern student of Socratic teaching is Allen Collins, who has observed a variety of Socratic dialogues and analyzed the strategies used (1977, 1982).

Basically, most Socratic teachers attempt to teach students to reason to general principles from specific cases. Collins (1977) gives 23 rules, such as the following:

1. Ask about a known case. For example, if I were trying to teach a group of teaching assistants about student cheating, I might say, "Can you describe a situation in which cheating occurred?"

2. Ask for any factors. "Why did the cheating occur?"

3. Ask for intermediate factors. If the student suggests a factor that is not an immediate cause, ask for intermediate steps. For example, if a teaching assistant says, "Students feel a lot of pressure to get good grades," I might say, "Why did the pressure for grades result in cheating in this situation?"

4. Ask for prior factors. If the student gives a factor that has prior factors, ask for the prior factors. For example, "Why do students feel pressure to get good grades?"

5. Form a general rule for an insufficient factor. For example, "Do all students who feel pressure cheat?"

6. Pick a counterexample for an insufficient factor. For example, "Do you think these students cheat on every test?"

7. Form a general rule for an unnecessary factor. For example, if a teaching fellow suggests that cheating occurs when tests are difficult, I might say, "Probably the pressure to cheat is greater when tests are difficult, but does cheating occur only on difficult tests?"

8. Pick a counterexample for an unnecessary factor. For example, "Is cheating likely to occur on college admissions tests, such as the SAT?"

9. Pick a case with an extreme value. For example, "Why is cheating minimized on SAT tests?"

10. Probe for necessary or sufficient factors.

11. Pose two cases and probe for differences. For example, "Why is there more cheating in large classes than in small ones?"

12. Ask for a prediction about an unknown case.

13. Trace the consequences of a general rule. For example, if the teaching assistants conclude that cheating will occur when tests are difficult and are not well proctored, I might say, "Engineering classes are considered difficult, and I understand that there is little cheating even though tests are unproctored." (The school has an honor code.)

In general, the rules involve formulating general principles from known cases and then applying the principles to new cases. Even if one does not use the Socratic method to its fullest, the questioning strategies described in Collins's rules may be generally useful in leading discussions.

WHAT CAN I DO ABOUT NONPARTICIPANTS?*

In most classes some students talk too much, and others never volunteer a sentence. What can the teacher do?

Unfortunately, most students are used to being passive recipients in class. Some of your students may come from cultures whose norms discourage speaking in class. To help students become participants I try to create an expectation of participation in the discussion section. You can start to do this in the first meeting of the course by defining the functions of various aspects of the course and explaining why discussion is valuable. In addition to this initial structuring, however, you must continually work to increase the students' awareness of the values of participation. Participation is not an end in itself. For many purposes widespread participation may be vital; for others it may be detrimental. But you want to create a climate in which an important contribution is not lost because the person with the necessary idea did not feel free to express it.

What keeps a student from talking? There are a variety of reasons—boredom, lack of knowledge, general habits of passivity, cultural norms—but most compelling is a fear of being embarrassed.

---

* Some students who are reluctant to participate orally will participate in a computer conference or by e-mail.

When one is surrounded by strangers, when one does not know how critical these strangers may be, when one is not sure how sound one's idea may be, when one is afraid of stammering or forgetting one's point under the stress of speaking—the safest thing to do is keep quiet.

What can reduce this fear? Getting acquainted is one aid. Once students know that they are among friends, they can risk expressing themselves. If they know that at least one classmate supports an idea, the risk is reduced. For both these reasons the technique of subgrouping helps; for example, you can ask students to discuss a question in pairs or small groups before asking for general discussion.

Asking students to take a couple of minutes to write out their initial answers to a question can help. If a student has already written an answer, the step to speaking is much less than answering when asked to respond immediately. Even the shy person will respond when asked, "What did you write?"

Rewarding infrequent contributors at least with a smile helps encourage participation even if the contribution has to be developed or corrected. Calling students by name seems to encourage freer communication. Seating is important too. Rooms with seats in a circle help tremendously.

Getting to know the nonparticipant is also helpful. For example, I have found that it is helpful to ask students to write a brief life history indicating their interests and experiences relevant to the course. These autobiographies help me to gain a better knowledge of each student as an individual, to know what problems or illustrations will be of particular interest to a number of students, and to know on whom I can call for special information. One of the best ways of getting nonparticipants into the discussion is to ask them to contribute in a problem area in which they have special knowledge.

The technique of asking for a student's special knowledge deals directly with one of the major barriers to class discussion—fear of being wrong. No one likes to look foolish, especially in a situation where mistakes may be pounced upon by a teacher or other students. One of the major reasons for the deadliness of a question in which the teacher asks a student to fill in the one right word—such as, "This is an example of what?"—is that it puts the student on the spot. There is an infinity of wrong answers, and obviously the teacher knows the one right answer; so why should the student risk making a mistake when the odds are so much against the student? And even if the answer is obvious: Why look like a pawn for the teacher?

One way of putting the student in a more favorable position is to ask general questions that have no wrong answers. For example, you can ask, "How do you feel about this?" or "How does this look to you?" as a first step in analysis of a problem. Students' feelings or perceptions may not be the same as yours, but as reporters of their own feelings, they can't be challenged as being inaccurate. While such an approach by no means eliminates anxiety about participation (for an answer involves revealing oneself as a person), it will more often open up discussion that involves the student than will questions of fact. Problem posting, the technique discussed in Chapter 4 as a method for establishing objectives during the first day of class, is an example of a discussion technique minimizing risk for students. It can be useful in introducing a new topic at the conclusion of a topic, or for analysis of an experiment or a literary work. An added advantage is that it can be used in large as well as small groups.

Another technique for reducing the risk of participation for students is to ask a question a class period before the discussion and ask students to write out answers involving an example from their own experience. Similarly, one can ask students to bring one question to class for discussion. This helps participation, helps students learn to formulate questions, and also provides feedback for you.

Finally remember that out-of-class learning is often more important than that in class. E-mail, computer conferencing, and other interactive technologies can support active learning, discussion, and debate.

All of these techniques will still not make every student into an active, verbal participant. Two group techniques can help. One is buzz groups; the other is the inner circle technique.

Buzz Groups—Peer Learning

One of the popular techniques for achieving student participation in groups is the buzz session. In this procedure, classes are split into small subgroups for a brief discussion of a problem. Groups can be asked to come up with one hypothesis that they see as relevant, with one application of a principle, with an example of a concept, or with a solution to a problem. In large classes I march up the aisles saying, "Odd," "Even," "Odd," "Even" for each row and ask the "odd" row to turn around to talk to the "even" row behind, forming themselves into groups of four to six. I tell them to first introduce themselves to one another and then to choose a person to report for the group. Next they are to get from each member of the group one idea about the problem or question posed. Finally they are to come up with one idea to report to the total class. I give the group a limited time to work, sometimes five minutes or less, occasionally ten minutes or more, depending on the tasks. Peer-led discussions need not be limited to five or ten minutes or even to the classroom (see Chapter 14).

The Inner Circle or Fishbowl

In using the inner circle technique I announce that at the next class meeting we are going to have a class within a class, with several of the students (6 to 15) acting as the discussion group and the others as observers. If the classroom has movable chairs, I then arrange the seating in the form of concentric circles. I am impressed that students who are normally silent will talk when they feel the increased sense of responsibility as members of the inner circle.

THE DISCUSSION MONOPOLIZER*

If you have worked on nonparticipation effectively, the discussion monopolizer is less likely to be a problem, but there will still be classes in which one or two students talk so much that you and the other students become annoyed. As with nonparticipation, one solution is to raise with the class the question of participation in discussion—"Would the class be more effective if participation were more evenly distributed?"

---

* Be sensitive to the fact that the most common monopolizer is the teacher. In our research, our observers reported that in a typical discussion class the teacher talked 70 to 80 percent of the time.

A second technique is to have one or more members of the class act as observers for one or more class periods, reporting back to the class their observations. Perhaps assigning the dominant member to the observer role would help sensitivity.

A third possibility is to audiotape a discussion, and after playing back a portion, ask the class to discuss what might be done to improve the discussion.

A fourth technique is to use buzz groups with one member chosen to be reporter.

Finally, a direct approach should not be ruled out. Talking to the student individually outside class may be the simplest and most effective solution.

APPRAISING PROGRESS

One of the important skills of discussion leaders is the ability to appraise the group's progress and to be aware of barriers or resistances that are blocking learning. This skill depends on attention to such clues as inattention, hostility, or diversionary questions.

Skill at appraising is of little avail if instructors don't respond to the feedback they receive. In some cases you may need to respond only by interposing a guiding question or by emphasizing a significant contribution. In other cases you may need to summarize progress and restate the current issue or point out the stumbling block or diversion that has stopped progress. In extreme cases, you may have to stop the discussion to begin a discussion of the reasons for lack of progress.

HOW CAN WE HAVE A DISCUSSION IF THE STUDENTS HAVEN'T READ THE ASSIGNMENT?

It's hard to have a discussion if students haven't studied the material to be discussed. What to do?

One strategy is to give students questions at the end of one class, asking them to get information on the questions before the next class. You might even give different assignments to teams of students. Another strategy is to ask students to bring one or more questions on the assignment to be turned in at the beginning of the next class.

If there are extenuating circumstances, you (or a student who is prepared) can summarize the needed points. Alternatively, you can give students a few minutes to scan the material before beginning the discussion. If used often, however, such strategies may discourage out-of-class preparation.

If the problem persists, present it to the students. What do they suggest? One likely proposal is a short quiz at the beginning of class—which usually works. However, you'd like to have students motivated to study without the threat of a quiz. Usually the quiz can be phased out once students find that discussion really requires preparation and that the assignments are more interesting as they develop competence.

BARRIERS TO DISCUSSION

A primary barrier to discussion is the students' feeling that they are not learning. Occasional summaries during the hour not only help students chart their progress but also help smooth out communication problems. A summary need not be a statement of conclusions. In many cases the most effective summary is a restatement of the problem in terms of the issues resolved and those remaining. Keeping a visible record on the chalkboard of ideas, questions, data, or points to explore helps maintain focus and give a sense of progress.

Barriers to Discussion

- Student habits of passivity
- Failure to see the value of discussion
- Fear of criticism or of looking stupid
- Push toward agreement or solution before alternative points of view have been considered
- Feeling that the task is to find the answer the instructor wants rather than to explore and evaluate possibilities

Another common barrier to good discussion is the instructor's tendency to tell students the answer before the students have developed an answer or meaning for themselves. Of course, teachers can sometimes save time by tying things together or stating a generalization that is emerging. But all too often they do this before the class is ready for it.

Agreement can be a barrier to discussion. Usually instructors are so eager to reach agreement in groups that they are likely to be happy when the students are agreeing. But agreement is not the objective of most educational discussions. Students come to class with certain common naive attitudes and values. Although the attitudes they hold may be "good" ones, they may be so stereotyped that the students fail to develop an understanding of the complex phenomena to which their attitudes apply. The teacher's task is often directed not so much toward attitude change as toward increased sensitivity to other points of view and increased understanding of the phenomena to which the attitude applies. As I suggested earlier, the instructor may sometimes need to assume a role of opposition.

When you oppose a student's opinions, you should be careful not to overwhelm the student with the force of the criticism. Your objective is to start discussion, not smother it. Give students an opportunity to respond to criticisms, examining the point of view that was opposed. Above all, avoid personal criticism of students.

HANDLING ARGUMENTS

In any good discussion conflicts will arise. If such conflicts are left ambiguous and uncertain, they, like repressed conflicts in the individual, may cause continuing trouble. The teacher helps focus these conflicts so that they may contribute to learning.

- Reference to the text or other authority may be one method of resolution, if the solution depends on certain facts.

- Using the conflict as the basis for a library assignment for the class or a delegated group is another solution.

- If there is an experimentally verified answer, this is a good opportunity to review the method by which the answer could be determined.

- If the question is one of values, your goal may be to help students become aware of the values involved.

- Sometimes students will dispute your statements or decisions. Such disagreements may often be resolved by a comparison of the evidence for both points of view, but since teachers are human, they are all too likely to become drawn into an argument in which they finally rest on their own authority. To give yourself time to think, as well as to indicate understanding and acceptance of the students' point, I suggest listing the objections on the chalkboard. (Incidentally, listing evidence or arguments is also a good technique when the conflict is between two members of the class.) Such listing tends to prevent repetition of the same arguments.

- In any case it should be clear that conflict may be an aid to learning, and the instructor need not frantically seek to smother it.

The Two-Column Method

Another of Maier's techniques, the two-column method, is a particularly effective use of the board in a situation in which there is a conflict or where a strong bias prevents full consideration of alternative points of view. Experimental studies (Hovland, 1957) suggest that, when people hear arguments against their point of view, they become involved in attempting to refute the arguments rather than listening and understanding. Disagreement thus often tends to push the debaters into opposite corners, in which every idea is right or wrong, good or bad, black or white. The truth is often more complex and not in either extreme.

The two-column method is designed to permit consideration of complications and alternatives. As in problem posting, before the issues are debated, all the arguments on each side are listed on the board. The leader heads two columns "Favorable to A" and "Favorable to B" or "For" and "Against" and then asks for the facts or arguments that group members wish to present. The instructor's task is to understand and record in brief the arguments presented. If someone wishes to debate an argument presented for the other side, the instructor simply tries to reformulate the point so that it can be listed as a positive point in the debater's own column. But even though an argument is countered or protested it should not be erased, for the rules of the game are that the two columns are to include all ideas that members consider relevant. Evaluation can come later.

When the arguments have been exhausted, discussion can turn to the next step in problem solving. At this point the group can usually identify areas of agreement and disagreement, and in many cases it is already clear that the situation is neither black nor white. Now the issue becomes one of *relative* values rather than good versus bad. When discussion is directed toward agreements, some of the personal animosity is avoided, and some underlying feelings may be brought to light. The next stages of the discussion are thus more likely to be directed toward constructive problem solving.

Challenges and disagreements may be an indication of an alert, involved class. But the instructor should also be aware of the possibility that they may be symptoms of frustration arising because the students are uncertain of what the problem is or how to go about solving it.

TEACHING STUDENTS HOW TO LEARN THROUGH DISCUSSION

I have already implied that classes don't automatically carry on effective discussions. To a large extent students have to learn how to learn from discussions just as they have to learn how to learn from reading. How can this occur?

First, they need to understand the importance of discussion for learning. Expressing one's understanding or ideas and getting reactions from other students and the teacher makes a big difference in learning, retention, and use of knowledge.

What skills need to be learned? One skill is clarification of what the group is trying to do—becoming sensitive to confusion about what the group is working on and asking for clarification.

A second attribute is the students' development of a willingness to talk about their own ideas openly and to listen and respond to others' ideas. It is important for students to realize that it is easy to deceive themselves about their own insights or understandings and that verbalizing an idea is one way of getting checks on and extensions of it. Teachers can encourage development of listening skills by asking one group member to repeat or paraphrase what another said before responding to it, and repeatedly pointing out the purpose and values students gain from discussion.

A third skill is planning. Discussions are sometimes frustrating because they are only getting under way when the end of the class period comes. If this results in continuation of the discussion outside the class, so much the better, but often learning is facilitated if students learn to formulate the issues and determine what out-of-class study or followup is necessary before the group breaks up.

A fourth skill is building on others' ideas in such a way as to increase their motivation rather than make them feel punished or forgotten. Often students see discussion as a competitive situation in which they win by tearing down other students' ideas. As Haines and McKeachie (1967) have shown, cooperative discussion methods encourage more effective work and better morale than competitive methods.

A fifth attribute is skill in evaluation. If classes are to learn how to discuss issues effectively, they need to review periodically what aspects of their discussion are proving to be worthwhile and what barriers, gaps, or difficulties have arisen. Some classes reserve the last five minutes of the period for a review of the discussion's effectiveness.

A sixth attribute is sensitivity to feelings of other group members. Students need to become aware of the possibility that feelings of rejection, frustration, dependence, and so on may influence group members' participation in discussion. Sometimes it is more productive to recognize the underlying feeling than to focus on the content of an individual's statement. One way of helping students develop these skills is to use student-led discussions preceded by a training meeting with the student leader.

Peer learning techniques, such as those discussed in Chapter 14, help in building the sense of community that enables students to confront one another openly and helpfully. Such community does not come overnight, but building a sense of community may be even more important for student learning than covering every chapter in the textbook.

TAKING MINUTES OR NOTES, SUMMARIZING

One of the problems with discussion is students' feeling that they have learned less than in lectures where they have taken voluminous notes. Thus I like to summarize our progress at the end of the period or ask students to contribute to a summary.

Boris (1983) suggests that a student be assigned each day to keep the "minutes" of the day's discussion and that each class period be initiated with a reading of the minutes. Such a procedure is probably particularly useful for the student taking the minutes, but it also has the value of starting the class with a review of where they have been so that there is a sense of building from one class period to the next.

IN CONCLUSION

The teacher's own needs are more evident in the conduct of discussion than in a lecture, for skillful discussion leading requires a quick awareness of individual and group needs.

In general, if an instructor is enthusiastic, friendly, and obviously interested in the subject, students also will be. Let me emphasize again that both lecture and discussion may have advantages at certain points in a course. But when discussion is appropriate, it can be both valuable and fun for the teacher as well as the students.

Supplementary Reading

S. D. Brookfield, *The Skillful Teacher* (San Francisco: Jossey-Bass, 1990).

J. H. Clarke, Designing discussions as group inquiry. *College Teaching*, 1988, *36* (4), 140–146.

A. Collins, Goals and strategies of inquiry teaching. In R. Glaser (ed.), *Advances in Instructional Psychology* (Hillsdale, NJ: Erlbaum, 1982).

A. Collins, Different goals of inquiry teaching, *Questioning Exchange,* 1988, 2 (1), 39–45.

J. T. Dillon, *Teaching and the Art of Questioning* (Bloomington, IN: Phi Delta Kappa Educational Foundation, 1983).

Barbara Scheider Fuhrmann and Anthony F. Grasha, *A Practical Handbook for College Teachers* (Boston: Little, Brown, 1983), Chapter 6.

S. L. Yelon and C. R. Cooper, Discussion: A naturalistic study of a teaching method, *Instructional Science,* 1984, *13,* 213–224.

6   Lecturing

The lecture is probably the oldest teaching method and still the method most widely used in universities throughout the world. Through the ages a great deal of practical wisdom about techniques of lecturing has accumulated. Effective lecturers combine the talents of scholar, writer, producer, comedian, entertainer, and teacher in ways that contribute to student learning. Nevertheless, it is also true that few college professors combine these talents in optimal ways and that even the best lecturers are not always in top form.

Why have lectures survived since the invention of print? Why have they persisted in the face of the intrusions of radio, television, computers, and other media? Is the lecture an effective method of teaching? If it is, under what conditions is it most effective? These questions will be answered not only in light of research on the lecture as a teaching method but also in terms of analyses of the information-processing techniques used by students in learning from lectures.

RESEARCH ON THE EFFECTIVENESS OF LECTURES

A large number of studies have compared the effectiveness of lectures with other teaching methods. When measures of knowledge are used, the lecture proves to be as efficient as other methods.

However, in those experiments involving measures of retention of information after the end of a course, measures of transfer of knowledge to new situations, or measures of problem solving, thinking, or attitude change, or motivation for further learning, the results show differences favoring discussion methods over lecture (McKeachie et al., 1990).

WHAT ARE LECTURES GOOD FOR?

We do not need to lecture when concepts are available in printed form at an appropriate level for our students. Print presents information in a form that can be covered more rapidly and in a way more accessible for retrieval than lectures. Students using printed materials can choose their own rate of learning: they can review, they can skip; they can vary the order.

The lecturer thus starts with some serious handicaps. However, not all information is available in printed form. For example, most printed sources available to college and university teachers for assignment to students are at least several years out of date by the time they are available for assignments. Lectures are particularly appropriate for helping students get up-to-date information on current research and theories relevant to topics they are studying. Moreover, lecturers may sometimes usefully summarize material scattered over a variety of printed sources, thus providing a more efficient method of conveying information than if students were to be assigned to cover these sources by their own reading. Finally, a lecturer can adapt material to the background and interests of a particular audience—material which in printed form is at a level or in a style not well suited to a particular class.

Lectures also can provide structures to help students read more effectively. In fact the lecture may help students learn to read. Readability of material depends on the expectations brought to material by the reader. Thus appropriate lectures can build structures and expectations that help students read material in the given subject matter area more effectively.

Lectures also have indirect values apart from their cognitive content. Many lectures have motivational functions. By helping students become aware of a problem, of conflicting points of view, or of challenges to ideas they have previously taken for granted, the lecturer can stimulate interest in further learning in an area. Moreover, the lecturer's own attitudes and enthusiasm have an important effect on student motivation. Research on student ratings of teaching as well as on student learning indicates that the enthusiasm of the lecturer is an important factor in effecting student learning and motivation. You may feel that enthusiasm is not learnable. Clearly some people are more enthusiastic and expressive than others, but you can develop in this area just as in others. Try to put into each lecture something that you are really excited about. Notice how your voice and gestures show more energy and expressiveness. Now try carrying some of that intensity and animation over into other topics. Like other learned behaviors, this takes practice, but you can do it. Murray (1997) showed that enthusiastic teachers move around, make eye contact with students, and use more gestures and vocal variation, and that teachers could learn these behaviors. Both research and theory support the usefulness of enthusiastic behaviors in maintaining student attention.

Not only is the lecturer a model in terms of motivation and curiosity, the lecturer also models ways of approaching problems, portraying a scholar in action in ways that are difficult for other media or methods of instruction to achieve. In fact there is some evidence suggesting that one of the advantages of live professors is the tendency of people to model themselves after other individuals whom they perceive as living, breathing human beings with characteristics that can be admired and emulated.

Finally, there are values in lecturing for professors themselves. Although there is little direct evidence on the point, there is certainly anecdotal evidence, as well as supporting psychological theory, suggesting that preparing and delivering a lecture is an important factor in the professor's ability to integrate and retrieve the subject matter.

A LITTLE BIT OF THEORY

The preceding section has included a good bit of theory of learning and motivation, but I want to be more explicit about one aspect of the cognitive theory of learning and memory. As I noted in the preceding chapter, memory depends heavily on the learner's activity—thinking about and elaborating on new knowledge. A key difference between modern theories of memory and earlier theory is that earlier theory thought of knowledge as single associations, in some ways like tucking each bit of knowledge into a pigeonhole. Now we think of knowledge as being stored in structures such as networks with linked concepts, facts, and principles. The lecture thus needs to build a bridge between what is in the students' minds and the structures in the subject matter. Metaphors, examples, and demonstrations are the elements of the bridge. Providing a meaningful organization is thus a key function of the lecture. Our research (Naveh-Benjamin et al., 1989) showed that students begin a course with little organization, but develop conceptual structures during a course that more and more closely resemble that of the instructor.

HOW CAN LECTURES BE IMPROVED?

The message of this chapter is that one way of improving lectures is to think about how students process lectures. What are students trying to do during a lecture?

As one looks at students at a lecture and observes their behavior, the most impressive thing one notices is the passive role students have in most classrooms. Some students are having difficulty in staying awake; others are attempting to pass the time as easily as possible by reading other materials, counting lecturer mannerisms, or simply doodling and listening in a relatively effortless manner. Most students are taking notes. Ideally, many students are attempting to construct knowledge by linking what the lecturer says with what they already know.

Attention

One of the factors determining students' success in information processing is their ability to attend to the lecture. Attention basically involves focusing one's cognitions on those things that are changing, novel, or motivating. Individuals have a limited capacity for attending to the varied features of their environment. The individual's total capacity for attention may vary with the degree of activation or motivation. At any one time, part of the capacity is devoted to the task at hand (in this case listening to the lecturer), part is monitoring other aspects of the classroom, and part of the attention capacity may be available for other uses—in other words, it is simply spare capacity.

Hartley and Davies' (1978) review of the research on attention of students during lectures reports that, typically, attention increases from the beginning of the lecture to ten minutes into the lecture and decreases after that point.

One of the characteristics of a passive lecture situation in which a lecturer is using few devices to get students to think actively about the content of the lecture is that attention tends to drift. Probably all of us have had the experience of listening to a speaker and finding with a start that we have not heard the speaker for some time because our attention has drifted on to thoughts that are tangential to the lecturer's theme. Bloom's (1953) studies of students' thinking during lectures and discussion indicated that more of students' thoughts were relevant to the content during lectures than during discussions, but that there was less active thinking in lectures than in discussions.

What Can Be Done to Get Attention?

In determining how to allocate attention, students use various strategies. Any lecturer knows that one way of getting attention is to precede the statement by the phrase, "This will be on the test." In addition, students listen for particular words or phrases that indicate to them that something is worth noting and remembering. Statements that enumerate or list are likely to be on tests and thus are likely to be attended to.

Changes in the environment recruit attention. The ability of changes to capture attention can work to the advantage of the lecturer. Variation in pitch, intensity, and pace of the lecture, and visual cues such as gestures, facial expression, movement to the blackboard, the use of demonstrations or audiovisual aids—all of these recruit and maintain attention to the lecture.

Auditory attention is directed to some extent by visual attention. As the eyes move, auditory attention tends to shift as well. Distracting movements in the classroom are thus likely to cause students to fail to recall what the lecturer has said. On the positive side, there is some evidence that students' comprehension is greater when the students can see the speaker's face and lips. Look at your audience; eye contact helps communication. When students are not highly motivated, spare capacity of attention is available. This spare capacity is very likely to be used for daydreaming or other tasks which may become more engrossing than listening to the lecture. Hence motivation is important in holding student attention. Linking lectures to student interests, giving examples that are vivid and intriguing, building suspense toward resolution of a conflict—these are all techniques of gaining and holding attention.

All of these devices will help, but recall the Hartley and Davies finding that students' attention tends to wane after ten minutes. A more radical device for maintaining attention requires breaking up the lecture rather than trying to hold attention for an hour or more. Student activities such as problem posting, the minute paper,* pairing, or small group activities can reactivate students' attention.**

TEACHING STUDENTS HOW TO BE BETTER LISTENERS

We assume that listening is an innate skill, but you can train your students to be better listeners. For example, you might begin by asking students to write for one minute on "What do I hope to get out of this lecture?" Then explain how this strategy will help them to be more effective listeners in any lecture.

---

* The minute paper (Wilson, 1986) is described later in this chapter in the section "How to Get Students Actively Thinking in a Lecture Situation."

** Brown and Atkins (1988, p. 29) list these and other student activities to get students' attention and thinking during lectures.

Another strategy is to tell students that you will give them five minutes at the end of the lecture to summarize the main points of the lecture for someone sitting near them. At the end of the class period, ask them what effect this had on their listening to the lecture, and point out that they can use this approach to lectures even if they summarize it only in their own notes.

SHOULD STUDENTS TAKE NOTES?

Note taking is one of the activities by which students attempt to stay attentive, but note taking is also an aid to memory. *Working memory,* or *short-term memory,* is a term used to describe the fact that one can hold only a given amount of material in mind at one time. When the lecturer presents a succession of new concepts, students' faces begin to show signs of anguish and frustration; some write furiously in their notebooks, while others stop writing in complete discouragement. Note taking thus is dependent on one's ability, derived from past experience (long-term memory), to understand what is being said and to hold it in working memory long enough to write it down. In most cases, when queried about their listening or note-taking habits, students report that they are primarily concerned about getting the gist of the lecture in order to be prepared for an examination. To do this they try to extract significant features from the lecture, to distill some of its meaning.

Hartley and Davies (1978) reviewed the research on note taking and student information processing during lectures. They report that students believe that there are two purposes for taking notes. One is that the process of taking notes will in itself help later recall; the other is that the notes provide external storage of concepts which may be reviewed when needed. The research results indicate some support for both beliefs.

Several studies show that students who take notes remember material better than a control group not taking notes, even though the note takers turned in their notes immediately after the lecture. Note taking involves elaboration and transformation of ideas, which increases meaningfulness and retention (Peper & Mayer, 1978; Weiland & Kingsbury, 1979). But note taking has costs as well as benefits. Student note-taking strategies differ. Some students take copious notes; others take none. We know that student information processing capacity is limited; that is, people can take in, understand, and store only so much information in any brief period of time. Information will be processed more effectively if the student is actively engaged in note-taking—analyzing and processing the information rather than passively soaking it up, but taking notes takes capacity that may be needed for comprehension if material is difficult. Thus, encourage students to take *fewer* notes and to listen carefully when you are introducing new, difficult material. They can then fill in their notes after class.

Students' ability to process information depends on the degree to which the information can be integrated or "chunked." No one has great ability at handling large numbers of unrelated items in active memory. Thus when students are in an area of new concepts or when the instructor is using language that is not entirely familiar to the students, students may be processing the lecture word by word or phrase by phrase and lose the sense of a sentence or of a paragraph before the end of the thought is reached. This means that lecturers need to be aware of instances in which new words or concepts are being introduced and to build in greater redundancy, as well as pauses during which students can catch up and get appropriate notes.

Snow and Peterson (1980) point out that brighter students benefit more from taking notes than less able students. We believe that this is because the less able students while they write their notes, keep what they hear in their memories, so that their note taking essentially blocks them from processing parts of the lecture. But this is not simply a matter of intelligence; rather, a student's ability to maintain materials in memory while taking notes and even to process and think about relationships between one idea and other ideas depends on the knowledge or cognitive structures the student has available for organizing and relating the material. Thus the background of the student in the area is probably more important than the student's level of intelligence.

Some faculty members hand out prepared notes or encourage the preparation of notes for students to purchase. Hartley's research, as well as that of Annis (1981) and Kiewra (1989), suggests that a skeletal outline is helpful to students, but that with detailed notes students relax into passivity. It is better simply to provide an overall framework which they can fill in by selecting important points and interpreting them in their own words. Because student capacity for information processing is limited and because students stop and go over a confusing part of a lecture again, you need to build more redundancy into your lectures than into writing, and you need to build in pauses where students can catch up and think rather than simply struggle to keep up.

One can train students to write better notes by collecting student notes, evaluating the degree to which they summarize, translate, and show relationships as opposed to simply representing more or less verbatim accounts.

HOW DO STUDENTS PROCESS THE CONTENT OF A LECTURE?

Let's assume that students are allocating attention appropriately to the lecture. This alone, however, does not ensure that the content of the lecture will be understood, remembered, and applied appropriately. Even though students are trying to meet the demands of the situation, they may differ in the ways they go about processing the words that they have heard.

Marton and Säljö (1976a, 1976b) and other researchers at the University of Göteborg have described differences in the way students go about trying to learn educational materials. Some students process the material as little as possible, simply trying to remember the words the instructor says and doing little beyond this. This would be described by Marton as a "surface approach." Other students try to see implications of what the lecturer is saying, relate what is currently being said to other information either in the lecture or in their own experience and reading, and try to understand what the author intended. They elaborate and translate the instructor's words into their own. They may question. This more thoughtful and more active kind of listening is what Marton and Säljö refer to as "deep processing."

Experienced students can probably vary their strategies from verbatim memory to memory of concepts, depending on the demands of the situation. Obviously there are times when exact recall of what the lecturer said is important, but in general, deep processing is more likely to yield long-term memory and retrieval of the kind of knowledge needed for solving problems.

Strategies of surface processing or deep processing are probably not fixed, and lecturers may be able to help their students process more material at a deep level and in addition help students to learn from lectures more effectively. Pointing out relationships, asking rhetorical questions, or asking questions to be answered by class members are ways of encouraging active thought. Teachers can also ask for examples of how students apply concepts to their own experiences, thus encouraging all students to realize that it is important to try to think about how concepts relate to oneself.

PLANNING LECTURES

A typical lecture strives to present a systematic, concise summary of the knowledge to be covered in the day's assignment. Chang, Crombag, van der Drift, and Moonen (1983, p. 21) call this approach "conclusion oriented." *Don't do it!* The lecturer's task in university teaching is not to be an abstractor of encyclopedias, but to *teach students to learn and think.*

I was a conclusion-oriented lecturer for 30 years. Now more of my lectures involve analyzing materials, formulating problems, developing hypotheses, bringing evidence to bear, criticizing and evaluating alternative solutions—revealing methods of learning and thinking.

One of the implications of the theoretical approach I have taken is that what is an ideal approach to lecturing early in a course is likely to be inappropriate later in the course. As noted earlier, the way students process verbal material depends on the structures that not only enable them to process bigger and bigger chunks of subject matter but also give them tacit knowledge of the methods, procedures, and conventions used in the field and by you as a lecturer. For, intentionally or not, you are teaching students how to become more skilled in learning from your lectures.

Because this is so, one should in the first weeks of a course go more slowly, pause to allow students with poor backgrounds time to take notes, and give more everyday types of examples. Pausing to write a phrase or sketch a relationship on the chalkboard will not only give students a chance to catch up but also provide visual cues that can serve as points of reference later. Later in the term, students should be able to process bigger blocks of material more quickly.

Adapting to the differences in students' knowledge from the beginning to the later stages of a course is but one example of the principle that one key to good lecturing is an awareness of the audience, not only in lecturing but in preparing the lecture. In every class there is student diversity—not only in background knowledge but also in motivation, skills for learning, beliefs about what learning involves, and preferences for different ways of learning.

PREPARING YOUR LECTURE NOTES

One of the security-inducing features of lectures is that one can prepare a lecture with some sense of control over the content and organization of the class period. In lectures the instructor is usually in control, and this sense of controlled structure helps the anxious teacher avoid pure panic.

But no matter how thoroughly one has prepared the subject matter of the lecture, one must still face the problem of how to retrieve and deliver one's insights during the class period. If one has plenty of time and is compulsive, one is tempted to write out the lecture verbatim. Don't! Or if you must (and writing it out may be useful in clarifying your thoughts), don't take a verbatim version into the classroom. Few lecturers can read a lecture so well that students stay awake and interested.

At the same time, few teachers can deliver a lecture with no cues at all. Hence you will ordinarily lecture from notes. Most lecturers use an outline or a sequence of cue words and phrases.

Day (1980) studied lecture notes used by professors at over 75 colleges and universities. She notes that extensive notes take the instructor out of eye contact with students so that students fall into a passive, nonquestioning role. Day suggests the use of graphic representations to increase teaching flexibility and spontaneity. Tree diagrams, computer flowcharts, or network models enable a teacher to have at hand a representation of the structure that permits one to answer questions without losing track of the relationship of the question to the lecture organization. Pictorial representations using arrows, faces, Venn diagrams, or drawings that symbolize important concepts may not only provide cues for the instructor but can also be placed on the board to provide additional cues for students. Color coding your notes with procedural directions to yourself also helps. I have a tendency to run overtime, so I put time cues in the margin to remind me to check. I also put in directions to myself, such as

- "Put on chalkboard." (usually a key concept or relationship)
- "Check student understanding. Ask for examples."
- "Ask students for a show of hands."
- "Put students in pairs to discuss this."

Whatever your system, indicate *signposts* to tell students what is ahead, *transitions* that tell students when you are finishing one topic and moving to the next, *key points* or *concepts*, and *links* such as "consequently," "therefore," and "because."*

ORGANIZATION OF LECTURES

In thinking about lecture organization, most teachers think first about the structure of the subject matter, then try to organize the content in some logical fashion, such as building from specifics to generalization or deriving specific implications from general

---

* These four types of signposts are discussed in George Brown, *Lecturing and Explaining* (London: Methuen, 1979).

principles. Too often we get so immersed in "covering" the subject that we forget to ask, "What do I really want students to remember from this lecture next week, next year?"

Some common organizing principles used by lecturers are cause to effect; time sequence (for example, stories); parallel organization such as phenomenon to theory to evidence; problem to solution; pro versus con to resolution; familiar to unfamiliar; and concept to application.

Leith (1977) has suggested that different subjects are basically different in the ways in which progress is made in the field. Some subjects are organized in a linear or hierarchical fashion in which one concept builds on a preceding one. In such subjects one must follow a particular sequence of ideas in order to reach a sophisticated level. Other subjects are organized more nearly in the manner of a spiral or helix in which the path from one level to the next is not linear but rather depends on accumulating a number of related ideas before the next level can be achieved; and any of the related ideas at one level need not precede other ideas at that level. Still other subjects are organized in the fashion of networks in which one may start at different points of the network and go in various directions. One may build up a network equally well by starting at any one of a number of places and proceeding through a variety of sequences to arrive at comprehension of the subject matter.

The logical structure of one's subject should be one factor determining the lecture organization, but equally important is the cognitive structure in the students' minds. If we are to teach our students effectively, we need to bridge the gap between the structure in the subject matter and structures in the students' minds. As is indicated in all of the chapters in this book, the learner's mind is not *tabula rasa*. The teacher is not making impressions on a blank slate. Rather our task in teaching is to help students reorganize existing cognitive structures or to add new dimensions or new features to existing structures. Thus the organization of the lecture needs to take account of the student's existing knowledge and expectations as well as the structure of the subject matter. Analogies linking new ideas to similar ones that students already know can help.

The Introduction

One suggestion for organization is that the *introduction* of the lecture should point to a gap in the student's existing cognitive structure or should challenge or raise a question about something in the student's existing method of organizing material in order to arouse curiosity (Berlyne, 1954a, 1954b). There is a good deal of research on the role of prequestions in directing attention to features of written texts. Prequestions in the introduction of a lecture may help students to discriminate between more and less important features of lectures. For example, before a lecture on cognitive changes in aging, I ask, "Do you get more or less intelligent as you get older?" and "What is a fair test of intelligence for older people?" Such questions may help create expectations that enable students to allocate their information processing capacity more effectively. If students know what they are expected to learn from a lecture, they learn more of that material (sometimes at the expense of other material; Royer, 1977).

Another approach is to begin with an example, case, or application that indicates the practical relevance of the topic. In many fields it is possible to begin some lectures with presentation of a problem or case from a current newspaper or television show, then ask students how they would think about it in the light of this course, or alternatively illustrate in the lecture how experts in this field would think about it.

The Body of the Lecture

In organizing the *body* of the lecture, the most common error is probably that of trying to include too much. Students' information processing capacities are limited, and a lecturer who is expert in the field is likely to overestimate the students' ability to grasp large blocks of material and to see relationships. An explanation that would be perfect for advanced students may be incomprehensible to beginning students. Lecturers very often overload the students' information processing capacity so that they become less able to understand the material than if fewer points had been presented. David Katz (1950), a pioneer Gestalt psychologist, called this phenomenon "mental dazzle." He suggested that, just as too much light causes our eyes to be dazzled so that we cannot see anything, so too can too many new ideas overload processing capacity so that we cannot understand anything.

Use the chalkboard, an overhead projector, or PowerPoint to give the students cues to the organization of the lecture. Placing a skeletal outline (or sequence of questions) on the board before the lecture may help; going to the board to construct an outline, fill in the skeleton, or simply write key words is useful in three ways:

1. It gives a *visual* representation to supplement your oral presentation. Using a diagram or other graphic representation will help visualization.

2. Movement (change) helps retain (or regain) attention.

3. It gives students a chance to catch up with what you've said (perchance to think!).

Using Examples   In order to link what is in your head with what is in the students' heads, you need to use examples that relate the subject to the students' experience and knowledge. I am not as effective a teacher today as I was decades ago because I do not know the students' culture and am thus limited in finding vivid examples of a concept in students' daily lives. Since no single example can represent a concept fully, you usually need to give more than one example. Concept formation research suggests that examples differing from one another are likely to be most effective if you point out the essential features of the concept exemplified in each example. And, most important, give students a chance to give examples.

Periodic Summaries Within the Lecture   From our knowledge of students' note-taking behavior and from our theory of information processing, it seems likely that students would be better able to learn from lectures if there were periodic summaries of preceding material. These give students a chance to catch up on material covered when they were not tuned in and also give them a check on possible misperceptions based on inadequate or misleading expectations. Moreover, such summaries can help make clear to students transitions from one theme to another, so that they are aided in organizing the material not only in their notes but in their minds. In fact, you might try thinking of your lecture as two or more minilectures separated by short periods for questions, discussion, or writing.

Probably one of the greatest barriers to effective lecturing is the feeling that one must cover the material at all costs. Although it may seem irrational to cover material when students are not learning from it, one should not underestimate the compulsion one feels to get through one's lecture notes. A remedy for this compulsion is to put into the lecture notes reminders to oneself to check the students' understanding—both by looking for nonverbal cues of bewilderment or of lack of attention and by raising specific questions that will test the students' understanding.

Most lecturers recognize that they need to check student understanding periodically; so they ask, "Any questions?" and after 3 to 5 seconds without response assume that everyone understands. Not so!

If you really want to know, give students a minute to write down a question, then have them compare notes with students sitting near them before asking for questions. You'll get some.

Once you have used this procedure a few times, so that students have found that questioning is not dangerous, you can simply say, "What questions do you have?"

The Conclusion   In the conclusion of the lecture, one has the opportunity to make up for lapses in the body of the lecture. Encouraging students to formulate questions or asking questions oneself can facilitate understanding and memory. By making the oral headings visible once again, by recapitulating major points, by proposing unanswered questions to be treated in the reading assignments or the future lectures, and by creating an anticipation of the future, the lecturer can help students learn. One good (and humbling) technique is to announce that you will ask a student to summarize the lecture at the end of the period. Another— less threatening—is to have students spend three minutes writing a summary of main points. Either method helps the process of elaboration which is critical for memory.

Having suggested all this, I must admit that my own greatest problem as a lecturer is that I never seem to be ready for the conclusion until it is already past time to dismiss the class.

HOW TO GET STUDENTS ACTIVELY THINKING IN A LECTURE SITUATION

As we have seen, a major problem with the lecture is that students assume a passive, nonthinking, information receiving role. Yet, if they are to remember and use the information, they need to be actively engaged in thinking about the content presented. One easy and effective device is the "Minute Paper." The Minute Paper is, as its title indicates, a paper literally written in a minute (or it can be a two-minute or three-minute paper). Announce at the beginning of the class period that you will interrupt your lecture midway through the period so that the students may write a one-minute paper on a topic derived from the lecture or that you will ask them at the end of the lecture to write the most important thing they have learned. Even better, you can ask them also to write the most important thing they learned from the previous week's lecture.

In Chapter 19, "Teaching Large Classes (You Can Still Get Active Learning!)," I describe other activities to stimulate thinking. Chapters 5 and 14 also describe methods for getting discussion in large classes.

Whatever the method, you ordinarily will want to end with a discussion of the complexity of the issue, the fact that there are pros and cons for each position, and perhaps that a resolution may be found other than a decision for one position and against the other. Since many students feel that the best way to learn is to listen to an expert, you will need here (as in other departures from lecturing) to explain why active thinking is vital for effective learning.

LECTURE AND DISCUSSION

Since discussion offers the opportunity for a good deal of student activity and feedback, it should, according to theory, be more effective than lecture in developing concepts and problem-solving skills.

DISTRIBUTION OF LECTURE AND DISCUSSION TIME

What research adds up to is the use of lecture for communicating information and modeling problem solving, and discussion for practicing problem-solving skills. One way of doing this is to schedule separate lecture and discussion periods. This administrative arrangement is supported by a study in the teaching of psychology in which discussion meetings were substituted for one-third of the lectures (Lifson et al., 1956). There were no significant differences in achievement. However, the partial discussion method, as compared with the all-lecture method, resulted in more favorable student attitudes, which persisted in a followup study two years later.

Warren (1954) compared the effectiveness of one lecture and four recitations to two lectures and three demonstrations per week. The four-recitations plan was superior. Superior students tended to prefer the two-lecture plan, whereas poorer students did not. On the other hand, in Remmers's comparison (1933) of two lectures and one recitation versus three recitations, the poorer students tended to do better in the lecture-recitation combination.

In a course in which the instructors must not only give information but also develop concepts, the use of both lectures and discussions would thus seem to be a logical and popular choice.

Sometimes you will be unable to schedule separate small-group discussions. Do not despair. Discussion is possible in large groups. As we shall see in Chapter 19 there are many practical methods for achieving the advantages of discussion in large groups.

IN CONCLUSION

What is the role of the lecturer in higher education? The lecture is sometimes an effective way of communicating information, particularly in classes where variations in student background, ability, or interest make feedback to the lecturer important. We have also shown that the organization and presentation of lectures may influence their effectiveness in achieving application of knowledge or in influencing attitudes. Discussion, however, may be more effective than lecturing in achieving some of the higher-level cognitive and attitudinal objectives.

Good lecturers probably do intuitively many of the things we have suggested. Becoming conscious of what is going on in the students' heads as we talk; being alert to feedback from students through their facial expressions, nonverbal behavior, and oral comments; adjusting one's strategies in reference to these cues—these will help the lecturer learn and help students to learn from the lecturer more effectively.

Supplementary Reading

A very practical guide for lecturers is George Brown's classic paperback, *Lecturing and Explaining* (London: Methuen, 1980).

Howard Pollio's Remembrance of lectures past: Notes and note-taking in the college classroom, *Teaching-Learning Issues*, 1990, *68*, Learning Research Center, University of Tennessee, not only reviews the research on note taking but also suggests ways to help students become better note takers.

Jerry Evensky's chapter The lecture, in L. Lambert, S. L. Tice, and P. Featherstone (eds.), *University Teaching* (Syracuse, NY: Syracuse University Press, 1996) is excellent. I like his statement "You should not think of the lecture as the passive period to be relieved by; 'Now we're going to do active learning.'"

7

Testing and Assessing Learning: Assigning Grades Is Not the Most Important Function

When we think about evaluating learning, most of us think about examinations—multiple-choice tests, essay tests, oral examinations, perhaps even performance tests. But there are other methods of assessment. In this chapter I will begin with suggestions for conventional testing, and then suggest other methods of assessing student learning.

Let me start with seven assertions:

1. What students learn depends as much on your tests as your teaching.

2. Don't think of tests simply as a means for assigning grades. Tests should facilitate learning for you as well as for your students.

3. Use some nongraded tests and assessments that provide feedback to the students and you.

4. Check your assessment methods against your goals. Are you really assessing what you hoped to achieve, for example, higher-order thinking?

5. Some goals (values, motivation, attitudes, some skills) may not be measurable by conventional tests. Look for other evidence of their development.

6. When the course is over, students will not be able to depend on you to assess the quality of their learning. If one of our goals is continued learning, students need practice in self-assessment.

7. To summarize: assessment is *not* simply an end-of-course exercise to determine student grades. Assessments can be learning experiences for students. Assessment throughout a course communicates your goals to students so that they can learn more effectively; it will identify misunderstandings that will help you teach better; it will help you pace the development of the course; and, yes, it will also help you do a better job of assigning grades.

Since grades in many courses are determined to a great degree by test scores, tests are among the most frustrating aspects of the course to many students and arouse a great deal of overt and covert aggression. If teachers attempt to go beyond the usual practice of asking simply for memory of information from the textbook or lectures, they are immediately deluged with the complaint, "These are the most ambiguous tests I have ever taken!"

REDUCING STUDENT FRUSTRATION AND AGGRESSION

To most beginning teachers the aggression that students direct against them after a test is very disturbing. It is likely to impair the rapport of the instructor with the class and may actually be a block to learning. Hence devices for reducing the aggression seem to be worthwhile.

The most obvious solution to the problem is to reduce the frustration involved in taking tests. An aid in this area is to emphasize the contribution the course can make to the students' long-range goals, so that the need of a good grade is not the only one involved in the situation.

Explaining how and why you test as you do will help. A nongraded practice test will provide guidance. Using periodic assessments of learning (not necessarily graded) to help students assess their own progress and to help you identify problems, with frequent explanations of why and how you test and assess learning, should reduce student anxiety and frustration about testing.

Yet, no matter how much you emphasize long-range goals, the tests will in large measure determine what students do. Do you want the students to memorize details? Then give the usual memory-of-details test.

BALANCING SPECIFIED OBJECTIVES WITH VARIOUS TYPES OF TEST ITEMS

The first step in constructing a test is to list your goals for the course. Once you have specified objectives you can determine how many test items embody each category of objective. You'll probably be surprised to find out how many of your test items pile up in certain categories.

One way of maintaining a balance is to construct a grid, listing objectives along the side of the page and content areas along the top. If you then tally items as you write them, you can monitor the degree to which your test adequately samples the objectives and content desired.

Because some course examinations emphasize recall of facts, many students demand *teaching* that emphasizes memorization of facts. One student wrote on a slip evaluating me, "The instructor is very interesting and worthwhile, but I have rated him low because he doesn't give us enough facts. The sort of job I get will depend on my grades, and I have little chance of beating other students out for an A unless I can get a couple of pages of notes each period."

Students may object at first to tests requiring them to think, but if you emphasize that the tests will measure the students' abilities to use their knowledge, you can greatly influence their goals in the course. This is indicated by a student comment we received: "More of the course should be like the tests. They make us apply what we've learned." Marton and Säljö (1976b) showed that questions demanding understanding rather than memory of detailed facts resulted in differing styles of studying for later tests and better retention. Foos and Fisher (1988) showed that tests requiring inferences enhanced learning more than those requiring memorized knowledge.

Admittedly it is more difficult to devise measures of the more complex, higher-level objectives. Yet the very effort to do so will, I believe, have an influence on student motivation and learning. Moreover, consideration of these objectives may help you break out of the conventional forms of testing. For example, in my classes in introductory psychology, the desired goals include developing greater curiosity about behavior, awareness of dimensions of behavior that might ordinarily be ignored, and increased ability to describe and analyze behavior objectively. To get at this I have sometimes used a film or videotape as a stimulus, with the test questions having to do with the students' reactions to the film; or I have asked students to leave the classroom for 15 minutes and then return and report on some interesting behavior they have observed. I have brought in scientific journals and asked students to find an article of interest and to write their reactions to it. I have asked for analyses of newspaper items to get at the degree to which students can read critically. Using materials with somewhat greater apparent relevance to course objectives than typical test items is more fun for the students taking the test—and more fun to grade.

WHEN TO TEST

Because tests are so important in operationalizing goals and influencing student methods of learning, I give an ungraded quiz during the first week and a graded test after the third or fourth week of a 14-week semester. To reduce the stress I weight early tests very little in determining the final grade. But an early test gets students started, in that they don't delay their studying until the conventional midterm examination, and it will help you to identify problems early, while they are still remediable. Thus early tests should demand the style of learning you expect and need to be constructed carefully, even though their purpose is more motivational and diagnostic than evaluative.

I usually also give midterm and final examinations, but the amount and frequency of tests should depend on the background of your students. In a first-year course in an area new to students, frequent short tests early in the term facilitate learning, as demonstrated in the Personalized System of Instruction (Keller, 1968). Generally, however, I want to wean students from studying for tests, so that they become lifelong learners who will be able to evaluate their own learning. This implies less frequent testing as learners become more experienced. It probably also implies questions requiring broader integration and more detailed analysis as the learners advance. For this reason my tests are all cumulative; that is, they cover material previously tested as well as material learned since the last test. A final note on planning the timing of tests and other assessment devices, such as papers or reports. Give the students a chance to comment. They may know of potential conflicting events that could influence due dates.

TEST CONSTRUCTION

In planning your tests you may want to use a mix of different types of questions in order to balance measurements of the varied goals of education. The following sections describe the strengths and weaknesses of each type of question, as well as tips on constructing items.

Choosing the Type of Question

The instructor who is about to give an examination is in a conflict situation. There are two time-consuming procedures involved in the administration of an examination: the first is the construction of the examination; the second is the grading. Unfortunately, it appears to be generally true that the examinations that are easiest to construct are the most difficult to grade and vice versa.

Teachers often choose questions solely in terms of class size, using multiple-choice tests for large classes, short-answer questions for medium-sized classes, and essay questions for small classes. Class size is obviously an important factor, but your educational goals should take precedence. This almost always implies use of some essay questions, problems, or other items requiring analysis, integration, or application.

Problems   In mathematics, science, and some other disciplines, a test typically consists of problems. The value of problems depends on the degree to which they elicit the sort of problem-solving skills that are your goals. Some problems are too trite and stereotypic to have much value as indicators of whether or not students understand the steps they are following. In other cases the answer depends to such a large extent on tedious calculations that only a small sample of problems can be tested. In such cases you might provide calculations leading up to a certain point and ask the student to complete the problem, or you might use a multiple-choice question about the proper procedure; for example, "Which of the following problems can be solved by procedure x?"

Short-Answer Items   An example of a short-answer item might be this: "Give one example from your own experience of the concept of elaboration." In responding, a student might describe an experience in explaining a concept to another student or in thinking of the relationship of a fact to a general principle.

Such a question is restricted enough that it is not often difficult to judge whether the expected answer is there. Furthermore, such questions can be presented in a format that allows only a small amount of space for the answer. The student's tendency to employ the "shotgun" approach to the examination is thus inhibited. Short-answer questions permit coverage of assigned materials without asking for petty details. Unfortunately, many short-answer questions test only recall of specific facts.

Short-answer questions can do better than testing facts. If you are trying to develop skill in analysis or diagnosis, for example, you may present case material or description of an experiment and ask the students what questions they would ask. You can then provide additional information that the students can use in an analysis. Or a short-answer question can ask students to solve a problem or propose a hypothesis relevant to information learned earlier. An example is the following question from a course on the psychology of aging:

1. Given the *differences* in ways in which men and women experience middle age, and the fact that depression rises as a psychiatric symptom in middle age, how might the *causes* of the depression differ for men and women at this time in life?

Essay Items   Although the short-answer examination is very useful in certain situations, I would recommend that, if possible, you include at least one essay question on examinations in most college courses. Experiments indicate that students study more efficiently for essay-type examinations than for objective tests (d'Ydewalle et al., 1983; McClusky, 1934; Monaco, 1977). Thus in addition to the values of essay tests as evaluation devices, you should take into consideration their potential educational value.

Where the tests can be returned with comments, essay examinations may give students practice in organized, creative thinking about a subject and an opportunity to check their thinking against the standards of someone with more experience and ability in the field. Moreover, they may, as we suggested earlier, orient students to work toward objectives beyond memorization of details. Johnson (1975) demonstrated that, when marginal comments on earlier tests emphasized creativity, creativity on the final exam was improved.

Finally, if you read the examinations yourself (or at least some of them), you get some excellent information on what students are learning. While the teacher can also learn from students' responses to objective tests, the impact on the teacher of what students are learning seems to be greater and more vivid in reading essay tests.

True-False Items   Although true-false examinations are rather easy to make up, I don't ordinarily advocate their use. This is partly a concession to student opinion. Students can usually figure out reasons why any particular item can be either true or false.

Multiple-Choice Items   It is improbable that most teachers can adequately measure all their objectives with a test made up entirely of multiple-choice questions. Nonetheless, for some purposes multiple-choice items are useful. They can measure both simple knowledge and precise discrimination. They can measure ability to apply concepts or principles; they can assess elements of problem solving. But they are not likely to assess organization of ideas, conceptual relationships, or many of the skills involved in higher-order thinking.

Good multiple-choice questions are difficult to construct. (As a matter of fact, the greater your experience in their construction, the more you realize how long it takes per item to construct a reasonably fair, accurate, and inclusive question.) Because of this difficulty, the construction of such items is probably not worthwhile unless they will be administered to several hundred students, either in a single year or in successive years. The box that begins on this page and continues to page 94 contains hints for their construction.

Constructing Multiple-Choice Items

1. Teachers' manuals that are provided for many textbooks contain multiple-choice items. You will not be able to rely on a manual as the source of all your questions, because it often will not contain many good questions and may cover only textbook material. You need to assess what students have learned in class as well as what they have read.

2. A second source of such items is the students themselves. This is not a particularly satisfactory source of test questions, because only about 10 percent of the items thus received will be usable. However, this technique is a useful pedagogical device because it gets the students to read their assignments more analytically. It also gives the instructor a good index of what the students are getting out of the various sections of their reading and gives you a chance to remind them of the goals of the course going beyond memory of details.

3. There are statistical methods for evaluating questions, but the best suggestions for improvement come from students themselves in their discussion of the test. It seems almost criminal to waste this experience with items; therefore I recommend a permanent file.

4. If you have a problem, but no good distractor (incorrect alternative), give the item in short-answer or essay form and use

(cont.)

the students' own responses for alternatives for a later use of the item in multiple-choice form.

5. Multiple-choice questions typically have four or five alternatives. Rather than wasting your and your students' time with extra alternatives that don't test a discrimination that is important, use only as many alternatives as make meaningful discriminations. Costin (1972) has shown that three-choice items are about as effective as four-choice.

6. For measuring understanding, I like questions that require the student to predict the outcome of a situation rather than those that simply ask the student to label the phenomenon.

7. Multiple-choice items need not stand alone. You can use a sequence of related items to measure more complex thinking.

8. Rules for stating the problem.

   a. The problem should be stated briefly but completely; the problem should not test the student's ability to understand complex sentence structure except when the teacher is deliberately measuring that ability.

   b. The problem should be stated in a positive, not a negative, form. Somehow, even intelligent adults often fail to see a "not" in reading a sentence. If you must use "not," underline it.

   c. It should be possible to understand the problem without reading the alternatives.

   d. The test is more interesting if the questions are worded in concrete rather than abstract terms. Such items are particularly worthwhile if you wish to measure the student's ability to apply concepts to concrete situations. In math and science, problems arising in the application of the math or theory are not only more interesting but also more likely to encourage students to generalize the concepts or algorithms to situations in which they will use them.

9. Grouping items under headings will improve student performance (Marcinkiewicz & Clariana, 1997).

10. Rules for developing the suggested solutions.

    a. The suggested wrong answers should represent errors commonly made by the students being tested.

    b. The right answer should be unquestionably right, checked by two or three colleagues.

(cont.)

c. The suggested answers should be as brief as possible.

d. The position of the right answers should be scattered.

e. Numerical answers should be placed in numerical order.

f. Even wrong alternatives should not contain words unfamiliar to students.

g. Use "all of the above" and "none of the above" rarely. Usually they are tossed in when you can't think of another good distractor.

h. The right answer should not be given away by irrelevant clues. A few examples of commonly occurring irrelevant clues are:

1. Alternatives that include absolute terms such as "always" and "never" are rarely right answers.

2. Alternatives that are longer and more elaborate than the others are frequently right answers.

3. If the lead of the item is an incomplete statement, then alternatives that do not complete it grammatically are obviously wrong.*

*Many of the foregoing rules are derived directly or indirectly from notes taken in the "Test Construction" class of Dr. R. M. W. Travers. For a more detailed exposition, see his book, *How to Make Achievement Tests* (New York: Odyssey Press, 1950), which is still an excellent source.

Even if you don't pretest the item on students, it is worthwhile to have someone take the test before it is in its final form. If you can persuade a skilled test taker who doesn't know the subject matter to take the test, you will probably be surprised at how many he or she gets right simply from cues you've provided in the questions.

How Many Questions Should I Use?

Obviously the number of questions depends on the type and difficulty of each question. I prefer to give tests without a time limit, but the constraints of class scheduling usually require that you clear the classroom so that the next class can begin. Thus you must plan the length of the exam so that even the slower students have time to finish before the end of the period. As a rule of thumb I allow about 1 minute per item for multiple-choice or fill-in-the-blank items, 2 minutes per short-answer question requiring more than a sentence answer, 10 or 15 minutes for a limited essay question, and a half-hour to an hour for a broader question requiring more than a page or two to answer.

Instructions to the Students

The test instructions should indicate whether or not students are to guess, what the time limit is, and any other directions that define the nature of the expected responses. Emphasizing in the multiple-choice test introduction that the students should choose the *best* answer may help prevent lengthy discussion with the student who can dream up a remote instance in which the correct alternative might be wrong.

In taking a multiple-choice examination, the student has a right to know whether there is a penalty for guessing. For the typical classroom examination, there is no point in a correction for guessing.

HELPING STUDENTS BECOME TEST-WISE

Particularly in the case of multiple-choice examinations, I have found that a good morale builder is spending 15 minutes or so the day before the first test telling students how to take a test of this sort.

Some of the points that I make in such a lecture follow.

Taking Multiple-Choice Tests

The student taking a multiple-choice examination is essentially in the same position as a poker player. The object is to get into a position where you are betting on a sure thing. If this is impossible, at least make your bet on the choice where the odds are in your favor. In poker, you are obviously in the strongest position if you know exactly what the opponent has; and in the examination situation, you are also in the strongest position if you know the material. There is no substitute for study. At the same time, it is unlikely that you will be absolutely certain of all the right answers. In these cases certain techniques may help.

What I recommend (to the student) is this: go through the examination a first time and answer all of the items you know. In addition to getting a certain amount of the examination done without wasting too much time on single, difficult items, it is frequently true that going through the complete test once in this way will suggest the answers to questions that might have been difficult had they been answered in serial order. When you have gone through the test once in this fashion, go through it again and answer any questions that are now obvious. There will still usually remain a few questions that have been left unanswered. It is in connection with these that certain tricks may be useful.

First of all, if the item is multiple choice, don't simply guess at this stage of the game. See whether or not it is possible to eliminate some of the choices as incorrect. In a four-choice multiple-choice item, the probability of getting the answer right by pure guesswork is one in four; if you can eliminate two of them, your chances are 50-50. So take advantage of the mathematics of the situation.

Once some of the answers are eliminated, there are still better ways of answering the questions than pure guesswork. One of these is to choose the answer that you first thought was right. A second is to choose one of the middle alternatives. If you have no notion at all as to the right answer, and if the "b" or "2" choice is one of the possibilities, use it. There are two reasons for this advice: (1) it gives you a rule of thumb by which you can answer all highly doubtful items, thus eliminating anxiety-building, trial-and-error behavior, and (2) it takes into account instructor behavior in constructing items.

When instructors set out to make up a multiple-choice item, they usually have (1) a bit of information for which they want to test, (2) a notion as to what is the right answer, and (3) one or more "seductive" alternatives. The tendency is, in listing choices, to make the first choice one of the seductive alternatives, the second choice the right answer, and the remaining choices anything else that they can think of. Instructors have a feeling that the right answer sticks out if it is first or last. Hence the correct answer on instructor-made tests tends to be in the middle.

Once the examination has been answered completely, it is a good idea to go through the whole thing again to check your choices on the various items to make sure that they are the ones you still regard as correct and to make sure that you have made no clerical errors in recording them. In this connection, it is worthwhile to point out the common misconception that, when you change your answers, you usually change from right answers to wrong ones. As a matter of fact, Mueller and Wasser (1977) reviewed 18 studies demonstrating that most students gain more than they lose on changed answers.

Taking Essay Tests

My instructions for essay exams are simpler. First, outline your answer before writing it. This provides a check against the common error of omitting completely one part of the answer. If a question completely baffles you, start writing on the back of your paper anything you know that could possibly be relevant. This starts your memory functioning, and usually you'll soon find that you have some relevant ideas. If you are still at a loss, admit it and write a question you can answer, and answer it. Most instructors will give you at least a few points more than if you wrote nothing.

Some will perhaps want to question whether it is wise to give away the secret of examination construction the way I am doing in this discussion. The answer to this question depends on your purposes in giving the examination. If you want to test for "test-taking" ability, you will not want to give the students these hints. At any rate, this orientation seems to have the effect of giving students the notion that you are not out to "outsmart" them, but that you are interested in helping them get as high a grade as their learning warrants. In this connection, it is a good idea to point out to the class that you are not out to trick them and that ordinarily the answer that they think is the right one will be the right one.

I also warn students that their grade will be affected by their writing.

Even if I intended not to grade on writing ability, my judgment is negatively influenced when I have to struggle to read poor handwriting or surmount poor grammar and sentence structure. Moreover, since I believe that every course is responsible for teaching writing, writing will enter into my grading.

It is amazing to me that, when I forget to mention writing, the essays are much less readable than when I announce that writing counts. Apparently my students can spell, punctuate, and write clearly if they need to, but don't bother if it isn't expected.

Research by McKeachie, Pollie, and Speisman (1955) and by Smith and Rockett (1958) has demonstrated that on multiple-choice tests the instruction "Feel free to write comments," with blank space by each question for the comments, results in higher scores, especially for anxious students.

Another technique I have tried is to permit students to bring a file card to class with as much information as they can cram onto it. Preparing the card requires students to think about what is important. This aids learning and memory; Steyn, Marais, and Rens (1996) showed that it reduces test anxiety.

ADMINISTERING THE TEST

Handing out a test should be a simple matter. Usually it is, but in large classes, simple administrative matters can become disasters. It is hard to imagine how angry and upset students can become while waiting only ten minutes for the proctors to finish distributing the test forms. And if this doesn't move you, imagine your feelings when you find that you don't have enough tests for all of the students. (It has happened to me twice—deserving a place among my worst moments in teaching!)

How can you avoid such problems?

1. If you are having tests duplicated, ask for at least 10 percent extra—more if the test is administered in several rooms. (Some proctor always walks off with too many.) This gives you insurance against miscounting and against omitted or blank pages on some copies.

2. Unless there is some compelling reason to distribute the tests later, have your proctors pass out the tests as students come into the room. This protects students from mounting waves of panic while they wait for the test to be distributed.

3. Minimize interruptions. Tell students before the exam that you will write announcements, instructions, or corrections on the blackboard. Some exam periods are less a measure of achievement than a test of the students' ability to work despite the instructor's interruptions.

Grading Essay Questions

I recommend that you use essay questions because of their powerful effect on the way students study, but there is a drawback. Instructors don't grade essay tests very reliably.

One of the problems is that standards vary. First papers are graded differently than later papers; a paper graded immediately after several poor papers is graded differently than one graded after several good papers.

There are eight procedures you can initiate to improve your evaluation of essay examinations—but they entail work.

1. Establish a set of criteria—not just a list of facts to be included. Are you looking for integration, for analysis, for rational arguments, for and against a conclusion? Be prepared to modify your criteria as you find student responses that you hadn't thought of.

2. Read exams without knowledge of the name of the writer.

3. Read all or several of the examinations in a preliminary fashion to establish some notion of the general level of performance.

4. Write (or choose after reading several papers) models of excellent, good, adequate, and poor papers to which you can refer to refresh your memory of the standards by which you are grading. This technique is particularly useful if an assistant is helping to grade or if grading is carried out over a period of time.

5. Having identified papers of differing levels of excellence, compare them to determine what the distinguishing features were.

You will find some characteristics that were not in your original criteria. Now set up the criteria you will use.

6. Write specific comments on the papers. One of the problems in using essay exams and in assigning term papers is that students feel that the grading represents some mysterious, unfathomable bias. The more that you can write helpful comments on the paper, the more students will learn. (I say more about this in Chapter 10, "Teaching Students to Learn through Writing: Journals, Reports, and Papers.")

7. Develop a code for common comments. For example, you might want to use a vertical line alongside paragraphs that are particularly good or "NFD" for "needs further development."

8. Give a global grade. Don't simply give points for each concept or fact mentioned. This simply converts the essay into a recall test rather than measuring higher-level goals of integration and evaluation.

9. If possible, do your grading in teams. My teaching assistants and I gather after administering a test. We bring in draft model answers for each question. We discuss what we expect as answers on each question. We then establish two- to three-person teams for each essay question. Each team then picks 8 to 12 test papers which are circulated among the team members, with each team member noting privately his or her grade for the question. The team then compares grades and discusses discrepancies until it has reached consensus. A second group of tests is then graded in the same way, with grades compared and discrepancies discussed. This procedure continues until the team is confident that it has arrived at common criteria. From this point on, each member grades independently. When a team member is not sure how to grade a paper, it is passed to another team member for an opinion.

We stay with the grading until all the papers are done, but we make a party of it to alleviate fatigue and boredom. Funny answers are read aloud. Sandwiches are brought in from a delicatessen. Teams help other teams for a change of pace or to balance the workload.

Grading papers is still time-consuming but does not become the sort of aversive task that makes for procrastination and long delays in providing feedback to students.

Helping Students Learn from the Test

The most important function of testing is *not* to provide a basis for grading. Rather, tests are an important educational tool. Not only do they direct students' studying, but they can provide important corrective feedback. The comments written on essay tests are far more important than the grade.*

What kind of comments are helpful? First of all, rid yourself of the usual teacher's notion that most inadequacies are due to a lack of knowledge, so that improvement rests simply on supplying the missing knowledge. Rather, we need to look for cues that will help us identify the students' representations of knowledge. Usually the students' problems arise from a lack of ability to see relationships, implications, or applications of material. There is always some discrepancy between the structure of knowledge in the student's mind and that in the instructor's. Students construct their own knowledge based on their individual past experiences and their experiences in the course. Thus comments on essay items are more likely to be helpful if they help students find alternative ways of looking at the problem rather than simply noting that something is wrong.

Comments that provide correction and guidance may not achieve their purpose if students become so discouraged that they give up. Thus the motivational as well as the cognitive aspects of comments need to be considered. Misconceptions need to be identified, but not in overwhelming number. Encouragement and guidance for improvement should set the overall tone. Feedback that helps students see their progress helps build self-efficacy and motivation for further learning.

---

*This holds true except for the final course examination. In my experience few do more than look at the grade on a final examination.

Helping Yourself Learn from the Test

Often we get so wrapped up in the pure mechanics of correcting and grading tests that we overlook the fact that measures of student performance not only can diagnose student weaknesses but also can reveal areas in which our teaching has failed to achieve its purposes. Once you've achieved some ease with the grading process, look back at the papers to see what they reveal about problems in student understanding. There may be some things about which the entire class seems a bit shaky; in addition there may be areas of difficulty experienced by certain sub-groups of students—perhaps those with background knowledge or experience different from the rest of the class. In short, think about what *you* need to do as well as about what the *students* need to do.

Grading "on the Curve": Don't Do It!*

The papers have been corrected, errors noted, comments written, but now you have to worry about grading. I'll have more to say about grading in Chapter 9, but for the moment let's consider grades given on a test when you are expected to convert a number of points into a letter grade such as A, B, C, D, or F.

Grading based on *relative* achievement in a given group may encourage an undesirably high degree of competition. Despite the absence of absolute standards in any very objective sense, I believe that attempts to avoid competitive grading systems are worthwhile. Grading on the curve stacks the cards against cooperative learning because helping classmates may lower one's own grade.

The problem of grading "on the curve" seems to arouse the most heated discussion around standards for assigning failing grades. Logically, it would seem that an instructor should be able to designate some minimal essentials, mastery of which would be necessary for a passing grade.

---

*Grading "on the curve" means to assign grades on the basis of how each student compares with other students who took the test rather than on the basis of the degree to which the student has achieved some standard of performance. For example, in grading on the curve one might give the top 10 percent of the scores A's, the next 25 percent B's, the next 35 percent C's, the next 20 percent D's, and the bottom 10 percent F's.

I tell my students that I'll grade in terms of percentage of a possible score. Thus if a test has 150 possible points, I say:

If you make 140 or over (93%+), I'll guarantee an A

135 to 139 (90%+) A–

131 to 134 (87%+) B+

125 to 130 (83%+) B

120 to 124 (80%+) B–, etc.

If everyone gets over 140 points, everyone will get an A, and I'll be very pleased if you all do well.

I tell the students that I may grade more generously than the standards I have announced but will promise not to be tougher than announced. As it turns out, my distribution of grades has not turned out to be more generous than that of my colleagues—which may indicate that I'm not teaching as effectively as I'd like.

My "percentage of possible points" system is fairly easy to apply but lacks the educational value of criteria or standards tied more directly to course goals. Royce Sadler (1987) describes the use of exemplars and verbal descriptions of quality to set standards for grading.

Returning Test Papers

Remember that tests are important tools for learning and that discussion of the test is worthwhile use of class time. You might begin by asking students what they learned from the test. Were they accurate in their assessment of how well they had done? (Helping students learn to assess their own learning is a worthy objective.) You don't need to discuss every question, but where there are common errors, try to find out why the error occurred and suggest strategies for avoiding such problems in the future (see Schultz and Weinstein, 1990).

Students do learn from their corrected papers (McClusky, 1934). Although you may not wish to spend class time quibbling over some individual items, you should make known your willingness to discuss the test individually with students who have further questions.

On multiple-choice questions that many students missed, I recommend this sort of procedure:

Read the stem of the item and each of the choices. For each of the incorrect choices give your reasons for regarding it as incorrect.

This procedure gives you the jump on the chronic criticizer. It is more difficult to maintain that a given choice is right under these circumstances than it would be if you had said nothing about the various alternatives, and students could argue that the correct alternative was not completely correct.

There will still be cases in which a legitimate argument arises. If some ambiguities have gotten through the screening process, and an item is really capable of two equally correct interpretations, admit it and change scores. But remember that you can't escape aggression simply by changing scores, because every time you admit a new right answer, the students who originally had the question right are likely to feel injured.

For essay tests I try to describe what we expected in a good answer and the most common inadequacies. I may read an example of a good answer (without identifying the student), and I might construct a synthetic poor answer to contrast with the good one.

Dealing with an Aggrieved Student

What about the student who comes to your office in great anger or with a desperate appeal for sympathy but no educationally valid reason for changing the test grade? First of all, listen. Engaging in a debate will simply prolong the unpleasantness.

Once you have heard the student out, if you have decided not to change the grade, try to convert the discussion from one of stonewall resistance to problem solving. Try to help the student find alternative modes of study that will produce better results. "What can we do to help you do better next time?" Encourage the student to shift from blaming you or the test toward motivation to work more effectively. Ask the student to summarize what he or she plans to do before the next test.

My colleague Deborah Keller-Cohen asks students coming to see her with complaints about grades to write a paragraph describing their complaint or point of view. She declares her willingness to go over the test of anyone who brings in such a paragraph, noting that she may change the grade either positively or negatively. She reports that this technique has a calming effect, resulting in fewer unfounded complaints and more rational discussion with those who do come in.

While these suggestions may save the instructor some bitter moments, they cannot substitute for the time (and it takes lots) devoted to the construction of good tests.

What Do You Do About the Student Who Missed the Test?

In any large class some students are absent from the test. Their excuses vary from very legitimate to very suspicious, but making that discrimination is not always easy.

Makeup tests can involve a good deal of extra work for the instructor. If you devise a new test, you may have trouble assigning a norm with which to grade the makeup comparable to grades on the original test. If you use the same test that the student missed, you cannot tell how much the student has learned about the test from students who took it at the scheduled time. I simply use marks from the tests the student did take to determine the grade, counting the missed test neither for nor against the student.

OTHER METHODS OF ASSESSING LEARNING

Performance Assessment

Over two decades ago, Alverno College instituted a student-centered curriculum and performance assessment plan that has been a significant model for American colleges and universities. Faculty members construct learning situations in which they can observe student performance and judge the performance on the basis of specified criteria. The faculty has defined developmental levels in each of several abilities that students are expected to achieve. Since no one situation is sufficient for assessing a complex ability, the assessment plan stresses multiple modes of assessment related to real-life contexts. In addition, faculty actively train students in methods of self-assessment, an important outcome if students are to continue learning when there are no longer teachers around to evaluate their work (see Alverno College Faculty, 1994; Mentkowski & Loacker, 1985).

Many other college teachers are now using methods of evaluating learning that are more authentically related to later uses of learning than are conventional tests. For example, in chemistry, mathematics, and engineering courses instructors now use fewer standard abstract problems that can be solved by algorithms and more problems describing situations in which more than one approach could be used and in which alternative solutions are possible.

Simulations (either on computers or role-played), hands-on field or laboratory exercises, research projects, and juried presentations (as are used in music, art, and architecture), are also examples of methods related more closely to later use of learning. Paper-and-pencil tasks may require similarity judgments, sorting, or successive choices or predictions following sequential presentation of information about a case, scenario, or situation.

Graphic Representations of Concepts

An organized framework of concepts is important for further learning and thinking. Graphic representations of conceptual relationships may be useful both for teaching and for assessing learning. Our research group (Naveh-Benjamin et al., 1986, 1989, 1991) has developed two methods (the "ordered tree" and "fill-in-the-structure," or FITS) that we have used to assess the development of conceptual relationships during college courses. In both of these methods the instructor chooses a number of concepts and arranges them in a hierarchical structure like that depicted in Figure 7.1 (which shows an example used in my Learning to Learn course). For the FITS task the instructor gives the students a copy of the basic structure with some concepts missing. The students are then asked to fill in the blanks.

Portfolios

Portfolios have traditionally been used in art or architecture classes, but they have become popular in a variety of subjects and

FIGURE 7.1   A Fill-in-the-Structure (FITS) Example

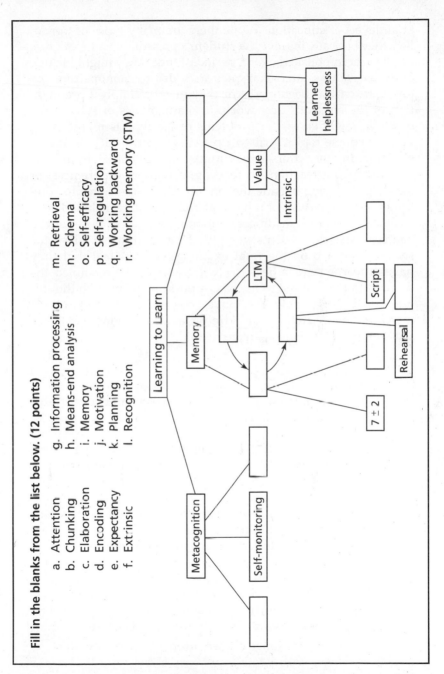

Fill in the blanks from the list below. (12 points)

a. Attention
b. Chunking
c. Elaboration
d. Encoding
e. Expectancy
f. Extrinsic
g. Information processing
h. Means-end analysis
i. Memory
j. Motivation
k. Planning
l. Recognition
m. Retrieval
n. Schema
o. Self-efficacy
p. Self-regulation
q. Working backward
r. Working memory (STM)

at all levels of education. While there are many types of portfolios, they basically involve the student's presentation of work that has been accomplished over a period of time. They might include early as well as later examples in order to demonstrate the progress that has been made, or they may be simply a presentation of the student's best work. In mathematics or science the portfolio might consist of problems or lab reports representing various course topics written up to show the student's understanding. In other courses they might include entries from journals describing reactions to reading, classroom experiences, or learning occurring outside the classroom. Papers, notes for presentations to the class, or other materials might be included.

One of the problems in conventional assessment in American courses is that the students who get a B on the first test, a B on the second, and a B on the final examination may feel that they haven't learned much because their grades have remained the same from the first test to the last. A portfolio helps both the students and me see how they have progressed. Students report increased self-awareness, and I frequently find evidence of learning that I would otherwise have missed.

Assessing Group Work

As teachers use more and more team projects and cooperative learning, one of the frequent questions is, "How can I assess group work?"

I've sometimes asked group members to write individual reports. Students are told that purely descriptive parts, such as the research design, may be the same on all papers, but that parts representing thinking are to represent the students' own thinking—although students are encouraged to read and discuss each other's papers before submitting them.

I've sometimes included an exam question relevant to the group projects; currently I ask each group to submit a single report which I evaluate. I also ask each student to turn in a slip of paper listing the members of his or her group and dividing 100 points in proportion to each member's contribution. Almost all groups apportion the points equally because I monitor the group's progress and try to get problems solved before the final product. In addition, students understand that the grade will be lowered for any student whose contribution is perceived to be less than that of other group members. Thus on a 100 point project I might give only 50 points to a student whose contributions were 10 percent or less as judged by his or her teammates. In most such cases I would have been aware of the problem earlier and discussed it with the group and the student, but even then I try to talk with the student before assigning the lower grade.

Classroom Assessment

As the title of this chapter indicated, the primary purpose of assessment is to provide feedback to students and teacher so that learning can be facilitated. *Classroom assessment* is the term popularized by Pat Cross and Tom Angelo to describe a variety of nongraded methods of getting feedback on student learning. I have already described minute papers in Chapter 6. Problem posting, discussed in Chapter 2, and the two-column method mentioned in Chapter 5 are ways of getting feedback as well as of facilitating student learning. Angelo and Cross (1993) describe a variety of classroom assessment techniques.

IN CONCLUSION

1. Learning is more important than grading.
2. Tests and other assessments should be learning experiences as well as evaluation devices.
3. Providing feedback is more important than assigning a grade. You can use nongraded evaluation as well as evaluation for assigning grades.
4. Try to assess attainment of all your objectives, even if some objectives (such as increased motivation for learning) are not appropriate criteria for grades.
5. Avoid evaluation devices that increase anxiety and competition.

Supplementary Reading

Paul Ramsden's chapter, Assessing for understanding, in his book *Learning to Teach in Higher Education* (London: Routledge, 1992) presents a wise perspective on assessment and gives examples from chemistry, anatomy, materials technology, engineering, history of art, statistics, medicine, and physics.

500 Tips on Assessment by Sally Brown, Phil Race, and Brenda Smith (London: Kogan Page, 1996) is a marvelous compendium of useful suggestions on all types of assessment, ranging from self-assessment through group assessment, multiple-choice tests, and assessment of performance, lab work, and dissertations.

Modern methods of assessing learner-centered courses are described in Graham Gibbs's book, *Assessing Student-centered Courses* (Oxford: Oxford Centre for Staff Development, 1995). Chapters give case studies illustrating assessment of group work, projects, journals, skills, and portfolios.

What to Do About Cheating

It may be hard for you to believe that your students would ever cheat—"Maybe other students cheat, but not mine!" Unfortunately, studies of cheating behavior invariably find that a significant percentage of students report that they have cheated. Most students would rather not cheat, but the pressures for good grades are so intense that many students feel that they, too, must cheat if they believe that other students are cheating. In my experience the most common excuse given by a student caught cheating is that other students were cheating and that the teacher didn't seem to care, at least not enough to do anything to prevent or stop cheating. Many students thus feel less stress when an examination is well managed and well proctored.

HOW DO STUDENTS CHEAT?

1. Students pass information to a neighbor; for example, they may loan a neighbor an eraser with the answer on the eraser.
2. Students use notes written on clothing, skin, or small note cards.
3. Students store answers in calculators or cassette recorders used during the exam.

4. Students peek at a knowledgeable neighbor's exam (sometimes seated in groups around the best student in the fraternity).

5. Students use a tapping or hand code.

6. Students accuse the teacher of losing an exam (which was not turned in).

7. Students pay someone else to take an exam or write a paper for them.

8. Students copy or paraphrase material for a paper without acknowledging the source.

PREVENTING CHEATING

"OK, so we want to prevent cheating. What can we do?"

An obvious first answer is to reduce the pressure. While you can't affect the general academic atmosphere that puts heavy emphasis on grades, you can influence the pressure in your own course, for example, by providing a number of opportunities for students to demonstrate achievement of course goals, rather than relying on a single examination.

A second answer is to make reasonable demands and write a reasonable and interesting test. Some cheating is simply the result of frustration and desperation arising from assignments too long to be covered adequately or tests requiring memorization of trivial details. In some cases cheating is simply a way of getting back at an unreasonable, hostile teacher.

A third answer is to develop group norms supporting honesty. I frequently give my classes a chance to vote on whether or not we will conduct the tests on the honor system. I announce that we will not use the honor system unless the vote is unanimous, since it will not work unless everyone feels committed to it. If the vote is unanimous, I remind the students of it on the day of the exam and ask whether they still wish to have the test under the honor system. While I haven't collected data on the success of this approach, I've never had a complaint about it. Although only a minority of classes vote for the honor system, a discussion of academic dishonesty is itself useful in helping students recognize why cheating is bad.

What else can be done?

One principle is to preserve each student's sense that he or she is an individual with a personal relationship both with the instructor and with other students. Students are not as likely to cheat in situations in which they are known as in situations in which they are anonymous members of a crowd. Thus, if a large course has regular meetings in small discussion or laboratory sections, there is likely to be less cheating if the test is administered in these groups than if the test is administered en masse. Moreover, if it is in their regular classroom, they may perform better because of the cues to their original learning (Metzger et al., 1979).

Even in small groups, cheating will occur if the instructor seems unconcerned. Graduate student teaching assistants often feel that any show of active proctoring will indicate that they do not trust the students. There is certainly a danger that the teacher will appear to be so poised to spring at a miscreant that the atmosphere becomes tense, but it is possible to convey a sense of alert helpfulness while strolling down the aisles or watching for questions.

The most common form of cheating is copying from another student's paper. To reduce this I usually ask to have a large enough exam room to enable students to sit in alternate seats. I write on the board before students arrive, "Take alternate seats." Some students fail to see the sign, so in large exams you not only need two proctors at each door passing out exams but at least one more to supervise seating.

In the event that you can't get rooms large enough to permit alternate seating, you probably should use two or more alternate forms of the test. Houston (1983) found that scrambling the order of items alone did not reduce cheating. Since I prefer to have items on a test follow the same order as the order in which the material has been discussed in the course, I scramble the order of items only within topics and also scramble the order of alternatives. I typically write separate sets of essay questions for the two tests. Since it is difficult to make two tests equally difficult, you probably will want to tabulate separate distributions of scores on each form of the test.

Whether you use one form or two, don't leave copies lying around your office or the typist's office. One of our students was nearly killed by a fall from a third-floor ledge outside the office where he hoped to steal the examination, and janitors have been bribed to turn over the contents of wastebaskets thought to contain discarded drafts of the test.

Plagiarism

If plagiarism occurs, sometimes it is simply the result of ignorance. Explaining what plagiarism is and indicating that it is a serious offense not only may prevent the naive student from plagiarizing but also may deter the intentional plagiarist. I discuss ways of preventing and handling plagiarism in Chapter 10.

All this advice will not eliminate cheating. It is a sad commentary on our educational system that it occurs, but recognizing and preventing problems is likely to be less unpleasant than ignoring them.

HANDLING CHEATING

Despite preventive measures, almost every instructor must at some time or another face the problem of what to do about a student who is cheating. For example, as you are administering an examination you note that a student's eyes are on his neighbor's rather than his own paper. Typically you do nothing at this time, for you don't want to embarrass an innocent student. But when the eyes again stray, you are faced with a decision about what to do.

Most colleges have rules about the procedures to be followed in case of cheating. Yet instructors are often reluctant to begin the procedure. The reasons for instructor reluctance vary. Sometimes it is simply uncertainty about whether or not cheating really occurred. Student's eyes do wander without cheating. Answers may be similar simply because two students have studied together. "If the student denies the charge, what evidence do I have to support my accusation?"

Again, unwillingness to invoke the regulations concerning cheating may be based on distrust of the justice of the eventual disposition of the case. Cheating is common in colleges; few teachers have not been guilty themselves at some stage in their academic careers. Thus most of us are understandably reluctant to subject the unfortunate one who gets caught to the drastic possible punishments that more skillful cheaters avoid. Such conflicts as these make the problem of handling a cheater one of the most disturbing of those a new teacher faces.

Unfortunately I've never been completely satisfied that I handle the problem adequately; so my "advice" should, like the rest of the advice in this book, be regarded simply as some ideas for your consideration rather than as dicta to be accepted verbatim.

First, let me support the value of following your college's procedures. Find out what they are and what legal precedents may affect what you should do. Even though it may not be long since you were taking examinations yourself, your role as a teacher requires that you represent established authority rather than the schoolboy code that rejects "tattlers." Moreover, your memories of student days may help you recall your own feelings when you saw someone cheating and the instructor took no action.

Further, student or faculty committees dealing with cheating are not as arbitrary and impersonal as you might expect. Typically, they attempt to get at the cause of the cheating and to help students solve their underlying problems. Being apprehended for cheating may, therefore, actually be of real long-term value to the students.

Finally, following college policies protects you in the rare case in which a student initiates legal action against you for an arbitrary punishment.

There still remain cases where the evidence is weak and you're not quite sure whether or not cheating actually occurred. Even here I advise against such individual action as reducing a grade. If you're wrong, the solution is unjust. If you're right, you've failed to give the student feedback which is likely to change his behavior. In such cases I advise calling the chairman of the committee handling cheating cases, the student's counselor, or some other experienced faculty member. It's surprising to find how often your suspicions fit in with other evidence about the student's behavior. Even when they don't, advice from someone who has additional information about the student will frequently be helpful.

Finally, let's return to the case of the straying eyes. Here you haven't time for a phone call to get advice; your decision has to be made now. Rather than arousing the whole class by snatching away the student's paper with a loud denunciation, I simply ask the student unobtrusively to move to a seat where he'll be less crowded. If he says he's not crowded, I simply whisper that I'd prefer that he move. So far no one's refused.

IN CONCLUSION

1. Prevention is preferable to punishment.
2. Dishonesty is less likely when students feel that the teacher and other students know them and trust them than in situations in which they feel alienated and anonymous.

Supplementary Reading

S. F. Davis, C. A. Grover, A. H. Becker, and L. N. McGregor, Academic Dishonesty: Prevalence, Determinants, Techniques, and Punishments, *Teaching of Psychology*, 1992, *19*(1), 16–20.

Jon McBurney, Cheating: Preventing and Dealing with Academic Dishonesty, *APS Observer*, January 1996, 32–35.

One might assume that it would be un-British to cheat. But Stephen Newstead, Arlyne Franklyn-Stokes, and Penny Armstrong found that British students are not much different from Americans in this respect. Their article Individual Differences in Student Cheating, *Journal of Educational Psychology*, 1996, *88*, 229–241, is consistent with American data.

The ABC's of Assigning Grades

Grading is currently in the news. Grade inflation, grading leniency, contract grading, mastery grading—all of these stimulate heated discussion and cries of dismay.* My own ideas of grading have become somewhat clearer as I have talked to my teaching assistants about grading policies, which may explain why I am less emotional about each of these issues.

Later in the chapter I will give you my viewpoint, but first let's agree that grades are fundamentally a method of communication. The question then becomes: What does the professor intend to communicate to whom?

When one puts grading into this context, three things become apparent:

1. Evaluation is a great deal more than giving a grade. In teaching, the major part of evaluation should be in the form of comments on papers, responses to student statements, conversations, and other means of helping students understand where they are and how to do better. A professor giving a course grade is

---

*Some definitions: *Grade inflation* The fact that the average grades in American colleges are now higher than they were 40 years ago. *Grading leniency* Giving higher grades than are usually assigned for a given level of achievement.

communicating to several groups—the student, professors teaching advanced courses, graduate or professional school admissions committees, prospective employers, and so on.

2. What professors communicate by a grade depends on the meaning of the grade to the person reading it—the effect that it has on that person.

3. Professors cannot change the meaning of grades unilaterally. The users' interpretations will be colored by their previous experiences with grades, and they are likely to be disturbed, or to feel that they are being misled, when a professor uses grades in new ways. This explains the strong emotional reaction to "grade inflation," "all A" grading, and other practices deviating from traditional meanings.

4. The meaning of A's, B's, and C's has changed over the 50 years I have taught. In 1946, C was the average grade. Today, B is more typical. But this is not a problem as long as those who assign and interpret grades understand the current meaning. Grading systems have changed periodically throughout the history of higher education.

What are grades used for? I suggest that the person reading a grade typically wants information with respect to some decision involving a judgment about the student's *future* performance. Mastery systems of grading, pass-fail grading, and other alternative systems are resisted because they may not be efficient conveyors of the information useful in predicting future performance. The box that begins below describes how three groups—students, professors, and employers—use grades.

What Do Students, Professors, and Employers Want from Grades?

Students

Students want to be able to use grades to assist them in decisions such as the following:

1. Will I do well if I take additional courses in this field?

(cont.)

2. Should I major in this field? Does it represent a potential career in which I'm likely to be successful?

3. Do I have the skills and ability necessary to work independently in this field—learning more, solving problems, able to evaluate my own work?

Professors

Professors advising the student or determining admissions expect the grade to tell them:

1. Does this student have the motivation, skills, knowledge, and ability needed to do well in advanced courses (insofar as the type of problems dealt with in the earlier course are relevant to the demands of the advanced courses or program)?

2. What kind of person is this? What does the pattern of grades tell us about this student's ability and work habits?

Employers

Similarly, prospective *employers* want to use grades to assist in decisions about whether or not the student will do well on the job.

1. How well will the student be able to solve problems on jobs related to the area of his or her coursework?

2. Does the overall pattern of grades indicate that this is the sort of person who will do well in our organization?

From this analysis it seems evident that grades are used not just as a historical record of what has happened but rather as information about what the student can do in situations outside the class for which the grade was awarded. For users, the grade is not so much historical as potentially predictive.

DO GRADES PROVIDE INFORMATION USEFUL FOR DECISION MAKING?

One of the arguments against conventional grading is that grades do not provide useful information for the major purposes for which they are usually used.

Most critics would grant that grades are useful for decisions about whether a student is likely to be able to succeed in an advanced course or in a further academic experience such as graduate or professional school, but they do not believe that they provide useful information for students or for potential employers, because the correlation with later occupational success are very low. (Pascarella & Terenzini, 1991).

Teachers assume that grades have some informational and motivational value for students. Critics argue that punishment and failure are not likely to be conducive to achieving the goal of continued enjoyment of learning, and that the threat of low grades is a crutch used to help inadequate teachers.

What about information for employers? Probably most personnel psychologists would agree that the best predictor of success on a job is successful performance on a similar job. For a young person entering the job market, the only previous employment has been in low-level part-time jobs. The employer's decision must then depend largely on other information, such as interviews, letters of recommendation, biographical data, family background, and test scores. Each source is only partially adequate. Insofar as the new job involves at least some expenditure for training, it seems likely that grades, representing the result of skills applied in study, learning, and problem solving, will add some useful information, albeit incomplete.

Since grades are commonly used in combination with other variables, however, one should not expect them to correlate with success for those selected. This is not simply a problem that only the top students were selected; it is a simple mathematical truism that, when one uses several selection criteria, each of which has some validity, one should expect low positive, zero, or even negative correlations between any one selection variable and the ultimate criterion of performance. This occurs because one will balance criteria against one another, selecting some people low in other important attributes because they have high grades and vice versa. Thus the common criticism that grades don't predict later performances is largely invalid since most of the studies cited have been carried out in situations where grades and other predictors have already been used in selection.

CONTRACT GRADING

In contract grading, students and instructors develop a written contract about what the student will do to achieve given grade levels. Contracts typically specify papers to be written, books to be read, projects to be completed, and so forth. With respect to the contract system of grading, it seems to me that the problem basically is that students often gain points, not for achievement, but rather for carrying out those activities, such as writing papers or reading books, that *should* be conducive to achievement. Thus, rather than measuring learning, you assess whether the student has engaged in activities that are the means to learning. I suspect that this means that in many cases there is a considerable gap between the points the student has earned and the points a similar student would earn if the student's achievement were assessed. If contract grading is used, criteria for *quality* as well as quantity of achievement are needed. See Table 9.1.

Assigning grades on the basis of the quantity of work done rather than the degree of competence achieved is not a problem restricted to contract grading. Many instructors subtract points for absences, tardiness, or other things they dislike. In psychology classes, points are sometimes added for participation in research studies, a very dubious practice unless it involves some assessment of what the students learned from research participation.

COMPETENCY-BASED GRADING

In "mastery," "competency-based," "performance-based," or "criterion-referenced" systems, the student is graded on a pass-fail basis for achieving mastery or competence in terms of carefully specified objectives. The real core of the problem may be in the use of the word *mastery*. The mastery concept essentially emphasizes reaching a particular finish line. In fact, however, most educational purposes in higher education have no end point, but are extensive in the breadth and depth of their possibilities. An achievement examination in a course is ordinarily designed to *sample* a domain of problems to solve, or concepts, or

	Pro	Con
Contract	Commitment to contract motivates students. May be individualized.	May reward quantity rather than quality.
Competency	Ties grade to course goals Encourages teacher and student to think about goals.	May be difficult to operationalize.
Both	Reduce student anxiety about competition and grades. Encourage student cooperation.	

TABLE 9.1   Contract Versus Competency Grading

generalizations, that the students will be able to generalize to a larger domain. The more limited the definition of those achievements that the students should "master," the less valid a test or grade is in terms of its ability to assess the students with respect to other problems, other concepts, or other generalizations in the total domain.

For example, suppose I give my students a list of five problems at the beginning of the semester and say, "My objectives are that you should be able to solve these five problems." In this situation most students will master the problems but differ substantially in their ability to solve other problems within the same general categories. Five problems that have *not* been specifically studied during the course would more likely be a reasonable sample of future problems students might encounter than five problems the students have already memorized, and a larger sample of problems from the domain would likely be even better.

Letting students turn in papers or book reports over and over again until they do them correctly is a fine teaching technique. However, the student who writes an acceptable book report after ten trials is probably less able to write a new report acceptably than the student who does it right in the first place. Thus the grade on such a rewritten paper should not be counted as equivalent to that of a paper that has not been rewritten.

Nonetheless, mastery learning has positive features. It forces the teacher to think about goals, and it focuses students' learning. Moreover, such a focus results in better retention (Kulik, Kulik, & Bangert-Drowns, 1988).

If all the work of the term has been done in groups, two approaches are possible (as discussed in Chapter 7).

1. Have each member of the group turn in a report, portfolio, or other evidence that can be assessed.

2. Have the group turn in such evidence, and ask each student to rate members of the group in terms of the percentage each contributed to the final product.

ASSIGNING GRADES

Because grades represent to many students a fearsome, mysterious dragon, anxiety can sometimes be reduced by encouraging the students to participate in planning the methods by which grades will be assigned. Students usually can recognize the instructor's need to conform to college policy in grade distribution, but the dragon seems less threatening if they have helped determine the system by which they are devoured (or rewarded). At the very least you should be clear about your criteria. Examples of previously graded work or tests may be helpful.

Some instructors have gone so far as to let students determine their own grades or to have groups of students grade one another. I like the idea that students should develop the capacity for self-evaluation, but I recognize that many students resist this procedure, either through modesty or fear that they'll underrate themselves. If you use it, I'd suggest thorough discussion of the plan with students and an agreed-upon, well-defined set of criteria that all students should use. Even if student participation is not possible, anxiety seems to be reduced if you explain the system you use and give your reasons for using this system.

You might also ask students to hand in their own estimates of their grades as an aid to knowing how to motivate them, and also in order to develop their abilities for self-evaluation. Atkinson and Litwin's (1960) theory of motivation suggests that the highest motivation to achieve occurs when the probability of success is moderate. This probably explains the finding of Means and Means (1971) that low-grade-point-average students achieved more when told that they had done well on an aptitude test, whereas high-grade-point-average students did better when told that they had done poorly. In general, motivation is not helped simply by giving high grades; nor is it helped by setting very tough standards. Students are most motivated when they feel that they can achieve success with a reasonable effort (Harter, 1978).

In keeping students informed during the course about where they stand, you probably are also helping them to control much of the anxiety they feel when the grading system is indefinite and unstructured. Sometimes it may seem easier to fight off grade-conscious students by being very indefinite about grades, but student morale is better when the students know the situation with which they must cope.

Whatever your grading strategy, being more generous in assigning grades to tests and papers than in the final distribution of grades guarantees visits from aggrieved students. One way in which you get yourself into this position is by providing opportunities for students to omit questions on an exam, to throw out the lowest test grade, or to submit extra work for a higher grade. Any of these procedures can have some educational justification, but if you expect to finish the course with grades representative of those for similar courses at your college, you need to devise a system of grading in which the constituents of the total grade will come out at an appropriate level in relation to the standards of grading at your college or university.

Professors sometimes devise systems of grading that allow students to drop out any test scores below A and are then surprised that their grade distribution is not comparable to that of other courses. You will find that your colleagues are not convinced that the students' level of achievement has improved so greatly in your class that they all deserve grades higher than those earned in other classes. Such grading leniency will not help your status in your department.

GRADING ON THE CURVE: A MILD REPRISE

In Chapter 7 we talked about grading a test on the curve. Now we extend our discussion to final course grades. One of the persistent controversies in college teaching is whether to grade "on the curve" or in terms of an absolute standard. In fact, these two positions are probably not as far apart as the argument would indicate. Even teachers who grade on the curve are influenced in setting their cutoff points between grades in terms of their feelings about whether this was a good or a poor class. Similarly, teachers who do not grade on the curve set their standards in terms of what previous experience leads them to regard as reasonable accomplishment in the course. As I indicated earlier, I believe that grading on the curve is educationally dysfunctional. If possible your grades should, both in the students' eyes and in actuality, be more nearly based on absolute standards than on relative standing in this particular class.

The use of an absolute standard is easier if you have formulated your major and minor objectives and tested their achievement. Travers (1950b) proposed one set of absolute standards:

- A: All major and minor goals achieved.
- B: All major goals achieved; some minor ones not.
- C: All major goals achieved; many minor ones not.
- D: A few major goals achieved, but student is not prepared for advanced work.
- E or F: None of the major goals achieved.

Ideally I should be able to list my goals for the course and at the end of the course have assessed each in such a way that I could use such a criterion-based system. In fact, however, my tests, papers, journals, research studies, and other elements of the assessment of learning are seldom pure measures of a single goal. For example, my tests assess knowledge and understanding of the major concepts and facts as well as ability to apply and think with these concepts. To separate out each component would be almost impossible. Consequently, I use the system described in Chapter 7—assigning points to each test, paper, and other assignments, and giving grades on the basis of the total percentage of points earned by the student over the term. This at least avoids the detrimental effects of grading students' performance relative to one another and probably approximates the outcomes described by Travers.

WHAT ABOUT THE STUDENT WHO WANTS A GRADE CHANGED?

If you have kept students informed of their grades on tests, papers, and other graded work during the term, you will have avoided most complaints. But there still may be some. My basic strategy is the same as that used in returning tests or papers: listen first, then go over the criteria used. Try to understand the student's reasoning. This may be a learning experience for both of you.

If students are worried about their grades in connection with their admission to a specialized school or because they are on probation, I may offer to write a letter to their advisor or other authorities describing their work in detail and pointing out any extenuating circumstances that may have influenced the grade. This may serve to cushion the refusal to change the grade.

In addition, of course, you may try to explain to the students the rationale of grades. Usually this doesn't seem to do much good. Both students and faculty sometimes confuse two possible criteria on which grades may be based. One of these is the relative amount of *progress* the student has made in achieving the goals of the course; the other is achievement of the goals of the course at the end of the term. In most classes, research has demonstrated a relatively low correlation between these two criteria. If you were to mark solely on progress, the students who came into the course with the least background might still be the poorest students in the class at the end of the course and get an A for their progress. Most employers, registrars, and professors interpret a grade in terms of achievement of course goals; hence professors who grade solely on the students' progress may send the students into advanced courses or jobs for which they lack the requisite skills and knowledge.

However, progress is also relevant to prediction. A student who has made a great deal of progress despite a poor background may do as well in a further course or job as some one with somewhat better performance at the end of the course who made relatively little progress. My own solution is to assign grades primarily in terms of achievement of course goals (total performance), but when a student's total points or overall performance is close to the boundary between grades, to assign the higher grade if there has been much progress.

No matter how you grade, some student will be unhappy. Be sympathetic, but beware! If you begin changing grades, the jungle drums of the campus will soon spread the word.

Don't finish reading this chapter with your own anxiety aroused by the dangers of grading. It is proper that good teachers should be humble as they see how great is the power they have over the happiness of their students by printing a simple A, B, C, or D. Nevertheless, one of the real satisfactions of teaching is giving a good grade to an ordinarily average student who has come to life in your course.

A List of Don'ts

These may look absurd, but they have all happened. Avoid making the same mistakes.

1. Never give students any idea of what their grades are before the final examination. The shock of seeing an F as the final grade will so stun them that they'll be incapable of protest. Or, better yet, tell them they had A's all the way through the course and got an A on the final, but you have given too many A's, so you're giving them B's.

2. Tell students that you really think they deserved a higher mark, but that you had to conform to department grading policies and hence had to grade them lower.

3. Tell students that their grades on the final exam were higher than their final grades in the course. (Of course they'll understand that the final examination is only one part of the total evaluation.)

4. Even though your school doesn't record pluses, tell students that their grades were D+, C+, or B+. They'll gladly accept the

(cont.)

fact that the C–, B– or A– was only a few points higher and will be proud that they did better than anyone else who got a D, C, or B.

5. If you make a distribution of total points earned on tests during the term, use large intervals, such as 80 to 90, 90 to 100. When you show a student her position on the distribution, she'll readily see that the person in the next interval above was really much superior.

6. Tell a student that grades are really very arbitrary, and that you could have split the B's from the C's in many different places, and that grades are so unreliable that you really can't distinguish your top B student from your low A student. He'll appreciate the aesthetic value of your choice of a cutting point.

RELEVANT RESEARCH

Not only do instructors control the pleasantness or unpleasantness of a good many student hours, but because of their power to assign grades they can block or facilitate the achievement of many important goals. The importance of this aspect of the teacher's role is indicated by studies of supervision in industry. In one such study it was discovered that workers were most likely to ask a supervisor for help if the supervisor did not have responsibility for evaluating his subordinates' (Ross, 1957). This implies that, as long as students are anxious about the grades the instructor will assign, they are likely to avoid exposing their own ignorance.

Students' anxieties about grades are likely to rise if their instructor's procedures make them uncertain about what they must do in order to attain a good grade. For many students, democratic methods seem unorganized and ambiguous. In an ordinary course students know they can pass by reading assignments and studying lecture notes, but in an extremely student-centered class they may find that the instructor doesn't lecture, doesn't make assignments, and doesn't even say which student comments are right or wrong. The student simply doesn't know what the instructor is trying to do. Thus, if your teaching or grading procedures differ from those your students are used to, you need to be especially careful to specify the procedures and criteria used in grading.

Some instructors have thought that the grade problem might be licked by using a cooperative system of grading. Deutsch (1949) found no differences in learning between students in groups graded cooperatively and those graded competitively, although the cooperative groups worked together more smoothly. Following up Deutsch's work, Haines and McKeachie (1967) also found no significant achievement advantages for students working cooperatively versus those working competitively for grades, but did find marked differences in group morale. Haines's work suggests that cooperative grading in the discussion can be successfully combined with individual grading on achievement tests. (See Chapters 7 and 14 for tips on grading groups.)

Complicating the problem of grading is the probability that low grades produce different effects on different students. Waterhouse and Child (1953) found that frustration produced deterioration in performance for subjects showing high interference tendencies (or anxiety) as measured by a questionnaire, but produced improved performance for those with low interference tendencies.

How do students learn to evaluate themselves? How do they learn to set goals for themselves? Do differing grading procedures facilitate or block such learning? To these questions we have few answers.

IN CONCLUSION

1. Grades are communication devices. Instructors cannot unilaterally change their meaning without distorting the communication process.

2. Grading standards differ from college to college and department to department, but there is some shared sense of the meaning of grades.

Supplementary Reading

What grades mean to faculty, parents, personnel directors, and students is described in H. R. Pollio, W. L. Humphreys, and O. Milton, Components of Contemporary Grade Meanings, *Contemporary Educational Psychology*, 1989, *14*, 77–91, and in O. Milton, H. R. Pollio, and J. Eison, *Making Sense of College Grades* (San Francisco: Jossey-Bass, 1986).

A fine vignette about the problem of assigning grades is Linc Fisch's "Students on the Line," in *The Chalk Dust Collection*, Stillwater, OK: New Forums Press, 1996, pp. 132–134.

Barbara Davis describes a number of systems for determining grades and gives sensible advice in her chapter Grading Practices (*Tools for Teaching*, San Francisco: Jossey-Bass, 1993).

Adding to Your Repertoire of Skills and Strategies for Facilitating Student Learning

CHAPTER

10

Teaching Students to Learn Through Writing: Papers, Journals, and Reports

· ·

When I began teaching, most courses in the social sciences and humanities required a term paper. Ordinarily papers were graded for the quality of the content and original thinking, disregarding the quality of writing (if this is possible). All too often, students looked at the grade on the term paper returned at the end of the term and paid little attention to helpful comments by the professor. The "writing across the curriculum" revolution taught us that thinking as well as writing is improved by the opportunity to get feedback on a first draft before turning in a paper for a grade. Thus more and more teachers are assigning several shorter papers with multiple drafts evaluated by peers or the teacher.

A LITTLE THEORY

Why does writing improve thinking? As I suggest in Chapter 27, skill in thinking is like musical and athletic skills. It takes practice to improve—particularly practice that enables one to see what works and what doesn't. Much of our thinking goes on in our minds, where it is not exposed to review. The very process of putting thoughts to paper forces clarification; seeing them on paper (or on the computer screen) facilitates our own evaluation; and receiving comments from peers or a teacher provides further help.

LOW-STAKES WRITING

One of the lessons I learned from training in "writing across the curriculum" is that students can learn a lot from low-stakes writing—writing that doesn't count for a grade. In fact, grading writing may interfere with learning. The "minute paper" described in Chapter 6 (and elsewhere) is a good example of low-stakes writing. Thus I begin this chapter with low-stakes writing and conclude with the traditional graded term paper.

THE STUDENT LOG OR JOURNAL

One example of low-stakes writing is a log or journal. My primary purpose in requiring a log or journal is to stimulate students to think about the course content outside the classroom context. A second goal is motivational. Choosing readings and experiences to write about ties course concepts to things that interest the student writer. A third goal is to develop habits and skills of using library resources which will be helpful when students run into problems or questions later in life.

Originally my journal assignment dealt only with readings chosen by the students outside the required assignments, but more recently I have encouraged students to write about anything in other courses or outside class that relates to the course. The log is described in my syllabus:

> The journal or log is not to be a "paper" in any formal way. It should demonstrate that you have thought about what you have read and experienced. How did it relate to other material of the course? Don't just summarize a reading. Write down your reactions, questions, comments, criticisms, and insights. Did you enjoy it?

Journals are turned in three times during the term. Students exchange journals the class period before each due date. The reader of the journal is encouraged to act as a coach rather than a critic. I write extensive comments both on the log and on the comments of the coach, pressing for active thinking. Thus the journal becomes a three-way dialog between the two students and me, as I give the pairs of students time to read each other's comments and mine when I return them.

Journals are not graded, but a specified number of points is allocated for writing the journal. However, I do tell students that full credit for the journals depends on an amount of reading and writing that is appropriate in relation to other course requirements (in my course, two to six hours a week). Over the course of the term, journals clearly improve in their quality of thinking, and I hope that the active observation and reading carries over to other courses and experiences after my course is over. Research evidence indicates that journals, as well as other writing, produce gains in learning, thinking, and motivation (Beach & Bridwell, 1984; Hettich, 1990).

THE TERM PAPER

When undergraduates are required to write a paper, they seem to face three alternatives:

1. Copy one from the World Wide Web, or borrow one from a friend or fraternity or sorority file. The student may have this retyped, and if there are no marks on it, simply retype the title page inserting his or her own name for that of the author.

2. Find a book in the library that covers the needed material. Copy it with varying degrees of paraphrasing and turn it in. Whether or not to list this book in the bibliography is a problem not yet adequately covered by student mores, although it is agreed that if it is listed in the bibliography it should be well hidden between two references with Russian (first choice) or German (second choice) authors.

3. Review relevant resources and, using powers of analysis and integration, develop a paper that reveals understanding and original thinking.

Most teachers prefer that their students adopt the third alternative. Few of us, however, have evolved techniques for eliminating the first two.

I start with the assumption that most students would rather not plagiarize. When they plagiarize it is because they feel trapped with no other way out. Typically in this situation the student feels that it is almost impossible to write a paper that will achieve a satisfactory grade. This may be because of self-perception of lack of ability or background. More often it results from a lack of planning; the student has arrived at the time the term paper is due with little preparation and no paper. The only way out seems to be to find an already-written paper.

How can one help students avoid such a trap? By pacing the student. I try to break the process of writing a term paper into a series of easy steps, such as:

1. Finding a topic

2. Gathering sources, data, or references

3. Developing an outline (I give my students a handout with an outline of the major sections to be included.)

4. Writing a first draft

5. Rewriting

In addition to an overall outline, I usually give my students advice about how to think about their paper. For example, I might ask students to choose an issue being discussed in the media to discuss from a psychological perspective. In this case I would say, "In writing your paper, first state the issue and explain its importance. Then assume that you are a prosecuting attorney presenting arguments and evidence for choosing one side of the issue. Then assume you are a defense attorney arguing the other side. Finally imagine that you are the judge stating your conclusions and the basis for them."*

I set deadlines for handing in a report at each step. When time permits, I meet with the student to discuss the paper at one of the

---

*I'm indebted to a British professor who described this in a faculty workshop I conducted at Oxford.

early steps. In the meeting I not only provide guidance, but also offer encouragement and motivation for doing well (and I can sometimes spot and discourage impending signs of plagiarism).

Other techniques I've used for discouraging plagiarism are:

1. Including on a test some questions that will require each student to use knowledge gained in preparing his or her term paper.
2. Having students give oral reports on their papers and answer questions from the class.

Dealing with Plagiarism

If, despite your preventive techniques, you suspect plagiarism, what should you do? Here you are in a conflict situation. Typically you don't want to reward plagiarism; yet it may be very difficult and time consuming to locate the original source. Without it you will probably not be able to take formal action. So should you forget it? No.

Ordinarily I recommend a conference with the student. You may use the indirect approach of discussing or questioning the student about the content of the paper to assess the student's knowledge, or you may be direct in expressing your suspicions. In many cases the student will admit plagiarism; in some cases you will encounter blustering anger. In any case you will need to arrive at a decision about (1) turning the case over to college discipline procedures, (2) permitting the student to write another paper, or (3) giving the paper full credit. Often I tell the student that I will consult my department chair or a respected colleague before making a final decision.

Giving a failing grade is probably the most frequent alternative chosen by teachers, but also the most problematic. The teacher is then vulnerable to a legal challenge of the grade for not following the college rules for disciplinary action.

Term Papers: A Reprise

If term papers are frequently inadequate, why would instructors bother to use them? As I see it, term papers attempt to gain two objectives:

1. To provide an opportunity for students to go beyond conventional course coverage and gain a feeling of expertise in some area. This is an important way in which students learn to value knowledge and learning.

2. To give students an opportunity to explore problems of special significance to them. In this way I hope to capture increased motivation.

TEACHING WRITING, GIVING FEEDBACK, AND CORRECTING PAPERS

"I'm teaching physics (or psychology or history). It's the job of the English Department to teach writing. It would be unfair to my students to evaluate their writing. Moreover, I've never had any training in teaching writing. I'm not even sure when to insert a comma in my own writing."

Such is the outcry in the professoriate when confronting the proposition that writing should be taught in all courses—across the curriculum.

There is some merit in the outcry. Few faculty members have been taught to teach writing—even fewer than have been taught to teach their own disciplines! But all of us have had substantial experience in writing—dissertations, reports, papers, books, and incidental letters. Writing is the very essence of academic life. "Publish or perish" is not an idle phrase. We write.

In addition to concerns about competence, faculty members have concerns about the time required. If one asks students to write more, how can one conscientiously comment on that writing without an impossible increase in time spent grading?

Here are some suggestions:

1. The professor is not the only person who can provide help on writing. Often peers can provide useful suggestions on their classmates' papers. To help students know what to look for, you can provide models—both of well-written papers on a given topic as well as of papers with your own comments about some common problems. Form subgroups of four or five students, and have each group read and comment on each other's papers.

2. A ten-page paper is not necessarily twice as valuable as a five-page paper. Short papers can be evaluated in less time than long papers and may provide sufficient stimulus for student thinking and sufficient opportunity for feedback.

3. Encourage students to revise their papers before turning them in, even if what is submitted is only a draft rather than the final paper. Developing the habit and skill of revising is worthwhile, and word processors make it easy. (And if the student takes time to revise, your time will be saved.)

4. Encourage students to submit a draft for feedback before submitting the paper for a grade. (The problem with the final version of papers is that, once a grade has been given, students sometimes ignore all other feedback.) Having a chance to try out ideas without risk helps free up students to be more thoughtful and creative. Hillocks (1982) found that focused teacher comments facilitate learning, but their effect is twice as great if students have a chance to revise their papers.

   When students submit their drafts, Barbara Cambridge (1996) asks them to attach three questions about what they'd like to know about the draft or what aspects they would like to improve. I like this because it encourages students to develop the ability to evaluate their own writing, and it gives us guidance about where to focus our comments.

5. Up to a point, more comments, and more specific comments, lead to greater learning. There are three kinds of qualifications to this statement:

   a. A student can be overloaded with feedback. There is a limited number of things a student can be expected to learn and remedy at one time.

   b. Motivation for improvement is affected by the balance of encouragement versus criticism. Feedback can be either helpful or detrimental (Kluger & DeKise, 1996). A heavy dose of criticism may cause a student to quit trying to improve.

   c. The type of comment makes a difference. Simply noting errors is not helpful if the student doesn't know how to correct the errors. Helpful comments provide guidance about how to improve.

6. Here are some examples of comments that might help:

"I don't quite follow your organization. Could you give me an outline along with your revision?"

"You state your position strongly, but you are weak in covering other positions. See if you can find others in class with a different position and listen to their arguments."

WHAT TO DO WHEN A PAPER IS TO BE GRADED

To help students learn to write and think, grades are of little value. Students need more information. Try to make your criteria clear. A good example of such a statement of criteria is the outline developed by Gary LaPree of Indiana University (LaPree, 1977) and contained in the box that begins below.

Criteria for Evaluating Term Papers

A. Content
1. Introduction
   a. Is the topic novel and original?
   b. Does the author state purpose, problem, or question to be considered?
   c. How does the author convince the reader that the paper is worth reading?
   d. Does the author present a preview of how the problem will be handled?
2. Body
   a. How are the statements made warranted? (Is there evidence that data collected have been analyzed and the literature reviewed? Are the assumptions logical?
   b. Presentation of evidence
      1. Is contradictory evidence dealt with adequately?
      2. Are multiple sources considered if available?

(cont.)

      3. Is the evidence discussed relevant to the purpose stated?

      4. Is the argument internally consistent? In other words, does one point follow from another?

      5. Is the argument plausible?

      6. Are the methods chosen for testing the argument convincing?

   c. Suitability of paper's focus

      1. Is the problem chosen focused enough to be adequately covered in the space of the paper?

      2. Is the problem chosen too specific for the author's sources of information?

   d. Background information

      1. Is enough information given to familiarize the reader with the problem?

      2. Is unimportant background material included?

   e. Is the presentation easy to follow and well organized?

   f. Does the author deal with the problem set up in the introduction?

 3. Conclusion

   a. Does the author summarize findings adequately?

   b. Is the conclusion directly related to the questions asked in the introduction?

   c. Does the author suggest areas where further work is needed?

B. Connections to class

1. Evidence that class materials have been read and understood

2. Application of lecture materials and assigned readings to paper

C. Form

1. Spelling

2. Grammar

3. Appropriate use of words

(cont.)

4. Paragraph form: Are ideas presented in coherent order?
5. Footnotes and bibliography: Are borrowed ideas and statements given credit? Is the form of the footnotes and bibliography understandable and consistent?

LaPree's list of criteria is not intended to be something one considers only after reading a paper, but rather is a guide to the teacher's active thought processes while reading student papers and for suggestions to be made to the student. Just as we teach students to read actively—questioning, relating, synthesizing— so we should be actively questioning the writer's thinking and expression as we read.

WHAT ABOUT DEADLINES AND STUDENTS WHO MISS THEM?

One of the banes of a teacher's existence is the paper or journal turned in after the due date. Some teachers refuse to accept late papers; more commonly we apply a sliding scale with increasing reduction of the grade the later the paper. Roberts and Semb (1990) let students choose their own deadlines, a method that should help motivation even though it failed to result in fewer late papers. I have sometimes asked the class to discuss the issue of deadlines and late papers, setting a due date that takes account of their schedules and mine. Regardless of the method you use, you need to leave yourself room for exceptions. Grandmothers sometimes really do die, and student illness and other emergencies may need to be recognized.

PORTFOLIOS

If you require more than one paper (perhaps short ones), you may want to reserve the grade for a portfolio (as I described in Chapter 1) rather than grading each paper separately. This gives the students a chance to show their development throughout the course.

IN CONCLUSION

1. Writing facilitates learning, memory, and thinking.
2. Development depends on feedback that provides guidance.
3. Feedback on nongraded writing or drafts of papers to be graded later contributes more to development than assigning a grade.
4. Prevent, in order to avoid punishing, plagiarism. If punishment is indicated, follow the procedures required by your institution.
5. Providing feedback takes time. Save time by encouraging peer feedback, self-evaluation, and shorter papers.

Supplementary Reading

Useful analyses of writing processes and implications for teaching may be found in:

L. W. Gregg and E. R. Steinberg (eds.) *Cognitive Processes in Writing* (Hillsdale, NJ: Lawrence Erlbaum, 1980). Note especially the chapter by Hayes and Flower.

E. P. Maimon, G. L. Belcher, G. W. Hearn, B. F. Nodine, and F. W. O'Connor, *Writing in the Arts and Sciences* (Cambridge, MA: Winthrop, 1981).

Ross MacDonald helpfully summarizes the research on feedback in Developing Students' Processing of Teacher Feedback in Composition Instruction, *Research in Developmental Education, 1991, 8 (5), 1–5.*

Writing to Learn: Strategies for Assigning and Responding to Writing Across the Disciplines—New Directions for Teaching and Learning, 1997, 69, edited by Mary Deane Sorcinelli and Peter Elbow, offers help on everything from types of assignments to grading.

E. M. White, *Teaching and Assessing Writing* (San Francisco: Jossey-Bass, 1994).

CommonSpace (Boston: Houghton Mifflin) is collaborative writing software developed for students and instructors who participate in the creation and revision of a document. This interaction might be between a professor and a student, a group of students working on a project, committee members revising a report, or an editor and author working on final changes in a manuscript. CommonSpace makes the inherent complexities of multiple inputs on multiple drafts easier to organize and track.

Teaching Students How to Learn More from Textbooks and Other Reading

11

· ·

While professors like to think that students learn from professors, it seems likely that students often learn more efficiently from reading than from listening. In Chapter 26 Claire Ellen Weinstein describes skills and strategies to improve learning and retention from reading. The journals described in Chapter 10 illustrate one attempt to get students into the library and reading primary sources. Nonetheless textbooks are still a basic tool for teaching most courses.

TEXTBOOKS

For decades the demise of the textbook has been eagerly predicted by advocates of each of the new panaceas for the problems of education. First television, then teaching machines, then the computer—each was expected to revolutionize education and free students and teachers from their longtime reliance on textbooks. But each of the new media has settled into its niche in the educational arsenal without dislodging the textbook. In fact, the greater availability of a wide variety of printed materials is probably as important as the technological revolution.

The introduction of open-stack libraries, paperback books, inexpensive reprint series, and the photocopier has given the college teacher the opportunity to choose from sources varying in style, level, and point of view. Many teachers are substituting paperback books, reprints, and collections of journal articles for the textbook as the sources of the basic information needed by students. But in most undergraduate courses there is little hope that bits and pieces will be integrated by students into a meaningful whole despite the valiant efforts of instructors to give assistance. Learning is facilitated by organization. Lacking organization, facts and concepts become so many nonsense syllables subject to interference, quickly forgotten and inaccessible. With input from field experience, discussion, paperbacks, reprints, the World Wide Web, and other sources, the student needs, more than ever, some frame of reference within which to assimilate the boomin', buzzin' confusion of points of view present in a modern course. Ideally, the textbook can provide such a structure.

Certainly, modern teachers should provide a variety of learning experiences for students. If individual differences are to be attended to in teaching, students need an opportunity to learn in laboratory settings, field experiences, discussion, lectures, or reading from diverse sources. Textbooks are an important part of the teacher's compendium of tools, and the newer teaching methods and aids supplement rather than supplant the textbook. In fact, a goodly part of higher education is education in how to read—how to read poems, how to read social science, how to read legal briefs, how to read the literature of our culture and our professions.

HOW DO YOU GET STUDENTS TO DO THE ASSIGNED READING?

The main reason students come to class unprepared is that they don't see what difference it makes. In many courses, textbook assignments and lectures are independent parts of the course, sometimes overlapping, sometimes supplementary, but often not perceived as interdependent. Thus the first strategy for encouraging reading is frequent use of the phrase "As you read in your textbook assignment for today, . . ." or the question "What was your reaction to [the author of the textbook]'s discussion of . . .?"

A second strategy is to have students write a "minute paper" at the beginning of occasional class periods on "The most important idea (or two or three ideas) I got from the assignment for today." Alternatively, you can have students write a question—either something they would like explained or something that was stimulated by the reading.

The basic problem often may be found in the meaning of the word *read*. To many, "read" is simply to pass one's eyes over the words as one does in reading a story. One has completed the assignment when one has reached the end of the assignment. We need to teach students how to read—how to read nonfiction with understanding, how to think about the purpose of the author, about relationships to earlier learning, about how they will use what they've read.

Research on Learning from Reading

A number of classic studies have compared printed materials with lectures, and the results—at least with difficult materials—favor print (Hartman, 1961). In fact Reder and Anderson (1982) found that students who studied textbook summaries scored better on achievement tests than those who read the entire text. The details in the text were distracting rather than supportive.

Study questions intended to guide the students' reading are often helpful. Marton and Säljö (1976b) found that questions designed to produce more thoughtful, integrative study were more effective than questions of fact.

Nevertheless, study questions do not automatically guarantee better learning. Students sometimes tended to look only for answers to the questions while disregarding the other content of the chapter (Marton and Säljö, 1976a). Andre (1987) reviewed meta-analyses and other studies of study questions and concluded that questions generally do aid learning and that higher-level questions, rather than low-level factual questions, increase the effectiveness of student processing of the reading. Similarly, Wilhite (1983) found that prequestions focusing on material at the top of the organizational structure facilitated learning, especially

Examples of Study Questions to Encourage Thought

Your assignment for Monday is to study the next chapter, "Memory." Here are some study questions:

1. How would you apply the idea of "depth of processing" to your learning from this chapter?

2. How does the limited capacity of working memory affect your learning in lecture classes?

3. How is the approach taken by researchers in memory like, and how is it different from, that taken by the researchers in learning you studied in the last chapter?

for the less able students. Instructors need questions that get students to *think* about the material.

Teaching Students to Learn More from Reading

We saw in Chapter 7 that students' study methods and learning were influenced by the sort of test questions they expected. Thus many students can read thoughtfully if tests require deeper understanding and thinking. But other students faithfully read and reread regardless of the type of assignment, memorizing definitions and facts without thought of the goal of the author and the relationship of this reading assignment to their previous learning. You can help by being explicit about why you chose the textbook and what you expect students to learn from it.

Recently I have put the students in my introductory psychology class into small groups on the first day of class to discuss what characteristics of textbooks help their learning. Then each student chooses two introductory psychology textbooks to compare before the next class meeting. At the next class the students report their findings, and each student chooses the textbook he or she prefers. This means that for the rest of the semester I need, in preparing for each class, to scan the three to six books that have been chosen, but this enriches the class discussions and seems to increase the meaningfulness of the students' study.

There is now ample evidence that students benefit from specific instruction in selecting main ideas, asking themselves questions, looking for organizational cues, and attempting to summarize or explain what they have read. Particularly in introductory classes you will help learning if you make explicit reference to your goal in assigning a particular chapter and discuss ways in which students can best achieve that goal (McKeachie, Pintrich & Lin, 1985; Weinstein & Mayer, 1986). Suggest that your students

1. Look at topic headings before studying the chapter.
2. Write down questions they would like to answer.
3. Make marginal notes as they read.
4. Underline or highlight important concepts.
5. Carry on an active dialog with the author.

For a fuller description of ways to help students become better learners, see Chapter 26.

IN CONCLUSION

1. Reading is an important tool for learning.
2. To facilitate learning, a teacher needs not only to choose appropriate reading materials but also to help students learn how to read them effectively.
3. Despite the availability of photocopies, coursepacks, paperbacks, and the World Wide Web, textbooks are still useful tools for teaching.
4. If material students need to learn is in print, in a form conveniently accessible for them, they will probably learn more efficiently from reading than from listening to you provide it in a lecture.

Supplementary Reading

Ference Marton, Dai Hounsell, and Noel Entwistle (eds.), *The Experience of Learning* (Edinburgh: Scottish Academic Press, 1984).

T. M. Chang, H. F. Crombag, K. D. J. M. van der Drift, and J. M. Moonen, *Distance Learning* (Boston: Kluwer-Nijhoff Publishing, 1983), Chapter 4.

C. E. Weinstein and R. E. Mayer, The Teaching of Learning Strategies, in M. Wittrock (ed.), *Handbook of Research on Teaching* (New York: Macmillan, 1983), pp. 315–327.

R. G. Crowder and R. K. Wagner. *The Psychology of Reading: An Introduction* (2nd ed.) (New York: Oxford University Press, 1992).

Laboratory Teaching: 12
Teaching Students
to Think Like Scientists*

The laboratory method is now so widely accepted as necessary for scientific education that it may seem heretical to ask whether laboratory experience is an effective way to achieve educational objectives. Fortunately there is evidence that laboratory instruction *can* be educational, but also evidence that it is often *not* effective.

Laboratory teaching assumes that first-hand experience in observation and manipulation of the materials of a science is superior to other methods of developing understanding and appreciation of research methods. Laboratory training is also frequently used to develop complex skills necessary for more advanced study or research and to develop familiarity with equipment, measures, and research tools.

From the standpoint of theory, the activity of the student, the sensorimotor nature of the experience, and the individualization of laboratory instruction should contribute positively to learning. However, information cannot usually be obtained by direct experience as rapidly as from abstractions presented orally or by

---

* This chapter deals with tradional "wet" labs. Computer simulation labs are discussed in Chapter 16.

printing. Films, demonstrations, science museums, and simulations may also shortcut some of the trial and error of the laboratory. Thus, one would not expect laboratory teaching to have an advantage over other teaching methods in amount of information learned. Rather one might expect the differences to be revealed in retention, in ability to apply learning, in actual skill in observation or manipulation of materials, and in understanding how scientists think and work. Unfortunately, little research has attempted to assess these special types of outcomes.

While reviews of research on laboratory teaching find that laboratory courses are effective in improving skills in handling apparatus or visual-motor skills, typical laboratories are generally not very effective in teaching scientific method or problem solving (Garrett & Roberts, 1982). Computer simulations can also effectively reach many of the objectives of laboratory teaching (Kozma, 1982). Involving students in faculty research projects also can help achieve these objectives (Davis, 1992), and is increasingly accepted as a vital part of a liberal education.

However, don't give up on the lab. Bainter (1955) found that a problem-solving method was superior to traditional laboratory manual methods in teaching students to apply principles of physics in interpreting phenomena. Lahti (1956) also found a problem-solving method to be superior to more conventional procedures in developing students' abilities to design an experiment. Lawrenz's cooperative-group inquiry-oriented lab produced gains in reasoning (1985). These studies point to the importance of developing understanding, rather than teaching problem solutions by going through a routine series of steps. Whether the laboratory is superior to the lecture-demonstration in developing understanding and problem-solving skills probably depends on the extent to which understanding of concepts and general problem-solving procedures are emphasized as opposed to "cookbook" methods.

TEACHING SCIENTIFIC PROBLEM SOLVING

In their book *Teaching in Laboratories* (1986), David Boud, Jeffrey Dunn, and Elizabeth Hegarty-Hazel point to scientific inquiry as the most important goal of laboratory teaching. The laboratory courses in chemistry supervised by my colleagues Nancy Koenigsberg Kerner, Seyhan Ege, and Brian Coppola offer good examples of modern problem-solving approaches. Students in Coppola's organic chemistry course work in groups on open-ended problems in which there may be several reasonable approaches and more than one possible satisfactory outcome. As compared with conventional courses, students in this course develop greater intrinsic motivation and better strategies for meaningful learning (Ege, Coppola, & Lawton, 1997). (See Chapters 14 and 16 for my discussions of cooperative and problem-based learning.)

In my own introductory psychology course, I have teams of three to five students design and carry out a research study. Since the study must be completed before the end of the semester, it obviously has to be limited, but the experience of developing a hypothesis and collecting data that will alter *a priori* probabilities with respect to the validity of the hypothesis is highly motivating as well as educational. Having students develop and carry out a research study is probably much easier in psychology than in other disciplines where the instructor's responsibility for safety is much more salient, but your success in giving students a sense that they are solving real problems rather than following a lab manual like a cookbook will determine, to a large extent, the degree to which you achieve the objectives of laboratory teaching.

IN CONCLUSION

1. Conventional laboratories have often failed to achieve their objectives.
2. Laboratories can teach scientific problem solving when the students have opportunities to work on open-ended problems in cooperative groups.

Supplementary Reading

The National Research Council Committee on Undergraduate Science Education, *Science Teaching Reconsidered* (Washington, DC: National Academy Press, 1997).

D. Boud, J. Dunn, and E. Hegarty-Hazel, *Teaching in Laboratories* (Guildford, Surrey, UK: Society for Research into Higher Education & NFER-NELSON, 1986).

S. N. Ege, B. F. Coppola, and R. G. Lawton, The University of Michigan Undergraduate Chemistry Curriculum: 1. Philosophy, Curriculum, and the Nature of Change. 2. Instructional Strategies and Assessment, *Journal of Chemical Education,* 1997, *74*, 74–94.

Many laboratory sections are taught by teaching assistants. Beverly Black, Martha Gach, and Nancy Kotzian have developed a useful *Guidebook for Teaching Labs* (Ann Arbor: Center for Research on Learning and Teaching, University of Michigan, 1996).

Experiential Learning: Service Learning, Fieldwork, and Collaborative Research

13

One of the valuable residues of the student revolution of the 1960s is the increased use of service learning and field experience as a part of undergraduate education. Not that field education was new. Cooperative education, in which periods of classroom education alternate with on-the-job experiences, had been successfully implemented well before the 1960s by Antioch College and several engineering and other colleges. Disciplines such as marine biology, forestry, archaeology, and geology had routinely required summer fieldwork.

But in the 1960s the educational value of direct experience converged with student idealism and desire for "relevant" meaningful service to produce numerous innovations in experiential education. At my own institution, the University of Michigan, "Project Outreach" became part of the introductory psychology program, and the sociology department initiated "Project Community." Students in these courses tutor schoolchildren, conduct recreational programs for patients in a mental hospital, visit and assist the elderly, and work with adolescents who are in detention for illegal activities. Both are still vital parts of our liberal arts curriculum.

Our department has also had a half-century tradition of involving undergraduates in collaborative research with faculty members. In recent years that program has expanded with university support for such collaborations. Service learning, fieldwork, experiential learning, and collaborative research all involve similar faculty-student relationships; the need to balance student independence and faculty guidance; the problem of preventing students from getting lost in the particulars of the project and missing the generalizable concepts, principles, and skills; and the need to give students experiences that build their sense of competence.

EXPERIENTIAL LEARNING

Experiential learning refers to a broad spectrum of educational experiences, such as community service, fieldwork, sensitivity training groups, internships, cooperative education involving work in business or industry, and undergraduate participation in faculty research. Clearly such experiences require new learning. But is such learning educational? To my mind the criterion is the degree to which the learning is transferable to other times and places. In deciding whether to develop an experiential "course" or to include experiential elements in an existing course, one must, as in making other educational choices, weigh the expected transferable outcomes derived from experience against the outcomes and costs likely from other educational activities.

WHAT ARE THE GOALS OF EXPERIENTIAL LEARNING?

Experiential learning has both cognitive and motivational goals. Educators hope that abstract concepts will become meaningful when students see that they are helpful in describing and understanding "real-life" phenomena. Similarly, we hope that experiences in the field or laboratory will stir up questions in students' minds that will lead to active learning. Such questions and students' reports of their experiences give students something to talk about in class discussions. Most importantly, actual experience can link learning, thinking, and doing. Teachers hope that field experiences will not only motivate students to learn current course materials but also increase their intrinsic interest in further learning. As a result of the experience, they learn both concepts and how the concepts relate to people; they learn both strategies for learning and strategies for dealing with social situations. Similarly, experience in collaborative research increases intrinsic motivation for research.

An associated goal, important to me, is to increase students' motivation to be of service to others. I am impressed that, even in the materialistic culture of the 1980s, students in my courses found great satisfaction in being helpful to older people, children, their peers, and other human beings. In the 1990s the *Chronicle of Higher Education* and other newspapers reported increased student involvement in volunteer work involving service to others.

ARE THESE GOALS ACHIEVED?

In the ninth edition of this book I said that there was little research evidence for the effectiveness of service learning. Since then a number of studies have reported positive findings. Markies, Howard, and King (1993) found positive effects on conceptual learning in a well-controlled study in political science. In another experiment comparing traditional instruction with the use of service learning. Kendrick (1996) found evidence of greater ability to apply course concepts to new situations and greater improvement in social responsibility and personal efficacy.

There is also evidence that service learning coupled with appropriate discussion can produce greater development in moral reasoning than discussion without service learning (Boss, 1994). Myers-Lipton (1994, 1996) found positive effects on racial prejudice and civic responsibility, but it took two years of service learning to produce significant effects.

HOW CAN WE GET BETTER OUTCOMES FROM EXPERIENTIAL LEARNING?

Supervising experiential learning requires finding a balance between student independence and teacher control. One needs to give the student sufficient freedom to make and learn from mistakes; yet you don't want students to lose so much time and become so frustrated that motivation disintegrates. As in other teaching methods, the ideal is to provide sufficient initial support and guidance so that the student can experience some progress, encouraging more independence as the student surmounts initial problems.

How does one ensure that the experience will be educational? Typically the answer is to require a journal or a written or oral report. The rationale for this is a good one. Generally speaking, research suggests that transfer is enhanced by verbalized concepts or principles. However, the key point, as in all education, is to think about the *goals* of the experience. Are students expected to learn how to apply concepts learned in previous or concomitant education? Are students expected to learn how to distill from real-life complexity generalizations or ideas useful in other situations? Is the experience designed to enhance motivation for learning and to facilitate personality development and altruistic values?

All too often, experiential learning is entered into as something obviously valuable without enough consideration of the values to be achieved. Consideration of goals is necessary if one is to work cooperatively with students to structure and evaluate the experiential learning. Diana Falk (1995) uses "preflection"—a discussion before beginning a service project in which students imagine what the experience will be like and express their feelings. This is also an opportunity for students to think about what they hope to learn and what they need to do to get the most out of this learning experience. You might even develop a contract (which can be revised as the experience develops) specifying the learning expected, the strategies (such as a journal) for achieving the goals, the deadlines, and the ways in which the students as well as the teacher can assess achievement of the goals.

As in the case of laboratories, the educational outcomes depend a great deal on the way field experiences are integrated with other educational experiences. Students in field experiences need to think about the meaning of the experience just as they need to think about their reading, classroom experiences, writing, and other educational activities. Discussions and lectures explicitly tied to field experiences, written reports and journals, oral presentations, and demonstrations are possible techniques for promoting long-term learning from field experiences. When service learning becomes an important part of the curriculum, reaching across several disciplines, institutions can have an important impact on their communities.

IN CONCLUSION

Experiential learning, whether in community service or in research, can be a powerful tool for enhancing both motivation and learning. But to be effective it requires careful planning, guidance, and evaluation.

Supplementary Reading

The classic book on the innovations in education in the 1960s is P. Runkel, R. Harrison, and M. Runkel (eds.), *The Changing College Classroom* (San Francisco: Jossey-Bass, 1972). Chapter 14 by Cytrynbaum and Mann is particularly relevant.

Another classic is Morris Keaton's book (with associates), *Experiential Learning: Rationale, Characteristics, and Assessment* (San Francisco: Jossey-Bass, 1976).

The two volumes of J. C. Kendall and associates (eds.), *Combining Service and Learning: A Resource Book for Community and Public Service* (Raleigh, NC: National Society for Internships and Experiential Education, 1990), provide both examples and practical advice.

Another set of two volumes is also a fine resource: J. Howard (ed.), *Praxis I: A Faculty Casebook on Community Service Learning* (Ann Arbor: OCLS Press, University of Michigan, 1993), and J. Galura, R. Meiland, R. Ross, M. J. Callon, and R. Smith (eds.), *Praxis II: Service Learning Resources for University Students, Staff, and Faculty.* (Ann Arbor: OCLS Press, University of Michigan, 1993).

14 Peer Learning, Collaborative Learning, Cooperative Learning*

One of the recurring criticisms of higher education is that it hasn't increased its productivity at the same rate as industry. By productivity critics typically mean that colleges should turn out more students using fewer teachers—as if colleges were factories producing shoes, automobiles, or soap.

The bottleneck in educational efficiency is that learning to think requires thinking and communicating the thinking through talking, writing, or doing, so that others can react to it. Unfortunately a professor can read only one paper at a time, can listen to only one student's comments at a time, and can respond with only one voice.

The problem is not one of communicating knowledge from professors to students more efficiently. Printed materials have done this very well for years, and for most educational purposes are still superior to any of the modern alternatives.

---

* This chapter deals with face-to-face peer learning. Diana Laurillard describes nonface-to-face discussion methods in Chapter 17. We shall use the term *peer learning* to include both "collaborative" and "cooperative" learning. Collaborative and cooperative learning involve peer learning in which there is interdependence of group members in working toward a common goal.

The problem is rather one of interaction between the learner and teacher. Fortunately, interactions that facilitate learning need not be limited to those with teachers. Often those with peers are more productive.

PEER LEARNING AND TEACHING

The best answer to the question: What is the most effective method of teaching? is that it depends on the goal, the student, the content, and the teacher. But the next best answer may be: Students teaching other students. There is a wealth of evidence that peer learning and teaching is extremely effective for a wide range of goals, content, and students of different levels and personalities (Johnson & Johnson, 1975; Johnson et al., 1981). Moreover, skill in working cooperatively is essential for most vocations. Miller and Groccia (1997) found that cooperative learning produced positive results in ability to work with others as well as better cognitive outcomes.

Suggestions for Students: How to Be an Effective Group

1. Be sure everyone contributes to discussion and to tasks.
2. Don't jump to conclusions too quickly. Be sure that minority ideas are considered.
3. Don't assume consensus because no one has opposed an idea or offered an alternative. Check agreement with each group member verbally, not just by a vote.
4. Set goals—immediate, intermediate, and long-term—but don't be afraid to change them as you progress.
5. Allocate tasks to be done. Be sure that each person knows what he or she is to do and what the deadline is. Check this before adjourning.
6. Be sure there is agreement on the time and place of the next meeting and on what you hope to accomplish.
7. Before ending a meeting, evaluate your group process. What might you try to do differently next time?

Here are some tips that may be helpful in initiating a variety of types of cooperative learning methods:

1. Explain why working together is important and valuable.
2. Make sure students know what their task is; for example, if it involves out-of-class work, give teams a few minutes before the end of the class period to make plans and to report to you what they plan to do.
3. For in-class group work, move around and listen in, to be sure students are not lost and confused.
4. Help students develop the skills they need for working together effectively.

STUDENT-LED DISCUSSIONS

In experiments in educational psychology and general psychology, Gruber and Weitman (1962) found that students taught in small, student-led discussion groups without a teacher not only did at least as well on a final examination as students who heard the teacher lecture, but also were superior in curiosity (as measured by question-asking behavior) and in interest in educational psychology. Romig (1972) and Beach (1960, 1968) report similar results in English and psychology classes: And Gruber and Weitman (1962) found that student-led groups in physics produced better complex problem solving.

Webb and Grib (1967) reported six studies in which significant differences in achievement and motivation favored student-led discussions over instructor-led classes. Webb and Grib also noted that students report that the sense of freedom to ask questions and express their own opinions is a major advantage of the student-led discussions.

How to Use Student-led Discussions

Do you just assign students to lead discussions of their peers? No. Student-led discussions don't give you a lot more free time. If the groups are to achieve the good results reported by researchers, you need to meet with the leaders to discuss issues that may arise and possible discussion-eliciting questions, and to make it clear that their status as leaders does not mean that they now have to play the role of experts. Questions that are not resolved can be referred back to you, to reading, or to World Wide Web resources.

PEER TUTORING

"Pay to be a tutor, not to be tutored" is the message from studies of peer tutoring. For example, Annis (1983a) compared learning under five conditions:

1. Students read a textbook passage.
2. Students read the passage and were taught by a peer.
3. Students did not read the passage but were taught by a peer.
4. Students read the passage and prepared to teach it to other students.
5. Students read the passage and taught it to another student.

The results demonstrated that teaching resulted in better learning than being taught. A similar study by Bargh and Schul (1980) also found positive results, with the largest part of the gain in retention being attributable to deeper studying of material when preparing to teach. These results fit well with contemporary theories of learning and memory. Preparing to teach and teaching involve active thought about the material, analysis and selection of main ideas, and processing the concepts into one's own thoughts and words. However, this does not mean that those being tutored fail to learn. Peer tutoring also helps those being tutored (Cohen, Kulik, & Kulik, 1982; Lidren, Meier, & Brigham, 1991). Hartman (1990) provides useful suggestions for training tutors.

THE LEARNING CELL

One of the best-developed systems for helping pairs of students learn more effectively is the "learning cell" developed by Marcel Goldschmid of the Swiss Federal Institute of Technology in Lausanne (Goldschmid, 1971). The learning cell, or student dyad, refs to a cooperative form of learning in pairs, in which students alternate asking and answering questions on commonly read materials.

1. To prepare for the learning cell, students read an assignment and write questions dealing with the major points raised in the reading or other related materials.

2. At the beginning of each class meeting, students are randomly assigned to pairs, and one partner, A, begins by asking the first question.

3. After having answered and perhaps having been corrected or given additional information, the second student, B, puts a question to A, and so on.

4. During this time, the instructor goes from dyad to dyad, giving feedback and asking and answering questions.*

A variation of this procedure has each student read (or prepare) different materials. In this case, A "teaches" B the essentials of his or her readings, then asks B prepared questions, whereupon they switch roles. Research by Goldschmid and his colleagues demonstrated that the learning cell is effective in a variety of disciplines (Goldschmid, 1975; Goldschmid & Shore, 1974). Training students to generate thought-provoking questions enhances learning (King, 1990; Pressley et al., 1992). Pairing can also be effectively used for interviews, discussion of an issue or questions, analyzing a case or problem, or summarizing a lecture or assigned reading.

TEAM LEARNING: SYNDICATE AND JIGSAW

The term *syndicate* has a faintly evil connotation in the United States, but in Great Britain and other countries, *syndicate* is used to describe a team-based system of learning that has proved to be effective. In syndicate-based peer learning, the class is divided into teams (or syndicates) of four to eight students. Each syndicate is given assignments (perhaps three or four questions).

---

* Students can also use the learning cell technique outside of class.

References are suggested, and members of the syndicate may divide up the readings. The findings may then be discussed by the various syndicates as they meet in small groups during the regular class period. The syndicate may then make a written or oral report to the class as a whole.

I have found that I get more interesting reports when I remind students that they have probably sometimes been bored by student reports. Hence they need to plan not only the content of the report but also how to make it interesting. I'm impressed by student creativity; my students have developed graphic and audio aids, skits, class participation, and other devices for motivating their classmates.

Hartman (1989) reports increased student motivation and student perceptions of deeper understanding as a result of the use of this method.

The *jigsaw* method, first developed by Elliot Aronson, begins like the syndicate by dividing a class into groups which are given assignments. Members of each group report back to their group, which agrees on what and how to present to the rest of the class. However, instead of a presentation to the entire class, each member of the group next meets in a new task group with one member from each of the other groups. In this new task group each student is responsible for teaching the students from the other groups what his group has learned. Since every student is thus in a group in which every group is represented, all students have the opportunity to learn the essence of all the assignments.

STUDENT CHARACTERISTICS AND PEER LEARNING

Peer learning works better for some students than others. Leith (1974a) found that introverts did about as well studying alone as in learning cells; extroverts did better in learning cells if their partners were also extroverts. A learning cell composed of an extrovert paired with an introvert was no more effective than individual learning. In summary, learning cells increase learning for some students and do not hurt the learning of any students.

When dealing with ability differences, however, it may be that heterogeneity is better than homogeneity. Larson, Dansereau, O'Donnell, Hythecker, Lambiotte, and Rocklin (1984) found that cooperative learners with partners with dissimilar vocabulary scores recalled more main ideas after studying a textbook passage not only on the passage studied cooperatively but on a passage studied individually.

Hall et al. (1988), in a review of studies on cooperative learning reported that cognitive differences among students affect learning in cooperative situations. Students strong in induction skill perform substantially better dyadically than individually, whereas the opposite was true for persons low in induction ability. In the case of field independence/dependence, pairs of heterogeneous abilities perform better than homogeneous pairs.

WHY DOES PEER LEARNING WORK?

Motivationally, peer learning has the advantages of interaction with a peer—an opportunity for mutual support and stimulation. (One piece of evidence for the motivational value of peer learning [Schomberg, 1986] is that it reduces absenteeism.) Cognitively it provides an opportunity for elaboration—putting material into one's own words—as well as a chance to begin using the language of the discipline. An effective partner can act as a model of useful strategies as well as a teacher. Several of the effective peer learning techniques involve alternating between listening and summarizing or explaining. Structures of peer learning that reduce the chance that one participant is simply a passive recipient seem likely to be better for both motivation and learning.

The task of the successful student in peer learning is to question, explain, express opinions, admit confusion, and reveal misconceptions; but at the same time the student must listen to peers, respond to their questions, question their opinions, and share information or concepts that will clear up their confusion. Accomplishing these tasks requires interpersonal as well as cognitive skills—being able to give feedback in nonthreatening, supportive ways, maintaining a focus on group goals, developing orderly task-oriented procedures, and developing and sustaining mutual tasks. It is little wonder that peer learning sometimes fails; the wonder is that it so frequently works. And it does.

Students are more likely to talk in small groups than in large ones; students who are confused are more likely to ask other students questions about their difficulties or failure to understand than to reveal these problems with a faculty member present. Students who are not confused must actively organize and reorganize their own learning in order to explain it. Thus both the confused and the unconfused benefit.

IN CONCLUSION

1. Students may learn more from interacting with other students than from listening to us. One of the best methods of gaining clearer, long-lasting understanding is explaining to someone else.
2. This does not mean that we can be eliminated or have time to loaf. More of our time will be spent in helping students work together effectively, less time in preparing lectures.

Supplementary Reading

The Johnson brothers at the University of Minnesota, D. W. Johnson and R. T. Johnson, are outstanding students of cooperative learning. Their book *Learning Together and Alone: Cooperation, Competition and Individualization* (Englewood Cliffs, NJ: Prentice-Hall, 1975) is a good summary of research at all levels of education.

One of the preeminent scholars of cooperative learning in higher education is Jim Cooper, who in 1991 initiated the newsletter *Cooperative Learning and College Teaching,* an excellent source of ideas for different ways of using cooperative learning. You can subscribe by writing:

Network for Cooperative Learning in Higher Education
Dr. Jim Cooper
HFA-B-316
CSU Dominquez Hills
1000 E. Victoria St.
Carson, CA 90747

Jim Cooper and Pamela Robinson have compiled an annotated bibliography of cooperative learning resources for science, mathematics, and technology courses.

A goldmine of helpful information is found in Philip Abrami's book *Classroom Connections: Understanding and Using Cooperative Learning* (Toronto: Harcourt Brace, 1995).

A good source for teachers as well as faculty developers is the article by L. K. Michaelsen, R. H. Black, and L. D. Fink, What every faculty developer needs to know about learning groups, in L. Richlin (ed.), *To Improve the Academy: Resources for Faculty, Instructional, and Organizational Development* (Stillwater, OK: New Forums Press, 1996).

In his book, *Collaborative Learning: Higher Education, Interdependence and the Authority of Knowledge* (Baltimore: Johns Hopkins Press, 1993), Kenneth Bruffee takes the position that knowledge is socially constructed. Whether or not you accept the social constructivist view, Bruffee's book is worth reading.

Project Methods, Independent Study, and One-on-One Teaching

15

If one goal of education is to help students develop the ability to continue learning after their formal education is complete, it seems reasonable that they should have supervised experience in learning independently—experience in which the instructor helps students learn how to formulate problems, find answers, and evaluate their progress themselves. One might expect the values of independent study to be greatest for students of high ability with a good deal of background in the area to be covered, since such students should be less likely to be overwhelmed by difficulties encountered. While this expectation contains some truth, motivation and work habits are also important. The material in this chapter is relevant to projects undertaken as part of a course, to senior and honors theses, and to supervision of graduate students.

Experiential learning (described in Chapter 13) also is aimed at the goal of leading students to view learning as going beyond classroom activities. Projects and independent study often include experiential learning experiences.

THE PROJECT METHOD

Independent study programs frequently involve the execution of projects in which a student, or group of students, undertakes to gather and integrate data relevant to some more or less important problem.

The results of research on the effectiveness of the project method are not particularly encouraging. One of the first "independent study" experiments was that of Seashore (1928). His course consisted primarily of guided individual study with written reports on eight projects, each of which took about a month to complete. Final examination scores, however, were no different for these students than for students taught by the usual lecture-discussion method (Scheidemann, 1929). Similar results were reported by Barnard (1936) for a "group study" method. In a study in a college botany course, Novak (1958) found that students in conventional classes learned more facts than did those taught by the project method. The project method was particularly ineffective for students in the middle third of the group in intelligence. Similarly, Goldstein (1956) reports that students taught pharmacology by a project method did not learn more than those taught in a standard laboratory.

With the support of the Fund for Advancement of Education, a number of colleges experimented with large programs of independent study. As with other comparisons of teaching methods, few large differences were found between achievement of students working independently and those taught in conventional classes. The expected gains in independence also often failed to materialize. Students taught by independent study did not always develop greater ability or motivation for learning independently. Nevertheless, a number of encouraging results emerged. One morsel of support comes from Thistlethwaite's (1960) finding that National Merit Scholars checked requirement of a term paper or laboratory project as one characteristic of their most stimulating course.

The student who completes a project often has a sense of mastery going well beyond that of completing a conventional assignment. Students working on a project have to solve real problems and to use their knowledge in new ways—characteristics of learning situations that both motivate and facilitate more lasting learning.

If we grant that projects sometimes fail to work well, what can we do to increase the probability of success? Here are three suggestions:

1. Be sure the student has a clear question, problem, or goal. This doesn't mean that the goal will necessarily be clear initially, but I do advocate monitoring students' progress in arriving at a goal that represents a problem that is meaningful for them.

2. Help students be explicit about the strategies they plan to use, about their time management, and how they will monitor their progress. This is a chance to get students to develop strategic learning.

3. Have students compare notes and get feedback on their progress from fellow students. Producing an independent product can be anxiety producing. Peer support can be helpful both substantively and emotionally.

But even if you use these strategies to help students prepare for independent study, a problem remains: your time. Supervision of independent study projects and theses takes time. Is there any way of reducing the time demands? Paradoxically, they involve reducing the one-on-one interactions assumed in independent study and using group strategies. In addition to the peer feedback in suggestion 3 above, you can do much of the planning and monitoring meetings with small groups of students. In fact, you can make the independent study project a small-group project—an alternative supported by research.

SMALL GROUP INDEPENDENT STUDY

Favorable results on independent study were obtained in the experiments carried out at the University of Colorado by Gruber and Weitman (1960). In a course in first-year English in which the group met only about 90 percent of the regularly scheduled hours and had little formal training on grammar, the self-directed study group was significantly superior to control groups on a test of grammar. In a course in physical optics, groups of students who attended class without the instructor but were free to consult him learned fewer facts and simple applications, but were superior to students in conventional classes in difficult applications and learning new material. Moreover, the areas of superiority were maintained in a retest three months later when the difference in factual knowledge had disappeared. In educational psychology, an experimental class of five or six students without the instructor was equal to a conventional three-lecture-a-week class in mastery of content, and tended to be superior on measures of curiosity. See Chapter 14 on peer learning for tips on guiding small groups.

RESEARCH ON VARIATIONS IN AMOUNT OF CLASSROOM TIME

Independent study experiments have varied greatly in the amount of assistance given students and in the patterning of instructional versus independent periods. For example, merely excusing students from attending class is one method of stimulating independent study. The results of such a procedure are not uniform but suggest that classroom experience is not essential for learning. However, different kinds of learning may take place out of class than in class.

The experiment reported by McKeachie, Lin, Forrin, and Teevan (1960) involved a fairly high degree of student-instructor contact. In this experiment, students normally met with the instructor in small groups weekly or biweekly, but students were free to consult the instructor whenever they wished to. The results of the experiment suggest that the "tutorial" students did not learn as much from the textbook as students taught in conventional lecture periods and discussion sections, but did develop stronger motivation both for course work and for continued learning after the course. This was indicated not only by responses to a questionnaire administered at the end of the course but also by the number of advanced psychology courses later elected.

The results of the studies in a child development course by Parsons (1957) and Parsons, Ketcham, and Beach (1958) were, in a sense, more favorable to independent study. In the latter experiment, four teaching methods were compared—lecture, instructor-led discussions, autonomous groups that did not come to class, and individual independent study in which each student was sent home with the syllabus, returning for the final examination. In both experiments, students working independently made the best scores on the final examination, which measured retention of factual material in the textbook. The instructor-led discussion groups were the lowest in performance on the final examination. There were no significant differences between groups on a measure of attitudes toward working with children. The authors explain their results in terms of the independent group's freedom from distraction by interesting examples, possible applications, or opposing points of view from those presented in the text.

Although the Parsons, Ketcham, and Beach results were favorable to independent study, they are not very satisfying to the advocate of this method, for they lead to the conclusion that if students know that they are going to be tested on the factual content of a particular book, it is more advantageous for them to read that book than to participate in other educational activities. But knowledge of specific facts is not the typical major objective of an independent study program. What instructors are hoping for is greater integration, increased purposefulness, and more intense motivation for further study. That independent study can achieve these ends is indicated by the Colorado and Michigan experiments. But the paucity of positive results suggests that we need more research on methods of selecting and training students for independent study, arranging the independent study experience, and measuring outcomes. Note that the Colorado and Michigan results came in courses in which a good deal of contact with the instructor was retained.

TIME IN CLASS

The independent study experiments demonstrate that education is not simply a function of time spent in a class with a teacher. Well-planned activities outside teacher-controlled classrooms can be at least as educational as conventional classes. But merely reducing time in class is not independent study. Generally speaking, the more time spent on learning, the greater the learning. Wakely, Marr, Plath, and Wilkins (1960) compared performance in a traditional four-hour-a-week lecture class with that in a class meeting only once a week to clear up questions on the textbook. In this experiment the traditional classes proved to be superior. Similarly, Paul (1932) found 55-minute class periods to be superior to 30-minute periods, as measured by student achievement. Shortening class periods, reducing the number of classes, and cutting the length of the academic term may be advisable as part of a planned educational change, but they should not be undertaken with the blithe assumption that the same educational outcomes will be achieved.

SENIOR PROJECTS

More and more departments require a project as part of a senior capstone course. The major problem departments encounter is a lack of faculty members and faculty time to provide adequate guidance and supervision. Even though senior projects usually involve the writing of individual theses, one can still gain some efficiency by grouping students with similar topics and encouraging cooperative work like that described in Chapter 14, "Peer Learning, Collaborative Learning, Cooperative Learning." Students can cooperate in digging out references for their review of previous research; they can provide frequent feedback to one another; they can support one another when barriers or blocks arise. The tips for term papers included in Chapter 10, "Teaching Students to Learn Through Writing: Journals, Reports, and Papers," as well as our discussion of projects earlier in this chapter, are also relevant here.

ONE-ON-ONE TEACHING

Independent study is only one example of teaching individual students. Music, art, physical education, dentistry, medicine, social work, and other fields all involve some individualized teaching one on one, and every teacher has occasions in which skills in tutoring or one-on-one teaching are needed.

There is relatively little research on one-on-one teaching methods, but several principles mentioned in earlier chapters are relevant:

1. Students are helped by a model of the desired performance. This may be provided by the instructor's demonstration of the technique, by a videotape, or by observation of a skilled performer. Generally speaking, positive examples are more helpful than examples of what not to do. When instructors perform, they should utilize the same techniques they use in presenting other visual aids, particularly in directing the student's attention to crucial aspects of the technique.

2. Students are helped by verbal cues or labels that identify key features of the skill. Students are likely to be distracted by irrelevant details.

3. "Bare bones," simplified simulations or demonstrations are more useful as starting points than complex real-life situations, which may overwhelm the student with too many details.

4. Permit students the maximum freedom to experience successful completion of a task or a part of a task, but give enough guidance so that they will not get bogged down in a rut of errors. This implies that the learning experiences of students go from the simple to the complex, with the steps so ordered that each new problem can be successfully solved.

5. Students need practice with feedback.

6. Feedback from the instructor or from peers may provide more information than the student can assimilate. Don't try to correct everything on the first trial.

7. Feedback can discourage students. Try to provide some encouraging feedback as well as identification of mistakes.

8. Feedback that identifies errors won't help if the learner doesn't know what to do to avoid the errors. Give guidance about what to try next.

9. High-level skills are developed through much practice. Simply reaching the point of successful performance once is not likely to achieve the degree of organization and automatization that is necessary for consistent success.

10. Practice with varied examples is likely to be both more motivating and more likely to transfer to out-of-class performance than is simple drill and repetition.

11. Coaching is not simply one-way telling and criticizing. Asking the learners about their perceptions of what they are doing and helping them evaluate their own performance is also important. In teaching self-evaluation, you may model the sort of analysis needed. As you evaluate work, verbalize the process you are using and the basis for your evaluation. Like other skills, self-evaluation is learned by practice with feedback. Thus students need many opportunities for self-evaluation with feedback *about their evaluation* as well as about the work being evaluated.

12. Peers can help one another. You don't need to monitor everyone all of the time.

IN CONCLUSION

There is an old saying that the ideal education would be Mark Hopkins on one end of a bench and a student on the other. Individualized instruction can be valuable, and in this chapter I have tried to suggest ways of maximizing its value. But there are many goals of learning that can be achieved as well or better in groups. Thus a good teacher should develop skills for using both.

Supplementary Reading

One of the most interesting, humorous, and wise books on teaching is Linc Fisch's *The Chalk-Dust Collection* (Stillwater, OK: New Forums Press, 1996). Chapter 1, "Coaching Mathematics and Other Sports," has much wisdom.

An excellent reference for project learning at all levels of education is P. C. Blumenfeld, E. Soloway, R. W. Marx, J. S. Krajcik, M. Guzdial, and A. Palinscar, Motivating Project-based Learning: Sustaining the Doing, Supporting the Learning, *Educational Psychologist*, 1991, *26*, 369–398. Although this article deals primarily with the project method in precollege education, the discussion of why projects help, how projects should be developed, and what kinds of difficulties occur is relevant for college teachers.

Problem-based Learning: Teaching with Cases, Simulations, and Games

16

PROBLEM-BASED LEARNING

Problem-based learning is (along with active learning, cooperative/collaborative learning, and technology) one of the most important developments in contemporary higher education. The ideas embodied in problem-based learning have a long history, ranging back at least to the use of cases in Harvard Medical School in the nineteenth century and extending through John Dewey's philosophy, Jerry Bruner's discovery learning, and the development of simulations in the 1960s. The current surge of interest, I believe, stems partly from McMaster University where, in 1969, the medical school replaced the traditional lectures in first-year basic science courses with courses that started with problems presented by patients' cases. A chemical engineering professor at McMaster, Don Peters, developed a problem-based approach for his courses, and another engineering professor, Charles Wales of West Virginia University, had a little earlier developed a problem-based method called "guided design." In a few years, courses and curricula in various disciplines in universities all over the world were using similar problem-based methods: In this chapter, I will describe guided design, the case method, and simulations—all variants of problem-based learning.

Steps in the Guided Design Process

1. State the problem and establish a goal that will be pursued in resolving it.

2. Gather information relevant to defining the problem and understanding the elements associated with it.

3. Generate possible solutions.

4. List possible constraints on what can be accomplished as well as factors that may facilitate getting a solution accepted.

5. Choose an initial or possible solution using criteria that an acceptable solution must meet. The criteria can include tangible and monetary costs and benefits, the likely acceptance of the solution by others, as well as discipline or other standard criteria normally applied to such problems.

6. Analyze the important factors that must be considered in the development of a detailed solution. What has to be done, who does it, when it should happen, and where the solution would be used are possible factors to explore.

7. Create a detailed solution.

8. Evaluate the final solution against the relevant criteria used earlier, to ensure that it meets at least those requirements and others that now appear to be necessary.

9. Recommend a course of action and, if appropriate, suggest ways to monitor and evaluate the solution when it is adopted.

Based on Wales & Nardi, 1982. Used by permission.

Problem-based education is based on the assumptions that human beings evolved as individuals who are motivated to solve problems, and that problem solvers will seek and learn whatever knowledge is needed for successful problem solving. Thus if an appropriate realistic problem is presented before study, students will identify needed information and be motivated to learn it. However, as in introducing any other method, you need to explain to students your purposes.

The steps involved in "guided design," described in the box above, are representative of those likely to be involved in many variations of problem-based learning.

In the McMaster model of problem-based learning, students meet in small groups with a tutor who acts as a facilitator. Although the facilitator is typically a faculty member, teaching assistants or peers can also be successful if trained. Typically, after the students have presented their recommendations, classroom discussion summarizes the learning that has occurred and integrates it with students' prior skills and knowledge.

THE CASE METHOD

As indicated earlier, the case method has been widely used in business and law courses for many years and is now being used in a variety of disciplines. Generally, case method discussions produce good student involvement. Case methods, like other problem-based methods, are intended to develop student ability to solve problems using knowledge, concepts, and skills relevant to a course. Cases provide contextualized learning, as contrasted with learning disassociated from meaningful contexts.

Cases are often actual descriptions of problem situations in the field in which the case is being used; sometimes they are syntheses constructed to represent a particular principle or type of problem. For example, in medicine a case may describe a patient and the patient's symptoms; in psychology the case might describe a group facing a decision; in biology the case might describe an environmental problem. Whatever the case, it typically involves the possibility of several alternative approaches or actions and some evaluation of values and costs of different solutions to the problem posed. Usually cases require that the students not only apply course content but also consult other resources.

Finding the Right Cases

You can write your own cases, but you may be able to find cases already written that are appropriate for your purposes and are motivating for your students. For example, Silverman, Welty, and Lyon (1994) have published cases for teacher education. Other cases can be found on the Internet.

Typically the case method involves a series of cases, but in some case method courses the cases are not well chosen to represent properly sequenced levels of difficulty. Often, in order to make cases realistic, so many details are included that beginning students lose the principles or points the case was intended to demonstrate. Teachers attempting to help students learn complex discriminations and principles in problem solving need to choose initial cases in which the differences are clear and extreme before moving to more subtle, complex cases. Typically, one of the goals of the case method is to teach students to select important factors from a tangle of less important ones which may nevertheless form a context to be considered. One does not learn such skills by being in perpetual confusion, but rather by success in solving more and more difficult problems.

The major problem in teaching by cases involves going from the students' fascination with the particular case to the general principle or conceptual structure. In choosing a case to discuss, the teacher needs to think, "What is this case a case *of*?"

Tips for Teaching with Cases

Usually cases are presented in writing, but you can use a videotape or you can role-play a problem situation. (Role playing is like a drama in which each participant is assigned a character to portray, but no lines are learned. The individuals portraying specific roles improvise their responses in a situation—a situation that presents a problem or conflict.)

Whatever method you use to present the problem, you should allow class time for students to ask questions about the process they are to use and to clarify the nature of the problem presented, but not about possible approaches or solutions to the problem.

You should clarify ways of going about the case study, such as:

1. What is the problem?
2. Develop hypotheses about what causes the problem.
3. What evidence can be gathered to support or discount any of the hypotheses?
4. What conclusions can be drawn? What recommendations?

Very likely you will want to form teams (as described in Chapter 14) and take time during class for the teams to agree on when to meet and to determine what they will do before their meeting. Some problems may involve work extending over several meetings in class and out of class.

When the teams report, your role is primarily to facilitate discussion—listening, questioning, clarifying, challenging, encouraging analysis and problem solving, and testing the validity of generalizations. You may want to use a blackboard or overhead to keep a running summary of points established, additional information needed, possible ethical or value considerations, and the evidence supporting alternative approaches.

If the case is one that actually occurred, students will want to find out what actually was done and how it worked out. You can have a productive discussion about how the actual process, variables considered, or strategies used differed from those in the class. Sometimes you might bring in someone working in the field so that the students cannot only see how an expert analyzes the case, but also ask questions about what really happens in practice.

GAMES AND SIMULATIONS

An educational game involves students in some sort of competition or achievement in relationship to a goal; it is a game that both teaches and is fun. Many games are simulations; for example, they attempt to model some real-life problem situation. Thus there are business games, international relations games, and many others. Whatever the topic, the planner of the game needs to specify the teaching objectives to be served by the game and then plan the game to highlight features that contribute to those objectives.

Early educational games often involved large-scale simulations in which participants played the roles of individuals or groups in some interpersonal, political, or social situation. Now many simulations are available on computers. Research and laboratory simulations are available for courses in the sciences, and interactive social simulations can be used to teach foreign languages. As I noted in Chapter 12 on laboratory teaching, the computer simulations are often more effective in teaching research methods than are traditional "wet labs." (Also see Chapter 17.)

As with other teaching methods, the effectiveness of simulations depends to some extent on the degree of instructional support or structure. Research on traditional as well as nontraditional teaching has shown that students with low prior knowledge tend to benefit from a higher degree of structure than students with greater knowledge or intelligence (Cronbach & Snow, 1977). Veenstra and Elshout's research (1995) on computer simulations in heat theory, electricity, and statistics found even more complex relationships. Structuredness made little difference for high-intelligence students; more structure enhanced learning for students with low intelligence and low metacognitive strategies (poor analysis, planning, evaluation, and work methods). But more structure impaired learning for low-intelligence students with high levels of metacognitive strategies.

The chief advantage of games and simulations is that students are active participants rather than passive observers. Students must make decisions, solve problems, and react to the results of their decisions. Lepper and Malone (1985) have studied the motivational elements in computer games. They found that key features are challenge, self-competence, curiosity, personal control, and fantasy.

There are now a number of well-designed games that have been used in enough situations to have the kinks worked out. Some use computers to implement the complex interaction of various decisions. One classic example is SIMSOC (Gamson, 1966), a sociology game in which students are citizens of a society in which they have economic and social roles; for example, some are members of political parties, and some have police powers. Games like this are useful in getting students to consider varied points of view relevant to the issues addressed in the game. Like the case method, an educational game may be either too simple or complex to achieve the kind of generalization of concepts or principles that the teacher desires. The biggest barrier to the use of games is logistic. Often it is hard to find a game that fits the time and facilities limitations of typical classes. Devising one's own game can be fun but also time consuming. Nonetheless, games are potentially useful tools for effective teaching.

IN CONCLUSION

Whether one uses cases, games, simulations, or other problems, problem-based learning is a valuable part of one's armamentarium of teaching strategies. In fact, even if you don't use problem-based learning in its traditional forms, the general principle that students like to solve problems that offer a challenge but are still solvable is important. And motivation isn't the only reason to use problems. If students are to learn how to think more effectively, they need to practice thinking. Moreover, cognitive theory provides good support for the idea that knowledge learned and used in a realistic, problem-solving context is more likely to be remembered and used appropriately when needed later.

There is a good deal of research on problem-based learning in its various forms, including case methods and simulations. My summation of the results is that, compared with traditional methods of teaching, problem-based learning may sometimes result in less acquisition of knowledge but typically shows little, if any, decrement. However, retention, application, and motivational outcomes are generally superior to those in traditional methods of instruction.

Supplementary Reading

Guided design is fully described in C. E. Wales and R. A. Stager, *Guided Design* (Morgantown: West Virginia University, 1977).

Donald Woods has published three useful books on problem-based learning: *Problem-based Learning: How to Gain the Most from PBL* (written for students), *Helping Your Students Gain the Most from PBL* (written for teachers), and *Resources to Gain the Most from PBL*. All three are published by Donald R. Woods, Department of Chemical Engineering, McMaster University, Hamilton, ON L85 4LT, Canada.

Practical help in using problem-based learning and in using role playing may be found in A. Grasha, *Teaching with Style* (Pittsburgh: Alliance Publishers, 1996).

LuAnn Wilkerson and W. H. Gigselaers (eds.), Bringing Problem-Based Learning to Higher Education: Theory and Practice, in *New Directions for Teaching and Learning*, No. 68 (San Francisco: Jossey-Bass, 1996), has chapters describing problem-based learning in a variety of courses.

Diana Laurillard has a good discussion of computer-based simulations in her book *Rethinking University Teaching: A Framework for the Effective Use of Educational Technology* (London: Routledge, 1993).

The Harvard Law and Business Schools were pioneers in using the case method. The following four references provide a good description of the methods they developed.

M. McNair (ed.), *The Case Method at the Harvard Business School* (New York: McGraw-Hill, 1954).

C. Argyris, Some Limitations of the Case Method, *Academy of Management Review*, 1980, 5, 291–298.

M. Berger, In Defense of the Case Method. A Reply to Argyris, *Academy of Management Review*, 1983, 8, 329–333.

C. R. Christensen and A. J. Hansen, *Teaching and the Case Method* (Boston: Harvard Business School, 1987).

A sophisticated description of the use of the case method in medical education as well as two experiments on activating and restructuring prior knowledge in case discussions may be found in H. G. Schmidt, *Activatie van Voorkennis, Intrinsieke Motivatie en de Verwerking van Tekst* (Apeldoorn, The Netherlands: Van Walraven bv, 1982). (Don't worry. Despite the Dutch title, the text is in English.)

A helpful general introduction to the case method is R. A. Weaver, T. J. Kowalski, & J. E. Pfaller, Case Method Teaching, in K. W. Prichard & R. McL. Sawyer (eds.), *Handbook of College Teaching: Theory and Applications* (Westport, CT: Greenwood Press).

Using Communications and Information Technology Effectively

17

There is often a sense of panic around the idea of learning technologies. It may be the panic of college administrators fearful of the capacity of commercial virtual universities to change higher education as we know it, or it may be the panic of the lecturers having to cope with a new method of teaching they have never experienced as learners. This chapter is an attempt to minimize the sense of panic and introduce some rationality.

WHY USE COMMUNICATIONS AND INFORMATION TECHNOLOGY FOR TEACHING?

There is no point in using communications and information technology (C&IT) unless it clearly improves the quality of learning in some way. Information technology is most importantly an *interactive* technology; it can be programmed to respond to a user's actions. This simple fact is the source of all our expectations of the value of C&IT in education. We know as educators that for students to learn they must be doing active cognitive processing (Grabe & Grabe, 1998). An interactive technology

This chapter was written by Diana Laurillard of the Open University.

provides a responsive environment, in which the student is invited to act and then receives some response. If we can program the electronic environment to invite the right kind of cognitive action, then we promote active learning, which is more productive and more stable than more passive forms of learning, such as listening to lectures.

We can usefully distinguish two different kinds of interaction: person-to-information via technology, and person-to-person via technology. The first includes the stand-alone information technologies of program on hard disk or CD-ROM, and networked technologies such as on-line databases and the web. The second includes communications technologies such as electronic mail, computer-mediated conferencing, and on-line discussion groups. Both kinds are of value in education, for different kinds of learning objectives.

Here are some examples of person-to-information interaction.

Person-to-Information Interaction

Learning Professional Practice   It is important for students to gain experience with the tools of their future trade, for computer-based application tools are now found in all professional work areas. Likewise, the curriculum of your subject area will necessarily be changing to reflect this change in the world of work, and your own professional updating will direct you toward what you should be offering your students. Examples of these tools are spreadsheets, data analysis, statistical analysis, computer-aided design, and project management tools.

Information-handling Skills   Information technology gives access to unmanageably large quantities of information, so an essential lifetime skill for our graduates is that they know how to search, evaluate, and select what they actually need from the mass of what is available. Both CD-ROM databases and the World Wide Web provide resources with which your students can practice information handling.

Rehearsal of Skills and Procedures   Rehearsal of this kind used to be known as "drill and practice," and although it is unfashionable, it is an ideal way to use a computer. What's more, students love it. For many types of topics, the software can automatically generate questions, and respond differently to right and wrong answers, and give the student plenty of practice in a series of examples. The feedback will not be sophisticated but can be sufficiently motivating to keep the student repeatedly working through examples. This gradually builds confidence in a non-threatening environment.

These are all examples of the student interacting with information, in its most general sense, in the program. No other person is involved, and the feedback from the program has to be designed in advance of the interaction.

Person-to-Person Interaction

The communications technologies are programmed to support interactions between people; the feedback is given by people, not a program; and the feedback is not designed in advance. Here are some examples of communications technologies used for teaching.

Practice in Discussion and Argument   Computerized communication can have surprising side-effects; we have found, for example, that some students are prepared to take a more active part in debates and tutorials if they can do so by electronic mail rather than face to face (Laurillard, 1993). This does not mean they are in danger of becoming isolated, unsocial individuals; rather, they are building up their confidence so that they are better able to cope with the difficulties of face-to-face interaction.

Articulating Ideas   The act of writing is good for clarifying ideas and understanding. E-mail and chat lines are already encouraging a greater degree of literacy simply by encouraging students to express themselves through the written word in order to communicate (Pea & Kurland, 1987).

Practice in Teamwork   Practice in working on a joint project by communicating on-line with the other students on their team will be especially useful for your students, since it is the way of working that will be found increasingly in the workplace. It will give them practice in file transfer between their systems, in using communications tools, in working to the discipline of a single shared master copy of any joint document, and in negotiating their work through the written word.

All of these uses of the technology offer ways of supporting more active learning. The feasibility of using them well depends to a great extent on the organization of your teaching program.

MAKING IT WORK

Introducing learning technology into a course is not a task a professor should undertake without proper support from the department and the institution. There are some brave folk known as "early adopters," who do this. We need them if innovation is ever to happen, and we thank them, but we do not all have to *be* them. For the sake of the students' sanity alone, it is important that most teachers who adopt learning technology in their teaching do so because it is robust, well supported, and well resourced.

There are five conditions under which it will be feasible for a professor to make effective use of C&IT:

1. All students have access to the technology at appropriate places and times to use it for study.

On campus this means no unreasonable waiting lines and reasonable availability if there are booking restrictions. For off-campus students it means being sure that they have their own access at home and do not have to rely on work-based computing which can impose restrictions on study. And it means *all* students—otherwise it cannot be a compulsory part of the course and becomes diminished in importance. Or it becomes an option, and that costs you time.

2. Students have access to the specified software applications and resources they will need for study.

Access and *specified* are the key words here. It may not matter much if students are using a variety of word processing formats, but if you were issuing a spreadsheet, say, then you have to specify the version of the software it works with and make sure they have access to it. If they need on-line access to a database, you have to be sure they are issued any necessary passwords. These are the kinds of additional tasks that C&IT requires which are just not there in the traditional methods of handouts and syllabi.

3. There is technical support available at study times for students who need it.

A campus-based computer center will usually have someone on hand to help, but students off campus, or working late at night in their rooms, will need a help line for those awful moments when they think they have lost a day's work, or the server seems to be down. Books and paper never treat you like that; it is another additional cost of the technology. Technical support is an institutional provision that you must make sure is available to your students. Not having it would be like running a library without library staff.

4. The department plans staff time appropriately for the requirements of C&IT.

Using the technology effectively means using it to reduce the amount of presentation you do and redistributing your time differently—moving from a focus on presenting to a focus on guiding. Suppose your students' workload were distributed as in the *classic* mode of teaching, across activities such as attending (lectures, reading), discussing (small-group sessions), practicing (practical exercises, projects, field trips), and articulating (writing assignments, presenting their work). A redistribution involving fewer lectures and using more interactive learning programs, guided resource-based learning, and communicative/collaborative activities would create a better balance between those learning activities in the *new* approach, as in Figure 17.1.

This redistribution of student learning time necessarily creates a redistribution of the professor's activities. That amount of attending to lecturing and books requires a certain amount of preparation and presentation time for the professor. That amount of small-group discussion and practical work requires a corresponding amount of professor time spent in guiding. That amount of articulating by the student requires corresponding professor time spent on assessing. The effect is modeled in Figure 17.2, assuming a class of 20 students (the number affects how much time is spent on assessing).

Now it is clear why departments must understand the effects on staff time of moving to interactive learning. If time spent presenting lectures were the indicator of staff workload, it would

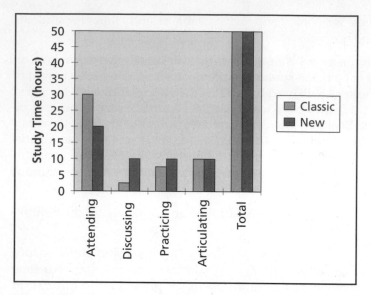

Figure 17.1   Redistribution of Students' Learning Activities

look as if they were spending less time on teaching. In fact, the total is very similar, but it is better distributed in the new approach, with the teacher doing less presenting and having more time for guiding. If you would like to put your own data into this model, you can download it from the following web site: http://watt.open.ac.uk/OTD/diana.htm as Sstime2.xls.

5. There is staff development time and resources available to enable professors to develop their skills in the use of C&IT.

These teaching methods are still innovative and will be for a generation to come. Few of us teaching now have spent much of our study experience on learning through new technologies, and there is little enough known by anyone about how to make the best use of them. We are in the equivalent of the early silent film era, when films echoed earlier media and began with curtains and a proscenium arch. We still talk about "pages" on the web, about making a "storyboard" for multimedia development. Even if the technology is robust, therefore, our use of it should still be seen as experimental. We all have to be reflective practitioners in

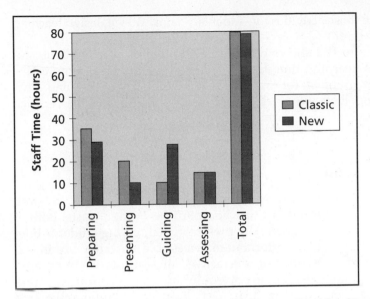

Figure 17.2 Effects of Redistribution of Student Workload on Staff Workload

our use of these media, expecting to fail and setting out the means by which to improve. That takes time, which should be recognized by the department and built into the professor's professional development time.

With all those conditions met, you are in a position to make effective use of C&IT. If any of them are missing, be very cautious about launching into it, unless you are prepared for the fun and the frustration of being an early adopter.

LEARNING ACTIVITIES

There is no point in using new technology unless it generates more productive learning experiences for students. Learning is an active process. Rothkopf (1970) has a nice phrase for it: "mathemagenic activities"; in other words, "activities that give birth to (-*genic*) learning (*mathema*)." That is exactly the teacher's task—to create those activities for students. So how do we design teaching to do that?

Figure 17.1 shows how we might attempt to redistribute students' learning time from a focus on attending to more active forms, grouped, for example, as discussing, practicing, and articulating. Here we consider how new technology can deliver each of these forms of learning activity.

Attending

The predominant forms of technology-based learning are web browsing and multimedia resource disks. What a waste! Both of these forms are essentially presentational, giving students bite-sized chunks of information accessible through an index. Frequently described as "interactive," these forms do not ask anything of students, and do not require any particular form of thinking or processing on their part. They are as interactive as a telephone directory. It can be valuable for a student to have access to indexed information, but access to an encyclopedia is not the cornerstone of a stimulating educational experience.

E-mail offers a simple solution for a more responsive form of presentation. With a distribution list of a group of students, you can set up an asynchronous question-and-answer session, using the "frequently asked questions" (FAQs) format. You know what those questions are from your existing experience with students. Set up a message with those questions as headers and a brief paragraph for an answer for each one. Put your e-mail address at the bottom so that students can e-mail you their additional questions, which you can progressively add to the list as necessary. If you have a web page, you can update the page with those questions and answers, and leave your e-mail address on the page. Either way, the technology makes it accessible at any time, as often as students wish, to as many students as you include, and makes it very easy for you to be responsive to their needs. For an even better service, you can get the web page to send an e-mail message to them with the most recent question and answer, automatically generated when you send it to the page. This essentially encourages "attending" by the student, but at least it is focused and well targeted.

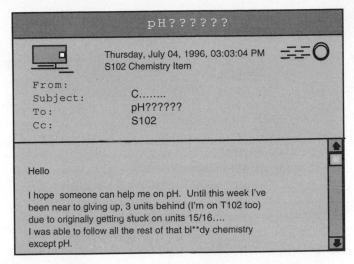

pH??????

Thursday, July 04, 1996, 03:03:04 PM
S102 Chemistry Item

From:
Subject: C........
To: pH??????
Cc: S102

Hello

I hope someone can help me on pH. Until this week I've
been near to giving up, 3 units behind (I'm on T102 too)
due to originally getting stuck on units 15/16....
I was able to follow all the rest of that bl**dy chemistry
except pH.

FIGURE 17.3   A Student (C...) Message to the Conference for the S102 Course

Source: Created with FirstClass Client Version 3.5 for Windows, by SoftArc, Inc. Reprinted by permission of SoftArc, Inc. All rights reserved.

Discussing

New technology can support discussing through a variety of formats, from conferencing (where the software supports a structured, asynchronous messaging environment for a group) to document discourse environments (where successive annotations can be embedded in a document, allowing a group to offer comments and debate). This is one of the easiest ways to encourage students to move from a passive to an active mode of learning, so we must look at an example of each format.

Figures 17.3 and 17.4 show a brief interchange between students in a chemistry course, using the FirstClass conferencing system.* The first sent a message asking for help on the concept of pH. The message was posted for all other students and the

FirstClass Client Version 3.5 for Windows is available from SoftArc Inc. (info@softarc.com).

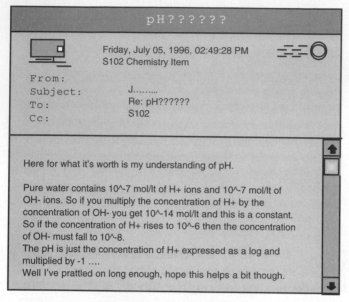

FIGURE 17.4   A Second Student (J...) Replies

Source: Created with FirstClass Client Version 3.5 for Windows, by SoftArc, Inc. Reprinted by permission of SoftArc, Inc. All rights reserved.

tutor to receive whenever they logged into the conference. One of the other students replied a day later (see Figure 17.4). The following day, the instructor logged in, saw the exchange, and put up a message saying that this was a good explanation, so students were reassured they were on the right track.

This simple exchange demonstrates the value of a system that encourages students to express their questions to each other and then to practice stating the answer, as J did. Conference formats of this kind increase the amount of input students make to this kind of tutorial, precisely because it is asynchronous. Without the pressure of time, students can take their time to frame their questions and replies. And the exchange is available for all to see, so there is still the same vicarious learning for the rest of the group, who also get to see the exchange. And they can see it several times over, if they wish. The messages in the conference can stay accessible on the network for as long as the course lasts. It is important, however, for the teacher to keep checking in, and for the students to know you are there in the background. You can set up private conferences for which students know you are not there, but there is a danger in a teacher-moderated conference, if students think you are checking and you are not, that they could reinforce each other's misconceptions.

We should also consider a very different form of networked discussion: a "document discourse environment." Figure 17.5 shows an example of how this works for an on-line journal, where submissions are published only on the web site, following

FIGURE 17.5   A Document Discourse Environment

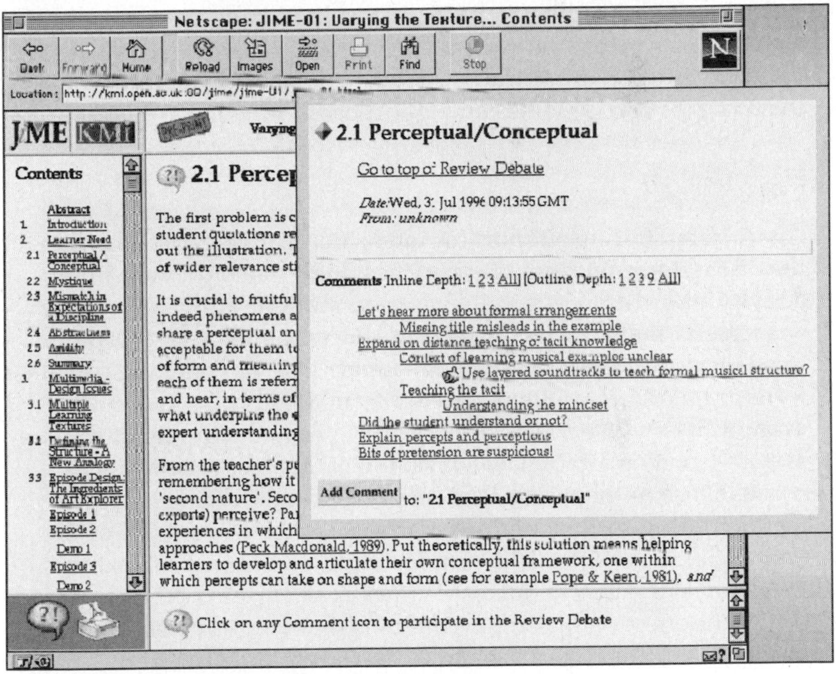

Source: Example taken from the *Journal of Interactive Media in Education* [www-jime.open.ac.uk], generated by the Digital Document Discourse Environment [d3e.open.ac.uk] (Summer and Buckingham Shum, 1998).

the usual refereeing process, and a debate can take place immediately, in the same software environment. A paper is presented on a web page with an index to each section, and a comment icon is associated with each topic in the index. When a contributing participant wishes to make a comment on a particular section, he or she clicks on the comment icon, which opens the second page, displaying the form of the discussion so far on that point. You can see what comments have been made and then add your own. A few days later, perhaps, you may rejoin to see how the discussion has developed.

The example in Figure 17.5 is from an electronic journal but takes exactly the same form as a reading group with your students, except that it is asynchronous and they have the opportunity to contribute much more than they normally would in such a group discussion.

Networked discussion groups of this kind have the additional virtue of providing you with a documented record of the quality of each student's contribution, which could be used, if you tell them in advance, for assessment purposes.

Practicing

Apart from offering support for interaction between people, as in the discussion environments, new technology also provides interactivity of a different kind—between student and data. These adaptive formats use the programmable capability of a computer to adapt its response to the user's input. This can take the trivial form of linking to an item selected from a menu, or, more interestingly, it can take the form of showing how the model of some system (such as a biological system or a business) behaves as a consequence of the user's decision. The program models the system according to the values of certain variables (a model of the national economy, to take a simple example), the student changes the value of a variable (increases interest rates), and the program shows the effect of this on, say, inflation or unemployment figures or the trade gap. You can see how powerful this format might be for helping students understand the behavior of certain systems, through practicing the control of them to achieve target end states. Simulations exist to model many different kinds of systems—environmental, biological, medical—but they are difficult to find and even more difficult to design. They have great potential, and there should be more of them, but they are complex forms of teaching to design, and we are a long way from the national library of such products that one day will be available.

There is another way to encourage practicing through IT: using commercial tools and databases to enhance IT skills across the curriculum. Employers expect graduates to enter the workforce equipped with an understanding of IT and able to use it. They should have the opportunity to do this embedded in the way they study. One example would be provided by your use of conferencing methods. Collaborative work on-line will be a skill to be mastered by all professionals, and this will give students valuable experience of it.

Another example would be to use a spreadsheet to provide a model of a system. We tend to think of spreadsheets modeling cash flows for business, but they could just as easily model the energy flows within a house, or population dynamics, or the quantifiable aspects of a chemical process. If you are not familiar with spreadsheets, find an Excel course, or something similar, and find out how to set one up. You then give your students the model, they change inputs to the model by changing values of certain cells, and they see the resulting outcome—whether it is the cost of heating due to the materials used in a house, population growth due to the resource availability, or the amount of hydrogen resulting from the type of acid chosen. The point is, through controlling the system to achieve a particular kind of result, the student begins to understand how it operates.

A further key skill, with which we must equip all our graduates, is information handling. The global information society will continue to challenge our skills in coping with the amount of information available to us, so graduates who can cope will be much sought after. The web is certainly the ideal training ground, as is the multimedia resource disk, but students will need your help if they are to achieve more than passive browsing.

Think of both the web and the multimedia resource disk exactly as you would encyclopedias, and give the students the corresponding support they would need to make good use of them. Clearly define the information they should seek, explain how they should use it, and describe what will count as high-quality performance. You have to provide the stimulus to encourage critical thinking or analysis, the support to help students do it, and the feedback and debriefing to help them see how to improve and develop their skills. Suppose, for example, you use a national newspaper on CD to get students to research and report on a hot topic. You should show them how to do different kinds of searches, how to constrain or expand their search, how to evaluate what they find, and give marks for completeness of coverage, how well they have synthesized the information, how well they have checked one source against another, and so on. The process will yield a close encounter with the material itself, but in a structured way, which in turn yields development of their information-handling skills. In this way, you begin to use IT to encourage the practice of their subject.

Articulating

Whenever students express their own representation of a subject, they are articulating it and in that way embedding it in their conceptual world in a memorable and retrievable way. That is why we set assignments, such as essays, problem sheets, lab reports, project work—in all these cases students are required to synthesize and articulate what they know. This could be seen as part of the discussion process—by responding to another student or to a question, students must articulate their view. It is worth keeping the two separate, however. Discussing requires some response to the ongoing debate constructed by the group dynamic, whereas articulating requires students to express their point of view as a coherent whole. Articulating plays a different role in the learning process.

New technology supports this activity in some very obvious ways—providing word processing tools, graphics tools, planning tools—all of which can be used to help students think through their point of view. Simply using the "outline" facility in a word processing program can make it easier for students to structure their thoughts for an essay, for example. The fact that a computer-based tool will produce professional-looking output will itself act as a motivator to do the work. But the assessment of it will still be the task of the teacher—we cannot yet get computers to make those kinds of judgments for us.

PLANNING THE DESIGN OF COURSE MATERIALS

The classic sequence of course design promoted by instructional designers goes like this: set objectives, select medium, design materials, test, redesign, implement. In practice, it is more likely to be select medium, design materials, implement, retrospectively define objectives if someone asks you to. There are good and bad reasons for this, and some of them are present in the use of IT. It is difficult to set objectives because the kinds of objectives that are appropriate for IT may be quite different from those you would set if restricted to other teaching methods. That is its unique value. There is an interrelationship between the medium and the objectives, and although it is important to start with objectives, you will probably iterate through that ideal sequence. The test-redesign phase tends to be omitted because the design phase took too much time. That we must avoid. But how? What are the key planning stages for designing your course materials?

1. Aim for Small but Perfectly Formed

Start small. This is difficult and complex, and there is much to learn about. If from the start you plan to take it right through to testing and redesign, then you can scale the ambitiousness of your design to fit that time. When we fail to test a teaching inno vation, it is as bad as a student's failing to test a hypothesis or check facts. Aim for an A grade in course design.

2. Build on Existing Work

You probably would not expect to write your own textbook, and you definitely should not expect to write a teaching program— one day, perhaps, but not as a matter of course. You want to build on what others have done, but how do you find something to fit your objectives? The educational sector has not yet evolved the equivalent of academic book publishing for learning technologies. We are in the equivalent of the Middle Ages prior to the invention of printing, like the medieval professor who is sure there is a very good book, beautifully hand-crafted, somewhere, but has no idea where or how to find it. So you have to be opportunistic. Use the web to find universities, colleges, and individual academics with something to offer; go to conferences; read the journals; use your professional association—it is as ad hoc as that. Although you will never find exactly what you want, you will find some ideas and some things you can build on. This is why the "set objectives, select medium" phase has to be iterative. The perfect textbook does not exist either—you build your teaching around what there is that is partway there.

3. Begin with What You Know

Bring technology into your learning activity design from whatever activity you use it in yourself. This is a technology-driven approach, because you begin with something other than the learning objectives, but at least you will be teaching a valuable skill which you understand well, so it is a good place to begin. If you use Powerpoint for lecturing, set students the task of using it to create presentations of their own. If you use e-mail, set up a distributed list for your students as an asynchronous discussion group, set a reading task, and get them to comment on-line.

4. Integrate the IT Method with Other Teaching

If you are offering an IT method to students, it is vital that you make it clear that this is an important part of the course. Brief them for their use of it, make the objectives clear, demonstrate it, suggest what they should do with it, define how much time they should spend on it, and, most important of all, explain how you will assess their work on it. This is how a teacher quantifies the importance of a piece of work for students—how many marks it will carry and what they are expected to do to gain them.

Building on others' materials carries with it the requirement to make sure that all the pieces appear coherent from the students' point of view. Just as textbooks have their quirks of vocabulary or symbolism, so do IT products. It will be important to check through the software being used to see what might cause problems. Use the briefing session to preempt these.

5. Test and Redesign

This does not have to be large-scale research. The best way to test the value of a learning experience of this kind is to make it small in scale but intensive. If you observe two pairs of students using the material you have put together, trying to carry out the activity you have set, you will understand more about the quality of the learning experience than from any number of questionnaires or test papers. Make it as realistic as possible for them, make it clear that you are testing the activity and not them, listen to what they say, watch what they do, take notes, and ask for their reflections on the process afterwards, not during.

The whole process need take only 30 to 60 minutes, depending on the amount of material. Using pairs of students allows you to hear how they are responding, what kinds of decisions they are making, what kinds of thinking they engage in. Using two pairs tells you whether there are great differences about which you need to find out more—perhaps using questionnaires that pick up on the contrasting observations you made. You should see from just two observation sessions the extent to which the activity achieves what you hoped for, and the kind of additional briefing or support notes you might prepare to improve it for students.

This is the minimalist approach to test-redesign, but for a busy teacher, that may be all that is feasible. Anything less gets nowhere near an A. If you can do further observation after the redesign, and use your findings to generate a short questionnaire, you get an A+. If you write up your experience and publish it in an educational journal, then you have made a contribution to furthering this very sparse area of knowledge, and that goes beyond mere grades.

IN CONCLUSION

We have looked at a range of mathemagenic activities here. New technology can support an impressive range, and we should aim to exploit it, while being sufficiently aware of our lack of experience that we always take an experimental approach. That means restraining our ambitions to designing activities that we can also test and redesigning until we are sure we know they are teaching well.

Very few of us have learned much through new technology. It's a little like trying to write a book when you've never read one. It's hard. But it's also easy to improve your performance if you take the trouble to do so.

Supplementary Reading

Pat Maier, Liz Barnett, Adam Warrne, and David Brunner *Using Technology in Teaching and Learning,* 2nd ed. (London: Kogan Page, 1998).

R. Pea and D. Kurland, Cognitive Technologies in Writing. In E. Rothkopf (ed.), *Review of Research in Education No. 14* (277–326) (Washington DC: American Educational Research Association, 1987).

Journal of Interactive Multimedia in Education website: http://www-jime.open.ac.uk/jime/

Author's website: http://watt.open.ac.uk/OTD/diana.html

Mark Grabe and Cindy Grabe, *Integrating Technology into Meaningful Learning,* 2nd ed. (Boston: Houghton Mifflin, 1998).

Diana Laurillard, *Rethinking University Teaching: A Framework for the Effective Use of Educational Technology,* (London: Routledge, 1993).

Class Size and Sectional Courses

18

CLASS SIZE

As budgets drop, more and more college teachers have to deal with large numbers of students enrolled in a single course.

In writing this book, I originally began with the topic "Class Size." I concluded that section by stating that more meaningful research on class size must take into account the methods of teaching classes of differing sizes. I thought this was a pretty insightful statement, but now I think that it was naive, for size and method are almost inextricably intertwined. Thus the research on class size and that on lecture versus discussion over lap. Large classes are most likely to use lecture methods and less likely to use discussion than small classes. Since discussion tends to be more effective than lecture for achieving changes in thinking and problem solving, we might expect large classes to be less effective than small classes.

Research on Class Size

The question of class size was probably the first college teaching problem approached by research. Are small classes really more effective for teaching than large classes? The professor's answer has generally been "yes." But the refreshing empiricism of the 1920s looked hard at many "self-evident truths" about human behavior; among them was the assumption that class size had something to do with educational effectiveness.

Among the first investigators were Edmondson and Mulder (1924), who compared the performance of students enrolled in a 109-student class with students enrolled in a 43-student class of the same course in education. Achievement of the two groups was approximately equal, with a slight edge for the small class on an essay and the midsemester tests, and for the large class on quizzes and the final examination. Students reported a preference for small classes. A number of experiments over the next six to seven decades generally supported these findings.

The Macomber and Siegel experiments at Miami University (1957a, 1957b, 1960) are particularly important because their measures included, in addition to conventional achievement tests, measures of critical thinking and problem solving, scales measuring stereotypic attitudes, and tests of student attitudes toward instruction. Statistically significant differences favored the smaller classes (particularly for high-ability students). When retention of knowledge was measured one to two years after completion of the courses, small differences favored the smaller classes in eight of the nine courses compared (Siegel, Adams, & Macomber, 1960). Meta-analyses of research on class size in classes ranging in level from elementary schools to universities also tend to support small classes (Kulik & Kulik, 1989).

Few instructors are satisfied with the achievement of knowledge if it is not remembered, if the students are unable to use it in solving problems where the knowledge is relevant, or if the students fail to relate the knowledge to relevant attitudes. If one takes these more basic outcomes of retention, problem solving, and attitude differentiation as criteria of learning, the weight of the evidence favors small classes.

Class Size: Theory

How can we account for these results?

Let's briefly return to theory. Insofar as information communication is a one-way process, size of group should be limited only by the audibility of the lecturer's voice. In fact, as Hudelson

(1928) suggested, a large class may have sufficient motivational value for instructors to cause them to spend more time in preparation of their lectures, resulting, I would hope, in better teaching and in greater student achievement.

But usually we have goals going beyond communication of knowledge. If educators are to make wise decisions about when and where small classes are most important, we need to analyze more carefully the changes in educationally relevant variables associated with changes in size. One lead comes from social psychologists Thomas and Fink (1963), who have reviewed research on face-to-face groups—not only classroom groups, but also laboratory, business, and other groups. They suggest that two types of input increase with increasing group size—*resource input* (skills, knowledge, and so on) and *demand input* (needs). It is clear that the larger the number of group members, the greater is the likelihood that some members will have resources of knowledge, intelligence, or other skills needed for the educational purposes of the group. It seems likely, however, that there is a limited amount of relevant knowledge and skills, so that beyond some point additional students contribute little that is not already part of the group's resources. A group's utilization of resources is constrained by the simple facts that (1) in a large group a smaller proportion of group members can participate orally, and (2) the larger the group, the less likely it is that a given person will feel free to volunteer a contribution. Because active thinking is so important to learning and retention of learning, constraints on oral participation are likely not only to induce passivity but also to be educationally harmful.

This chapter and the following chapter suggest strategies to use to achieve better learning. Clearly, large classes can be effective. The problem is that most faculty members lack the skills to compensate for large size. They use less discussion, require less writing, are less likely to use essay exams—in short, the way we teach large classes is different (and usually less effective) than the way we teach small classes.

Determining When Small Classes Are Needed

In order to apply these general propositions to teaching, we need to ask the following questions:

1. In what teaching situations is the amount of information in the group important?
2. What kinds of students benefit most from small sections?

In What Teaching Situations Is the Amount of Information in the Group Important?   One might, for example, hypothesize that in most courses in which knowledge is the primary goal, the relevant information is contained in books and the instructor's mind, and the amount added by students is likely to be inconsequential; thus class size should be unimportant for this goal. On the other hand, if application is an important goal, varied knowledge of application situations contributed by students may well be significant; thus, if Thomas and Fink's principles are valid, there may be groups too small, as well as too large, to be maximally effective for this goal.

What Kinds of Students Benefit Most from Small Sections?   Both Ward (1956) and Macomber and Siegel report results suggesting that the ablest students are most favorably affected by being taught in small classes. Siegel and Siegel (1964) report that personal contact with the instructor was particularly important for acquisition of concepts by three types of students: (1) those with low motivation; (2) those who are unsophisticated in the subject-matter area; and (3) those who are predisposed to learn facts rather than to apply or synthesize.

Wulff, Nyquist, and Abbott (1987), however, found that many students liked the lack of pressure, the independence, and the freedom to skip meetings in large classes.

Many students feel more comfortable being anonymous where there is no threat of exposure—no discussion, no writing—just taking notes and answering objective test questions. But these may be the very students who need most to find that others respect their ideas, that they can carry through a project, or can write a paper successfully.

Class Size: Conclusions

It is commonplace to suggest that the effect of class size depends on the method used, and it is probably true that the size of the group is less critical for success of lecture, for example, than for that of discussion (Attiyeh & Lumsden, 1972). But most important, analysis of research suggests that the importance of size depends on educational goals. In general, large classes are simply not as effective as small classes for retention of knowledge, critical thinking, and attitude change. Note, however, that large-group discussion methods can be used effectively, and pairing, buzz groups, and other peer learning techniques increase the effectiveness of learning in large classes (see Chapters 5 and 14).

MULTISECTION COURSES

Unfortunately, there are seldom enough funds to teach all courses in small groups. As a compromise solution, I have scheduled large courses for two hours of lecture (in large sections) and two hours of discussion (in small sections). The assumption here is that lectures are valuable for certain purposes, such as communicating information, and that the effectiveness of the lecture method is not greatly affected by class size. Furthermore, large-group class meetings are economical for test administration, guest lecturers, and some films or videotapes. By teaching the students in large sections part of the time, it becomes economically feasible to keep the discussion sections small enough to permit wide student participation. Thus, rather than offering 5 sections of 45 students each, you might consider the possible advantages of a 225-student lecture section and 9 discussion sections of 20 to 30 students.

In universities these sections are usually taught by graduate student teaching assistants; if faculty or graduate students aren't available, don't be afraid to use undergraduate students. As we saw in Chapter 14 both the student discussion leaders and the students being taught benefit from this arrangement.

Coordinating Multisection Courses

In any multisection course taught by several different instructors, the problem of coordination inevitably arises. The first approach to coordination is enforced uniformity of course content, sequence of topics, testing, grading, and even anecdotes. Such a procedure has the advantage that students who later elect more advanced courses can be presumed to have a certain uniform amount of background experience. It also is efficient in that only one final examination must be constructed, only one course outline devised, and students can transfer from section to section with no difficulty in catching up.

The disadvantage of this approach is that such uniformity often makes for dull, uninteresting teaching. If the teaching assistants are unenthusiastic about the course outline, they are likely to communicate this attitude to the students. If the course can be jointly planned, this may make for greater acceptance, but may also take a great deal of time.

A second approach to this problem is to set up completely autonomous sections, with all the instructors organizing and conducting their sections as they wish. Although this means that Psychology 1 with Professor Smith may be quite different from Psychology 1 with Professor Jones, proponents of this solution point out that transfer students who are accepted for advanced work are likely to differ even more from local students than local students differ from section to section under this plan, and that the difference in student learning between instructors is relatively small when compared with the total range of differences between students at the end of a course.

Whether or not variation between sections is permitted, a frequent sore spot in multisection courses is the tendency for students to leave or avoid sections taught by certain instructors and to crowd into others. Some instructors intentionally depict their sections as being more difficult in order to drive away less motivated students. If this produces large disparities in the numbers of students taught by "popular" and "unpopular" instructors, the cohesiveness of the instructional staff is likely to be threatened. On the other hand, from the standpoints of both student learning and instructor satisfaction, it would seem wise to give students some opportunity to select the section they feel will be most valuable (or pleasant) for them.

Conflict may be minimized and education enhanced if certain sections are specifically labeled as being for a particular purpose. For example, certain sections may be labeled Honors sections or for graduate students; certain sections may be labeled as placing greater emphasis upon theory; certain other sections may be taught entirely by discussion and so labeled. One of the advantages of a multisection course is the opportunity it provides for establishing groupings with similar interests or backgrounds.

Training and Supervising Teaching Assistants

Most large universities use graduate or undergraduate student assistants to teach discussion or laboratory sessions in large courses. As the course coordinator, you are responsible for the quality of education your students receive, and to a large extent this depends on the motivation and skill of the teaching assistants.

Your responsibility begins well before the first class meetings, for your teaching assistants need to know what you expect in terms of attendance at lectures, participation in weekly planning and training sessions, testing and grading, office hours, and such. But even more important than the formal requirements are the aspects of preparing the teaching assistants for meeting their first classes, establishing a good working relationship with their students, and developing the skills needed for leading discussions, answering questions, and carrying out other teaching responsibilities.

Here are some suggestions for assisting teaching assistants:

1. Hold weekly meetings to discuss teaching problems and plans.
2. Collect feedback from students early in the term.
3. Observe classes and discuss your observations with the TA.

To get student feedback, you can use simple open-ended questions, such as:

"What have you liked about the class so far?"
"What suggestions do you have for improvement?"

Visiting classes or videotaping can provide useful information about nonverbal characteristics of the teacher and reactions of the students. But observation or videotaping takes time. If you have time, visit classes, but if you are short of time, there is little evidence that videotaping or observation results in significantly greater improvement in teaching than consultation on student ratings collected early in the term (and perhaps repeated a little later). So if you're short of time, invest it in consultation.

IN CONCLUSION

Class size is important.

When taught appropriately, small classes are likely to be better than large classes for achieving long-term goals, such as retention and use of knowledge, thinking, and attitude change.

Nonetheless, when dealing with large classes, you can come closer to the outcomes of small classes by

1. Providing discussion sections taught by trained teaching assistants.

2. Using teaching methods that facilitate active, meaningful, learning (see the next chapter).

Supplementary Reading

Because almost every large university now has a program for training teaching assistants, there is a biennial meeting on training, and the papers from the meeting are typically published. The first volume is still one of the best:

J. D. Nyquist, R. D. Abbott, D. H. Wulff, and J. Sprague (eds.), *Preparing the Professoriate of Tomorrow to Teach: Selected Readings in TA Training* (Dubuque, IA: Kendall/Hunt, 1991).

Teaching Large Classes (You Can Still Get Active Learning!)

19

While sectioning is preferable to a large class without sections, you may at some time be faced with teaching an unsectioned large class. Often one assumes that a large class simply requires skills in lecturing and writing objective tests. These are important, but one can do more. Large classes need not constrain you as much as you might expect. You don't need to lecture, or at least you don't need to lecture all the time.

FACILITATING ACTIVE LEARNING

The most commonly used method of stimulating active learning is questioning and encouraging student questioning, as discussed in Chapters 5 and 6. But there are many other tools in your active learning kit that are usable in large classes. Remember that, in Chapter 14, on peer learning, I reported the research showing that students learn more in student-led discussions, or in learning cells, than they learn in traditional lectures. Thus you can get the advantages of a multisection course by organizing students to meet in class or out of class for discussion.

Techniques such as buzz groups, problem posting, and the two-column method of large-group discussions were also described earlier. Buzz groups (described in Chapter 5) can be formed and asked to discuss how the material might be used or applied. Simply pausing occasionally to give students a couple of minutes to compare their notes can activate thinking (Ruhl, Hughes, & Schloss, 1987). Maier (1971) gives examples of the use of such techniques.

Encouraging Student Writing in Large Classes

One of the most important drawbacks of large classes is the lack of student writing. Because grading essays is so time-consuming, most faculty members reduce, or eliminate, writing assignments in a large class. Take heart! You can get some of the educational advantages of writing, and at the same time improve attention to the lecture, without being submerged by papers to grade.

The "minute paper," described earlier, is one valuable tool.* At an appropriate point in the lecture, announce the paper and the topic or question you want students to address; for example, you might ask the students to summarize the major point or points made so far in the lecture. Or you might give the students a choice of topics, such as a summary, a question, an application, or an example. When the minute is up, you may either collect the papers or break the class into pairs or subgroups to review and discuss one another's papers.

If you wish, you can evaluate and comment on the papers as you would any other student papers. If the class is exceptionally large, you may announce that you'll read and return only a sample of the papers. Students can be motivated to think and write without the threat of grades, and this technique not only gets students thinking actively during the lecture but gives you feedback about what students are learning from the lecture.

Similar to the "minute paper" is the "half-sheet response" (Weaver & Cotrell, 1985). In this technique students tear out a half-sheet of notebook paper to respond to a question or instruction such as:

"What do you think about this concept?"
"Give an example of this concept or principle."

---

* The minute paper need not be one minute, it can be two, three, or as many minutes as needed for a particular topic.

"Explain this concept in your own words."

"How does this idea relate to your own experience?"

"What are some of your feelings as you listen to these ideas?"

"How could you use this idea in your own life?"

Both the minute paper and the half-sheet response can help initiate a large-group discussion.

Other Ways to Maintain Student Involvement

There are a variety of techniques that can help break the deadly routine of lectures day after day: debates, fishbowl, interviews.

In addition to the large-group discussion and subgrouping techniques discussed in Chapters 5 and 14, you can enliven your class with debates either between faculty members or between student teams.

If you use student debaters, you need to provide a clear structure, probably using a handout describing the issue, the length of talks, opportunity for rebuttal, and the goal of the debate as a learning device.

How do you choose the debaters? One option is to divide the class into six- to eight-person teams who prepare their arguments and evidence and coach a representative to participate in the debate. (I also like to allow the team time for coaching before the rebuttals.)

The "fishbowl" can be used in small, as well as large, classes. Tell the students that at the next class meeting you will choose six students (or any convenient number) to be "in the fishbowl." You will then conduct a discussion (based on the work to date) with the students in the fishbowl. The rest of the students are to act as observers and recorders, noting both the process and the content of the discussion. Before the end of the class period, observers will write a brief summary of the discussion and raise questions that remain or answer the question, "What would you have said that wasn't said?"

Another break in lectures can be provided by an interview—perhaps of a colleague with special expertise, someone from outside the university, or one of the students with special experience. A variant might be a dialog on a topic in which you and a colleague have somewhat different views.

Reducing Students' Feelings of Anonymity

1. Announce that you'll meet any students who are free for coffee after class. (You won't be swamped.)
2. Pass out invitations to several students to join you for coffee and to get acquainted after class.
3. Pass out brief student observation forms to several students at the beginning of class and ask them to meet you to discuss their observations.
4. Circulate among early arriving students to get acquainted before class starts.
5. Use a seating chart so that you can call students by name when they participate.
6. During your lecture, move out into the aisles to solicit comments.
7. If you can't use regularly scheduled discussion sections, set up an occasional afternoon or evening session for more informal discussion of an interesting question or for review before an examination.
8. Have students fill out an autobiographical sketch with name, hometown, year in college, and what they hope to get out of the course (Benjamin, 1991).

If you use these methods, some students will be frustrated. They came to hear you tell them the TRUTH, which they can then memorize for tests. To handle this frustration, two things may help:

1. Explain how active participation contributes to better understanding and memory.
2. Make sure that your students realize that your tests will require thinking, not just rote memory.

STUDENT ANONYMITY

A major problem of teaching a large class is that students not only feel anonymous, they usually *are* anonymous. And as social psychological research has shown, people who are anonymous feel less personal responsibility—a consequence not only damaging to morale and order but also unlikely to facilitate learning. Moreover, the sense of distance from the instructor, the loss of interpersonal bonds with the instructor and with other students—these diminish motivation for learning.

What can we do? The fact that with increasing class size it becomes less and less possible to know students as individuals is likely to make us feel that it is not worth trying to do anything. I think this is a mistake. In my experience the students appreciate whatever efforts you make even if they do not take advantage of them. The box on page 212 shows some things I've tried.

GIVING TESTS IN LARGE CLASSES

In classes of 200 or more, unwary instructors are likely to run into problems they would never dream of in teaching classes with an enrollment of 20 to 30. Most of these problems are administrative. For example, course planning almost inevitably becomes more rigid in a large class because almost anything involving the participation of the students requires more preparation time.

Perhaps you're used to making up your tests the day before you administer them. With a large class this is almost impossible. Essay and short-answer tests that take relatively little time to construct take a long time to score for 200 students; so you may spend long hours trying to devise thought-provoking objective questions for a part of the test. But once you've made up the questions your troubles are not over, for secretaries require a good deal of time to make several hundred copies of a test. Thus spur-of-the-moment tests are almost an impossibility, and by virtue of the necessity of planning ahead for tests, other aspects of the course also become more rigid.

As I indicated in Chapter 7, essay examinations are superior to typical objective examinations in their effect on student study and learning. Thus you are likely to regret the loss of the opportunity to give essay tests in a large group. But this loss is not inevitable. To some extent it can be compensated for by greater care in the construction of objective test items. But it is also possible to use essay items without increasing your load beyond reason. In a

500-student lecture course, I regularly included an essay item on the final examination with the stipulation that I would read it only if it would affect the student's letter grade for the course. Since the majority of the students were fairly clearly established as A, B, C, or D students on the basis of other work and the objective part of the final examination, the number of essays I needed to read was not excessive. My subjective impression was that knowledge of the inclusion of an essay item did affect the students' preparation for the exam.

OUTSIDE READING

The testing problem is just one of several factors structuring the conduct of large classes. Another is the assignment of readings in the library. With a small group you can assign library work with little difficulty, only making sure that the materials needed are available and, if necessary, reserved for the class. With a class of several hundred students a library assignment without previous planning can be disastrous. The library's single copy of a book or journal is obviously inadequate. Thus a library assignment must be conceived far enough in advance (usually several months) that enough copies of the book can be obtained, and the librarian can prepare for the fray.

IN CONCLUSION

Large classes are probably generally less effective than small ones for higher-level goals. Nonetheless, they are not likely to disappear, and they can be very effective when taught by methods that stimulate students to active, mindful thinking rather than passive absorption.

You'll probably spend some time lecturing. This does not mean that the students can now slip into passivity. Active learning does not necessarily involve only student talking, writing, or doing; what is important is active *thinking*. The techniques described in this and preceding chapters can lead in to continued active learning and thinking during the periods of lecture.

Supplementary Reading

M. G. Weimer (ed.), *Teaching Large Classes Well* (San Francisco: Jossey-Bass, 1987).

Graham Gibbs, *Improving the Quality of Student Learning* (Estover Plymouth, England: Plymouth Distributors, 1992).

Tracey Sutherland and Charles Bonwell (eds.), *Using Active Learning in College Classes: A Range of Options for Faculty*, New Directions for Teaching and Learning, No. 67 (San Francisco: Jossey-Bass, 1996).

Charles Bonwell and James Eison, *Active Learning: Creating Excitement in the Classroom*, ASHE-ERIC Higher Education Report No. 1, 1991.

Understanding Students

20 Taking Student Social Diversity into Account

Traditional discussions of student differences have focused on variations in cognitive style, cognitive development, motivation, speed, and preferred physiological modality. In the past decade or so, discussion of difference with respect to learning during the college years has centered as well on student social diversity—the ways in which students are different by virtue of their socioeconomic class, race, ethnicity, sex, age, sexual identity, and ability. The discussion of social identity has been exploratory—and often explosive. The present setting is one of increased awareness of the issues, but continued uneasiness about them.

There are several reasons why it is important to attend to student diversity. These reasons are clustered into moral, intellectual, and social grounds for multicultural teaching (Karenga, 1995). The moral grounds focus on mutual respect between teachers and learners as people. The intellectual imperative highlights the importance to any intellectual endeavor of multiple perspectives, of seeing things from the fullness of human experience, of growth through challenge and contrast. Socially, the call is for justice and equity among people, both while they are in formal learning environments and as they subsequently live their lives. Sutton

This chapter was written by Nancy Van Note Chism of Ohio State University.

(1993), referencing the contributions of Henry Giroux and Paulo Freire, states, "Education is part of a larger ethical, social and cultural enterprise in which teachers are morally responsible to help students engage in a struggle for a more humane world" (p. 163).

In addition to these fundamental considerations, the growing social diversity of the current and projected student populations is forcing consideration of the need for attention to a different kind of teaching (Upcraft, 1996). Students who are older than the traditional 17- to 22-year-old range now constitute the majority of the higher education population. Women are now the majority sex at many institutions and nationally account for 54 percent of all bachelor's degree students. Students of color are a greater presence on campus (following a decline in participation during the 1980s), and the changes in their representation (see Table 20.1) show a marked difference in the past 20 years (Chronicle of Higher Education, 1997). Students with physical or learning disabilities are attending and self-identifying in higher numbers, reported as 10 percent in 1996 (American Council on Education, 1996), and legislation, such as the Americans with Disabilities Act of 1990, requires educational settings to address the needs of the disabled. Gay, lesbian, and bisexual students (who have heretofore been a largely "invisible" population) are becoming increasingly articulate about their participation. In summary, these trends show that, "Whether we are prepared to deal with it or not, it is happening. It does not matter whether we are liberals or conservatives, the future of this country is going to be multicultural" (Hodgkinson, 1995, p. 3).

Disappointing retention rates and discouragement on the part of many traditionally underrepresented students are indicators that higher education has not been successful in serving new learners. Although financial aid, residential life, and a host of other factors are important, the weight of past research evidence suggests that faculty are critical to student educational attainment: positive in- and out-of-class relationships with their teachers can enable students to overcome constraints and achieve academic success. (Astin, 1975; Ferguson, 1990; Pascarella & Terenzini, 1991). One step to helping students from diverse groups to succeed, then, is becoming aware of the tremendous influence that we can have on student success.

Group	Percentage growth
American Indian	73%
Asian American	309
African American	41
Hispanic American	187
White American	14
International	87

TABLE 20.1   Change in the Racial/Ethnic Composition of the Undergraduate College Population (1976–1995)

While student success is a deep concern to us, some faculty members are unconvinced that there are any teaching issues surrounding social diversity. Some of us have many anxieties about multicultural teaching (Weinstein & Obear, 1992). We wonder whether attention to difference will fragment and irritate social relations and prevent rather than encourage student success. We argue about "canon" issues, fearing a watering down of the curriculum. We may fear that the purposes of social diversity will call upon us to treat students preferentially—a practice that we have always been careful to avoid. We may also feel that we are walking on eggshells, that whatever action we take will be misinterpreted. But it is clear that the problems need to be addressed openly. The payoff is not only for our students themselves, but also for our colleges and universities as they profit from truly embracing the opportunity to let previously unheard or unheeded voices enrich and broaden ways of thinking and knowing.

The main teaching issues connected with social diversity fall into two broad categories: curriculum and instructional strategies. The first, curriculum issues, is the most frequently debated. The claim is that the content of most courses very narrowly focuses on the Western intellectual tradition, specifically the experience of the mainstream European-descended male. Thus students from other cultural traditions feel marginal to the academic experience. They see no role models and feel that their experience is not valued. Second, classroom interactions, academic discourse, cognitive style, and other aspects of teaching and learning also exhibit a male European cultural style that constrains full participation by students from other backgrounds and excludes insights from other cultures. Majority as well as minority students, then, experience an education that is far too narrow, given the possibilities.

The literature on multicultural teaching bears several messages for us to consider: (1) all students need to feel welcome; (2) they need to feel that they are being treated as individuals; (3) they need to feel that they can participate fully; and (4) they need to be treated fairly (Adams, 1992, Border & Chism, 1992; Bowser, Jones, & Young, 1995; Schoem et al., 1993; Wlodkowski & Ginsberg, 1995).

FEELING WELCOME IN THE CLASSROOM

Feeling included is a key to student motivation to learn (Wlodkowski & Ginsberg, 1995). It is important, then, that students not encounter overt hostility, ignorance, and insensitivity, as well as more subtle messages that their cultural heritage is not valued. Although they report that most faculty do not voice such overt hostility, students pick up on more subtle clues, often entangled in our attempts to be humorous, such as jokes about sexual orientation or physical disabilities or women. The message received is that there is an underlying resentment about the presence of the students who "don't fit." Many times, well-meaning but ignorant statements are the cause for discomfort. If we follow our slips into profanity with "My apologies to the ladies," we could be seen as patronizing by women students; if we address a student with a learning disability with exaggerated enunciation, we could make the student feel that it was assumed that he was dull-witted. In order to become more sensitive, we must look within ourselves for lingering biases that are a pervasive result of modern socialization. We must be patient with ourselves and our students while several generations try to unlearn some deep-seated prejudices.

Language is a cue to our stance for many students. Preferences on terminology continue to change as social groups explore their identity. Presently, for example, "gay and lesbian students" is more preferable than "homosexual students"; "Asian" is preferred to "Oriental"; and "women" is preferred to "gals" or other diminutives. When we listen to the dialog around common terms or ask students about their preferences, we avoid using terms that offend and demonstrate our care and sensitivity.

Welcoming not only involves being personally sensitive as the instructor, but also helping all students to display welcoming behavior toward each other in the classroom. We play a critical role in monitoring classroom behavior and addressing problems as part of the learning experience when they occur. Rather than hurriedly passing over the comment of a student who refers to "colored people on welfare," it is important for us to openly discuss issues surrounding the negative image and language choice of the response, even if embarrassment is a possibility. Teaching for diversity is not only being more welcoming to diverse groups but also increasing the sensitivity of majority students to cultural differences.

For students from diverse groups to feel valued, we must go beyond neutrality. Frequently, the students experience alienation because their presence is not acknowledged at all. They often use the term *invisible* to describe how they feel. Although majority students sometimes describe the same feeling, it is experienced more deeply by students who are from a group that has traditionally experienced exclusion, because they are more likely to take it personally. To avoid having students interpret the impersonal, businesslike behaviors of the traditional classroom as instances of personal rejection, we can take care to call students by name, engage in formal greetings or "small talk" before moving on, or allow for the personal to enter the domain of the scholarly as appropriate. When we acknowledge diversity at the beginning of a course by indicating that we welcome different perspectives and want to accommodate different needs, we set the tone for students to feel respected and free to communicate with us.

One of the biggest problems with helping underrepresented students feel welcome is large class size. They can feel lost and may also feel that the peer environment is more likely to get out of hand because classroom management is more of a challenge. Students of color, for example, often say that they are very hesitant to speak out on issues about people of color in large-group settings because they fear physical violence and slurs that the instructor will not witness. Our attempts to manage large-class environments well and to increase personal contact with students by walking throughout the room, scheduling out-of-class visits with students, or working closely with small groups of students on a rotating basis are especially important gestures that can be made to students experiencing the "outsider" syndrome. The use of collaborative learning, peer teaching, focus groups, and other methods can help students feel included (Wlodkowski & Ginsberg, 1995).

Feeling Welcome Through the Curriculum

Alienation also occurs frequently when students look in vain for mention of their social group or evidence of their perspective throughout the curriculum. For example, works by or about people of color or gay, lesbian, or bisexual people should not be noticeable only by their absence. Often we do not realize the effect of emphasizing only traditional content. In data collected for a study of gay and lesbian issues in the college classroom (lopez & Chism, 1993), one gay student reported looking forward to the day when his American history instructor would lecture on a section of the text that dealt with the gay pride movement, only to hear the instructor say that he would not deal with the "so-called Stonewall Riots." Another student in the same study reported that a human sexuality instructor said that the class would skip the chapter on homosexuality because the course was only about "normal" sexuality. The students reported that examples used in classes and assignments consistently presumed a heterosexual orientation. When such things happen, students feel that their point of view, their culture, their heritage is not welcome. They look for role models of scholars, practitioners, and artists in their field of study and find few examples that would encourage them to persist in school. Simple attempts at inclusion can be of enormous importance to students seeking validation. They can also increase the breadth of exposure of majority students.

As many scholars have noted, rethinking the curriculum often begins with including references to or about scholars or issues connected with socially diverse groups, but ultimately involves a transformative approach whereby the entire assumptions and content of a given field are reconsidered from the perspectives of diverse people (Gay, 1995; Kitano, 1997; Sleeter, 1991; Toombs & Tierney, 1992). Transformation in sociology, for example, could begin with attention to eliminating stereotyped references that occur or including mention of the work of some current sociologists of color, but would move on to rethink some basic ways of doing or thinking about sociology in light of feminist epistemology or other paradigms. Often the scholarship necessary to revise courses is hard to access or undeveloped. It takes both personal and institutional commitment and much original scholarship to do this work. Excellent advice on curriculum transformation is now available in such works as *Creating an Inclusive Curriculum* (Friedman, Kolmar, Flint, & Rothenberg, 1996). The rewards of investing in curricular change are powerful: the enrichment of the scholarship as well as the increased engagement of students from diverse social groups.

In sum, if we wish to create a welcoming climate, we can:

- Display authentic concern for students and avoid patronizing behaviors.

- Attend to terminology preferences of social groups by reading and listening to discussions as well as asking directly.

- State explicitly that diversity is valued in the classroom and deal promptly with biased student comments rather than ignore them.

- Personalize classroom interactions as much as possible by engaging in informal discussion before class, using students' names, and encouraging students to visit during office hours.

- Enrich course content by drawing on perspectives, examples, and references that reflect the fullness of human inquiry.

Being Treated as an Individual

While students from diverse groups are very eager that their social groups feel welcome on campus, they also want to be treated as individuals. One barrier that prevents this is stereo-typing. Images of the African-American student as a "dumb jock" or "special admissions" student; of the female sorority student as a "fluffhead"; or of the lesbian student as an "argumenta-tive dyke" influence our expectations, often in unconscious ways. Stereotypes that are ostensibly positive, such as the "math whiz" Asian American or the "wise" older student, are also problematic because they may place unrealistically high expecta-tions on some students. We do not have to voice these stereo-types for students—they often get the message indirectly. For example, we may lavish excessive praise on an American Indian student, causing the student to feel that the expectations for him are low because of his ethnicity. We might consistently ask female students, rather than males, to take notes for students who are ill, or ask males, rather than females, to head up lab groups. Since early socialization into these stereotypes is very powerful, we are often unaware of the biases we exhibit. Attending to these requires that we engage in a continual process of "unlearning" through careful reflection on our past assumptions in light of present understandings.

Tokenism, paying attention to a person solely because of a cho-sen demographic characteristic of interest, can also get in the way of treating students individually. Students feel uncomfortable when we say such things as, "John, how do disabled people feel about this issue?" John may not have an opinion; he may feel that there is likely to be a range of opinions on the topic across stu-dents with disabilities; and he might feel put on the spot. While it is understandable that we might want to include the student in the treatment of a topic and hear the voice of the "local expert," most students want to be respected as individuals and to con-tribute on their own volition when these issues are addressed.

Individual nurturing through mentoring relationships is also important, yet women and students of color report much lower instances of being mentored than male European Americans (Blackwell, 1990; Hall & Sandler, 1982). In commenting on the rea-sons for the lack of mentoring and graduate associateships reported by minority graduate students, Blackwell concludes that faculty do not choose students who are different from themselves, as there is a "tendency for faculty members to consciously or sub-consciously attempt to reproduce themselves through persons chosen as their protegees" (p. 8). Keeping an open mind about having work go in a new direction or appreciating stylistic differences as potentially complementary or liberating are often involved in mentoring previously underrepresented students.

In sum, to treat students as individuals, we can

- Look beyond stereotypes to appreciate individual characteristics.

- Allow students to volunteer opinions rather than asking them to serve as representatives of their social group.

- Cultivate mentoring relationships with students from underrepresented or marginalized groups.

FULL PARTICIPATION IN LEARNING

Valuing people who think and act in ways that are consistent with the traditional culture of the institution often leads to inadvertent or deliberate exclusion of those who are different. Usually we are unaware that we are operating within a cultural perspective, since the dominant culture is taken for granted. As Adams (1992) describes, while this culture is natural and invisible to some, it is uncomfortable for any students from socially diverse groups, because in its most extreme form, it is "narrow in that it rules out nonverbal, empathic, visual, symbolic, or nuanced communication; it neglects the social processes by which interpersonal communication, influence, consensus, and commitment are included in problem solving, it overlooks the social environment as a source of information . . . ; it ignores the values and emotions that nonacademics attach to reasons and facts" (p. 6).

The disjuncture between the dominant classroom culture and the culture of many students can be extreme. For students who have not had a great deal of mainstream culture experience and whose native language is not English, the differences are enormous (Collett & Serrano, 1992). Many scholars have enumerated differences between particular cultures and academic culture. Hofstede (1986), for example, talks about differences in whether the individual or the group is valued, whether there are large or small power distances between people, whether the culture seeks certainty or tolerates ambiguity, and whether the culture stresses the "masculine" characteristics of material success and assertiveness or the "feminine" characteristics of quality of life and interpersonal relationships. He describes the classroom culture as very different from the cultural expectations of many groups. Much has been written about the differences between an afrocentric versus eurocentric worldview (Asante, 1987, 1988; Karenga, 1995). These studies portray the afrocentric worldview as stressing harmony, egalitarian social relations, a fluid notion of time and space, the social world, nonverbal communication, holistic thinking, intuitive reasoning, and approximation and the eurocentric worldview as stressing competition, power, numerical precision, abstract thinking, verbal communication, analytical thinking, logic, and quantitative accuracy. This literature portrays American classrooms as valuing the eurocentric worldview.

Learning Style Dimensions of Full Participation

There is not a clear consensus on whether one can draw implications on learning styles from cultural styles or whether particular learning styles are associated with particular groups. In the case of some of the populations being discussed, such as gay, lesbian, and bisexual students, there is no present evidence to indicate that there are clear patterns. For some other groups, such as students with learning disabilities, there are clear differences (by definition) connected with the disability. In some of the remaining categories of students, such as nontraditional age students, women, and students of color, several studies suggest that there are patterns. These descriptions must be viewed with caution, since talking about broad patterns across groups of people who have many intragroup differences can lead to stereotyping and overgeneralization. On the other hand, if descriptions of styles are considered as tools to illustrate differences rather than as applicable to every individual in the categories described, they can be helpful. Irvine and York (1995) provide an excellent overview of this topic.

When scholars talk about major differences in cognitive and social-interactional styles across various cultures, they often use the work of learning style theorists and apply their constructs, which are usually polar opposites, such as abstract versus concrete thinking, to a particular cultural group. Anderson and Adams (1992), for example, use Anderson's categories of relational and analytical and Witkin and Moore's (1975) categories of field independence and field dependence (also termed "field sensitivity") to illustrate differences in style. They argue that women from the European-American culture and men and women from American Indian, Hispanic-American, and African-American cultures often exhibit a style that is relational and field dependent. They suggest that many people from these groups are more improvisational and intuitive than sequential and structured; more interested in material with social or concrete content than abstract material; more holistic than analytic; and more cooperative than competitive. Most European-American males (most faculty members) and Asian-American males would tend to fall into the opposite categories. They have been socialized through their culture and the academic tradition to value analytic, structured, abstract approaches. The danger that this research warns against is that we might view differences from the traditional norm as deficits, devaluing the work of some students and preventing them from learning well.

Similarly, a body of literature on cognitive development discusses patterns in the way in which women take in and process information (Baxter Magolda, 1992; Belenky et al., 1986). These studies have looked closely at epistemological development, resisting the strict association of one pattern with male students and one with females, while at the same time identifying contrasting styles that are gender related. They find that development in the women they studied culminates in levels of thinking that are as complex as those described in studies of men but are qualitatively different at each stage in gender-related ways. Baxter Magolda, for example, describes four levels of epistemological reflection: absolute, transitional, independent, and contextual knowing. Within each of the first three levels, however, students demonstrate contrasting approaches, generally termed "relational" and "abstract." For example, transitional knowers, the most prevalent type of knowers among traditional-age college students, demonstrate two patterns: the interpersonal pattern, found more frequently in women, and the impersonal, found more frequently in men. Although both genders are transitional

Interpersonal	Impersonal
Want to exchange ideas with others	Want to debate ideas
Seek rapport with the instructor	Want to be challenged by the instructor
Want evaluation to take individual differences into account	Want fair and practical evaluation
Resolve uncertainty by personal judgment	Resolve uncertainty by logic and research
Source: Baxter Magolda, 1992.	

TABLE 20.2   Gender-related Patterns of Thinking in Traditional-Age College Students

knowers in that they view knowledge as uncertain, at least in some areas, and understanding as more important than acquiring and remembering information, they demonstrate the different gender-related patterns in Table 20.2.

One area of research that documents how different ways of knowing affect classroom learning is the literature on classroom participation. Several researchers have found in empirical studies that in classroom discussion white males speak more frequently and for longer periods than white females and than males and females of color and that they are treated deferentially by teachers (Allen & Niss, 1990; Sadker & Sadker, 1992; Trujillo, 1986). Clearly, the style associated with European-American males is dominant in many American college classrooms, making it difficult for others to participate.

Physical and Learning Disabilities

Students with mobility impairments, problems with vision or hearing, and students who learn differently because of attention issues, dyslexia, or a host of other characteristics must also be allowed full participation. Although such students are encouraged to speak with instructors about their needs, teachers can pave the way for this interaction by opening each course with a general statement on caring about students' individual needs and inviting students to speak with them about these as well as inserting statements about alternative formats and practices in the syllabus for each course. Rojewski and Schell (1994) suggest specific ways in which instructors can adapt or modify their teaching to serve students with disabilities. Instructors who cultivate a good relationship with the campus units that serve students with disabilities can make good recommendations and provisions for full participation.

Age Differences

Full participation for students older than the traditional 17- to 22-year-old college student can be fostered by attending to students' need for relevance to life experiences and being flexible when the personal responsibilities of students with child care issues or workplace pressures call for different learning arrangements. When the age of the student entails some physical limitations, such as hearing loss or diminished memory, provisions similar to those extended to students with physical disabilities, such as alternative formats, permission to audiotape class, and extended time for tests, can be offered.

Increasing Opportunities for Full Participation

In general, then, we can increase opportunities for participation in several ways. First, we can be aware that different cultural and learning styles exist. We can reflect on their own styles and on the extent to which our preferences for a style or grounding in a culture leads to teaching practices that exclude others. Similarly, we can be alert to these differences among our students.

Second, we can use varied instructional approaches. Moving between lecture, discussion, small-group work, experiential learning, simulations, and other strategies allows more possibilities for students to find learning opportunities for all to expand their own stylistic repertoires. Similarly, we can use redundancy in teaching modalities and provide for options in assignments.

Third, we can evaluate work from multiple perspectives. For example, rather than viewing a personal narrative by a non-traditional-age student as "subjective, emotional, and unscholarly," we can see it as an alternative kind of contribution to the traditional footnoted and impersonal paper, each valuable in a different way.

Increasing Motivation

In addition to attending to differences in style, culture, and physical ability, a very powerful way that we can enable full participation in learning is to attend to the motivational aspects of learning. Wlodkowski and Ginsberg (1995) enumerate ways in which this can be done:

- *Establishing inclusion* focuses on conveying a sense of respect for the student and working to connect students through communicating a sense of confidence in the student and encouraging collaboration and ownership. Practices that foster inclusion include collaborative and cooperative learning, peer teaching, writing groups, and exercises that create opportunities for reframing knowledge from different perspectives.

- *Developing attitude* speaks to the importance of students' need for personal relevance and self-determination. Strategies that attend to attitude include engaging students in goal setting, allowing choices in learning, and encouraging experiential learning.

- *Enhancing meaning* stresses the need for engagement and challenge through promoting higher-order thinking in real-world applications. Meaning can be enhanced though the use of critical questioning, decision-making exercises, research on student-generated questions, and creative activity.

- *Engendering competence* addresses a central finding of motivation theory research, the need for the learner to feel that success is possible. Here, the focus is on multiple ways to represent knowledge and effective assessment methods, including frequent feedback, self-assessment on the part of the learner, and alternatives to pencil-and-paper tests that are grounded in the context of the skills or knowledge being assessed.

BEING TREATED FAIRLY

Egalitarian treatment of students is a very valued norm in American higher education. Grading anonymously, giving all students the same amount of time to complete a test or assignment, and requiring the same number and type of assignments by each student are common practices. We often say, "I treat all students the same." Yet a closer look reveals that we do not treat all students the same, nor should we. Students with disabilities are often allowed more time for exams, the help of a reader, or a special setting for taking the test. Nonnative speakers may be allowed to use dictionaries during test taking, and their work may be graded more for content than for expression of ideas. Equal treatment involves not necessarily same treatment, then, but treatment that respects the individual needs of particular learners.

While we may readily accept different treatment for students who are disabled, nonnative speakers, or even those older students who have hearing impairments or work slowly, we might find it much more difficult to justify different treatment based on gender or cultural characteristics. Once again, however, beginning with the individual student is important. It is important to have expectations that are appropriate to the student. Some disjuncture between the student's point of entry and the dominant culture may occur, and balance should be sought. For example, students coming from cultures where time is viewed fluidly may have difficulty understanding that due dates will be interpreted literally or that class begins promptly on the hour. Most students have learned to be bicultural and to operate under different sets of assumptions based on the cultural context. Others, however, may need help. It may be necessary to have individual conversations with such students, emphasizing the expectations or making reminders about due dates. It may be important to tolerate a few mistakes before penalizing students or to rethink the cultural-embeddedness of the rule. A conversation at the start of the course on expectations and standards, coupled with a clear syllabus, can help communications immeasurably.

We can also consider cultural or gender-related issues that may affect class discussion. Many female students or men and women students from American Indian or Asian-American backgrounds have been socialized to value listening more than speaking. For them, a class participation grading scheme based on number of contributions in class may be problematic. Fair treatment might be based on quality of comment rather than quantity or on performance in dyad or small-group, rather than whole-class, conversation. Students who are from more reflective than spontaneous cultures can be helped by giving the class time for silent thought before responses are solicited. They may need to learn the culture. Conversely, students from the dominant culture may learn from them, incorporating the strengths of silent reflection into class routines. Myra and David Sadker (1992) recommend that teachers ask an observer to record participation levels in their classes to give them a sense of the patterns that are occurring so that they may avoid the pitfall of unequal discussion.

Inherent in all discussions about fairness is mutuality. The need for order and routine must be balanced by appreciation for variation and richness of perspective. Strongly forcing students from nontraditional backgrounds to acculturate to the institution in order to succeed prevents the institution from learning and expanding its potential. Pervading considerations of social diversity are issues involved in the ongoing revitalization of colleges as places of learning.

IN CONCLUSION

As faculty, we play a crucial role in the success of students from socially diverse groups. To help these students succeed and to help the institution benefit from their talents and perspectives, we can

1. Make the students feel welcome by displaying genuine interest, personalizing our interactions with them, and honoring and including their perspectives and experiences.
2. Treat students as individuals, rather than as representatives of social groups.

3. Ensure that students from diverse social groups have ample opportunity to participate fully through providing options for different learning styles and modes of expression.

4. Strive for fair treatment by communicating appropriate expectations and making instructional decisions with inclusion in mind.

Supplementary Reading

L. B. Border and N. V. N. Chism, eds., *Teaching for Diversity*, New Directions in Teaching and Learning, 49 (San Francisco: Jossey-Bass, 1992). This collection of essays treats the following topics: the culture of the classroom, learning styles of diverse learners, gender equity in the classroom, feminist pedagogy, and developing programs to promote inclusive teaching. Descriptions of successful programs and a resource guide are included.

B. P. Bowser, T. Jones, and G. A. Young, eds., *Toward the Multicultural University* (Westport, CT: Praeger, 1995). This collection focuses on the rationale for multicultural teaching and curriculum, but also identifies the issues of key populations and addresses such organizational considerations as technology, strategic planning, assessment, and institutional structure.

D. Schoem, L. Frankel, X. Zúñiga, and E. A. Lewis, eds., *Multicultural Teaching in the University* (Westport, CT: Praeger, 1993). This collection of thoughtful essays explores the meaning and function of multicultural teaching in higher education through conceptual pieces as well as reports of the actual experiences of instructors from various disciplines and perspectives working to enact new curricula and teaching practices.

R. Wlodkowski and M. Ginsberg, *Diversity and Motivation: Culturally Responsive Teaching.* (San Francisco: Jossey-Bass, 1995). The authors approach multicultural teaching from the perspective of motivation, identifying norms and structural conditions that will help students feel included, establish a productive attitude toward learning, derive meaning from their learning, and feel competent as learners.

Problem Students (There's Almost Always at Least One!)* 21

Periodically during my weekly meetings with teaching assistants, I suggest that we discuss problem students or situations in their classes as an agenda item for the next week. I have never found that the next week's discussion ended early for lack of examples. It is reassuring to know that one is not alone in having a particular problem and that it is probably not due solely to one's inadequacy as a teacher. This chapter will discuss some of the common problems that have been raised by my teaching assistants and will suggest some strategies to try. But first a word of general advice.

It is human nature for us to perceive the problem as the student; but before focusing on changing the student's behavior, take a few moments to look at what you are doing that might be related to the student's behavior. Interpersonal problems involve at least two people, and in many cases the difficulties are not one-sided.

---

* Note that strategies for dealing with some problems have been discussed in earlier chapters; for example, students who don't do their share of the work are discussed in Chapter 14, on peer learning.

ANGRY, AGGRESSIVE, CHALLENGING STUDENTS

Every once in a while a class will include one or more students who seem to have a chip on their shoulder—who convey, both verbally and nonverbally, hostility toward you and the whole enterprise. Sometimes the attitude is not so much hostility as a challenge to your authority. What can you do?

Probably the most common strategy we use is to try to ignore them. This strategy often succeeds in avoiding a public confrontation and disruption of the class. However, it may not result in better motivation and learning for the student.

I try to become better acquainted with the student. If I have had students turn in minute papers or journals, I read the angry student's writings more carefully to try to understand what the problem is. I may ask the student to come in to see me and discuss the paper, leading to questions about how the student feels about the course, what things he enjoys, what topics might be interesting to him. (I use the male pronoun because these students are most likely to be males, although I have also encountered hostile female students.) Sometimes you will feel in such a conversation that you have to drag each word from the student; yet the student will accept your invitation to come in for another discussion. Sometimes you may need to invite a small group of students to meet with you (including the hostile student) in order to make the situation less threatening for the hostile student who hides fear with aggressiveness.

Whatever your strategy, it seems to me important to let the student know that you recognize him as an individual, that you are committed to his learning, and that you are willing to listen and respond as constructively as possible.

What about overt hostility—the student who attacks your point of view during a lecture or class discussion, or the student who feels that your poor teaching or unfair grading caused students' poor performance on a test?

First of all, *listen* carefully and respectfully. Nothing is more frustrating than to be interrupted before your argument or complaint has been heard. Next, acknowledge that there is a possibility that the student may be right or at least that there is some logic or evidence on his or her side. Recognize the student's feelings. Then you have at least two or three alternatives:

1. State your position as calmly and rationally as you can, recognizing that not everyone will agree. If the issue is one of substance, ask the class what evidence might be obtained to resolve or clarify the issue. Don't rely on your own authority or power to put the student down or to make it a win-lose situation. If the issue is one of judgment about grading, state your reason for asking the question, what sort of thinking you were hoping to assess, and how students who did well went about answering the question. Note that your judgment may not be perfect, but you have the responsibility to make the best judgment you can, and you have done so.

2. Present the issue to the class. "How do the rest of you feel about this?" This has the obvious danger that either you or the aggressor may find no support and feel alienated from the class, but more often than not it will bring the issues and arguments for both sides into the open and be a useful experience in thinking for everyone. This might be a place to use the two-column method described in Chapter 5, listing on the chalkboard, without comments, the arguments on both sides.

3. Admit that you may have been wrong, and say that you will take time to reconsider and report back at the next class session. If the student really does have a good point, this will gain you respect and a reputation for fairness. If the student's argument was groundless, you may gain the reputation of being easy to influence, and have an increasing crowd of students asking for changes in their grades.

What about the student who comes into your office all charged up to attack your grading of what was clearly a very good exam paper?

Again, the first step is to listen. Get the student to state his or her rationale. As suggested in Chapter 7, you may gain some time to think if you have announced that students who have questions or complaints about grading of their tests should bring a written explanation to your office of their point of view and the rationale for their request for a higher grade.

But, once again, don't be so defensive about your grading that you fail to make an adjustment if the student has a valid point. I have on rare occasions offered to ask another faculty member to read the paper or examination to get an independent judgment.

If you don't feel that the student has a valid point and your explanation is not convincing, you may simply have to say that, although the student may be right, you have to assign the grades in terms of what seem to you the appropriate criteria. If you have been clear about the rubric you use in grading, both before giving the assignment or test and when you returned the papers, grievances should be rare.

ATTENTION SEEKERS AND STUDENTS WHO DOMINATE DISCUSSIONS

In their book *The College Classroom,* Dick Mann (1970) and his graduate students describe eight clusters of students, one of which is "attention seekers." Attention seekers talk whether or not they have anything to say; they joke, show off, compliment the teacher or other students—they continually try to be noticed (Mann et al., 1970).

At the beginning of the term, when I am trying to get discussions started, I am grateful for the attention seekers. They help keep the discussion going. But as the class develops, both the other students and I tend to be disturbed by the students who talk too much and interfere with other students' chances to talk. What do I do then?

Usually I start by suggesting that I want to get everyone's ideas—that each student has a unique perspective and that it is important that we bring as many perspectives and ideas as possible to bear on the subject under discussion. If hands are raised to participate, I call first on those who haven't talked recently.

If the problem persists, I may suggest to the class that some people seem to participate much more than others and ask them for suggestions about what might be done to give all students a chance to participate.

Alternatively, I might ask two or three students to act as "process observers" for a day, to report at the end of the class or at the beginning of the next class on their observations of how the discussion went, what problems they noticed, and what suggestions they have. (I might even ask the attention seeker to be a process observer one day.) Or you might audiotape or videotape a class and play back one or more portions at the next class period for student reactions.

If all else fails, I ask the student to see me outside class and mention that I'm concerned about the class discussions. Much as I appreciate his involvement it would be helpful if he would hold back some of his comments until everyone else has been heard.

In the preceding comments I may have assumed that the attention seeker was not making good, helpful comments. There are also dominant students who are knowledgeable, fluent, and eager to contribute relevant information, contribute real insights, and solve problems. We prize such students; yet there is still the potential danger that other students will withdraw, feeling that there is no need to participate, since the dominant student is so brilliant or articulate that their own ideas and questions will seem weak and inadequate. Here subgrouping may help, with the stipulation that each student must present his or her question, idea, or reaction to the task of the group before beginning a general discussion.

In his newsletter *The University Teacher* Harry Stanton (1992), consultant on higher education at the University of Tasmania, suggests that each student be given three matches or markers at the beginning of the class. Each time they speak they must put down one of their markers and when their markers are gone, their contributions are over for the day. Perhaps subgroups could pool their markers or one could borrow or bargain for an extra marker for a really good idea that needs to be presented at this time.

SILENT STUDENTS

What to do about the students who never participate in class discussions? If we believe that it is important for students to practice thinking and get reactions to their ideas, students who fail to participate are perhaps more of a problem than the attention seekers. You may argue that students have the right to remain silent, and I have some sympathy for that position; yet it seems to me that we do not suggest that students have a right to omit tests or to opt out of writing papers or other assignments that we believe contribute to learning. Students have a right to expect that we tell them why we expect active participation or why other assigned activities will contribute to learning, but this does not mean that they should be able to omit anything that they wish to.

In earlier chapters I discussed some techniques of getting participation, such as minute papers, pairing, buzz groups, and problem posting. These techniques, useful for all students, are also helpful for students who would otherwise be silent. But there may still be students who, despite having written a minute paper and participated in a buzz group, remain silent in general class discussions. What can we do?

One aid involves getting to know the students' interests or special experiences well enough that you can call on them for some item on which they have special expertise. We have discussed such techniques as papers or file cards filled out the first week of class with information about relevant student experiences. A silent student's research paper may give the student expertise or information useful at some point in a class discussion. A student panel in which students prepare presentations on different aspects or sides of some theoretical or applied issue may provide an opportunity to involve one or more silent students. (If you use such a panel, it is probably wise to meet with them to give support and guidance both in preparation of the content and in planning how to make the presentation interesting and informative.) And, as in dealing with the aggressive and attention-seeking students, getting to know the student outside of class is likely to help you generate strategies for facilitating learning. Sometimes the student who is silent in class feels freer to participate in e-mail or computer conferencing discussions.

Both nonparticipants and discussion monopolizers have been discussed in Chapter 5, which presents some of these and other strategies for dealing with such students.

INATTENTIVE STUDENTS

Periodically I have a class in which two or three students in the back of the classroom carry on their own conversations. This is annoying not only to me but to students sitting near them. What to do?

Think back to my first word of advice. Is the lecture material too difficult? too easy? Is the topic of discussion one that arouses anxiety? Assuming that the answer to these questions is "no" and the behavior persists despite changes in topic or level of difficulty, what next?

My first attempt is typically to break the class into buzz groups assigned to work on some problem or to come up with a hypothesis, and to move around the class to see how the groups are progressing, making sure that I get to the group including the disruptive students to see that they are working on the group task. Usually this works, and sometimes this gets the students reengaged in the class for the rest of the class period.

But suppose that in the next class period the same problem recurs? This time I might have the class write minute papers and call on one of the inattentive students to report what he or she has written, or alternatively call on someone seated near the inattentive group, centering activity toward that part of the classroom.

Another possibility is to announce that, because research evidence indicates that students who sit in front get better grades (and you can explain why seeing an instructor's face and mouth improves attention and understanding), you have a policy of rotating seats periodically so that next week you will expect those sitting in the back row to move to the front row and all other rows to move back one row.

If all else fails, I might have a general class feedback discussion on what factors facilitated and what factors might have interfered with learning in the class thus far in the term. Alternatively, I might ask one or more of the students to see me outside of class to ask about their feelings about the class and to express my concern about not being able to teach in a way that would capture their attention.

UNPREPARED STUDENTS

There are often good reasons why students come to class unprepared, but there are also students who are chronically unprepared for no apparent reason. What can we do?

In my introductory course I try to communicate from the beginning that I expect students to read the assignments before class by announcing that I will give a brief quiz the second day of class based on the first lecture or discussion and the assignment for the next class. I give the quiz and then ask students to correct their own papers, indicating that this quiz had two purposes: to start the habit of reading the assignment before class, and to give them an idea of whether or not they were getting the main points of the assignment. I give a second quiz a week later and a longer one three weeks later. By this point I hope that my students have established a routine for keeping up with their assignments.

Such a procedure assumes that students know what is expected of them. One of the most common causes of under-preparation is that students don't really know what is expected. Often instructors say something like, "You might want to look at the next chapter of the book before the next class," or they state that the next lecture will be on topic X, without indicating that this is also the topic of the next reading. Giving students some questions to think about as they study the next assignment can help, as will announcements of an activity in the next class that depends on the assignment. One of the advantages of a well-written syllabus is that it communicates your expectations. You also need to communicate expectations by frequent use of such phrases as "As your assignment for today demonstrated" or questions such as "What does X (the textbook author say about . . . ?" or "What evidence from the assigned readings would support (or not support) your position?"

THE FLATTERER, DISCIPLE, CON MAN (OR WOMAN)

If one is new or somewhat insecure, it is tempting to respond positively to anyone who tells you that you are the best teacher he or she has ever had, or who is impressed with the depth of your knowledge and wants to learn more about your special research interests. In fact, one does not need to be new or insecure; we all relish compliments and interest in our work. More often than not such interest is genuine and can be genuinely enriching both for you and the student; but there are students for whom such an approach is a conscious strategy for winning better grades or getting exceptions from deadlines for papers or other requirements.

The real danger presented by such students is that you will begin to mistrust all students and lose compassion for students who really need an extension of time or some other indication of flexibility. I would rather be conned a couple of times than to turn off by cold rigidity a student who is in real need. Thus my advice is to start with an assumption of honesty; nonetheless, in general, don't change the rules of the game unless you are willing to change them for everyone or unless you are convinced that there are reasonable grounds for a special exception.

DISCOURAGED, READY-TO-GIVE-UP STUDENTS

Often after the first few weeks you will spot some students who seem depressed and discouraged. Sometimes they come to class late or miss class; often their papers are constricted and lack any sense of enthusiasm or creativity. In my introductory classes, some students begin with great enthusiasm and energy and a few weeks later seem to have lost their energy; interestingly, we spot the same phenomenon in our proseminar for beginning Ph.D. students.

In both cases the transition to a new level of education brings demands greater than those students have experienced in the past. Often their familiar supports from family and friends are no longer available; they begin to doubt their own ability to achieve their goals.

There is a magic elixir for this problem that research has demonstrated to be surprisingly effective. This is to bring in students from the previous year who describe their experiences of frustration and self-doubt during their first year and report that they surmounted them and survived. The theory explaining why this works basically states that the task is to convince the discouraged students that their problems need not be attributed to a lack of ability that cannot be changed but rather is a temporary problem. By developing more effective strategies, investing more effort, or simply becoming less worried, better results are likely to follow (Van Overwalle, Segebarth, & Goldchstein, 1989; Wilson & Linville, 1982, 1985).

STUDENTS WITH EXCUSES

As indicated earlier, I believe that it is better to be taken in by a fraudulent excuse than to be seen as unfair in response to a legitimate excuse. Nonetheless, one doesn't want to be seen as so gullible that students come to rely on excuses rather than doing their assignments. Caron, Whitbourne, and Halgin (1992) studied excuse making and in their sample found that about two-thirds of their students admitted having made at least one false excuse while in college. From these students' reports it appears that fraudulent excuses were about as frequent as legitimate ones. In most cases the excuse was used to gain more time for an assignment.

The Caron et al. data do not give many clues about what one can do to prevent or detect false excuses. If the problem is one of time, one might build in checks on the progress of a paper or other assignment to reduce the tendency to put off work until the last minute—you could, for example, have students turn in an outline or bibliography some time before a paper is due.

Sometimes I have announced in the syllabus that there would be a graded series of penalties depending on how late a paper was, indicating that this was to make up for the advantage the late students had in having extra time to look up more sources, get comments and feedback from other students, and so forth. An alternative that I have not used, which might be more advantageous psychologically, would be to offer a bonus for papers turned in early.

It might also be wise to put in your syllabus that you want to be flexible on deadlines and recognize that unforeseen events may prevent students from being able to meet a deadline. But in making exceptions you will require evidence supporting the request for an extension.

STUDENTS WHO WANT THE TRUTH AND STUDENTS WHO BELIEVE THAT EVERYTHING IS RELATIVE

You have just given a superb lecture comparing two competing theories. A student comes up after class and says, "That was a great lecture, but which theory is right?"

All too many students feel that the teacher's task is to tell students the facts and larger truths and the student's task is to listen to the truth, learn it, and be able to give it back on exams. This conception seemed to William Perry of Harvard University to be particularly common among first-year students.

Perry (1981) suggested that individual differences in student responses to teaching may be conceptualized in terms of student stages of cognitive development. Students at the lower stages are characterized by a dualistic view of knowledge. Things are either true or false, right or wrong. The teacher knows the truth; the student's job is to learn the truth. Students in the middle stages have learned that authorities differ. There seems to be no settled truth; everyone has a right to his or her own opinions. This stage is succeeded by the recognition that some opinions and generalizations are better supported than others. The student's task is to learn the criteria needed for evaluating the validity of assertions in different subject matter fields. The final stages involve student commitment to values, beliefs, and goals with the recognition that despite the lack of complete certainty one must make decisions and act on one's values. Barbara Hofer (1997) found that dualists are now rare. Rather, college students are more likely to believe that multiple perspectives are equally valid. So what should teachers do?

Perry and Hofer would agree that teachers need to help students understand how knowledge is arrived at in their own disciplines, what counts as evidence, and how to read critically and evaluate knowledge claims. For development in epistemological beliefs students need to debate and discuss issues in which competing ideas are challenged and defended; they need to write journals and papers that are responded to by the teacher or by peers.

STUDENTS WITH EMOTIONAL REACTIONS TO SENSITIVE TOPICS

In almost every discipline there are some topics that will arouse strong feelings in some of your students. In a psychology class it might be "group differences in intelligence"; in biology it might be "evolution" or "animal experimentation"; in sociology it might be "the role of birth control and abortion in population policy." Often we are hesitant to open such topics up to discussion.

But if the topic is relevant and important, it is probably wise to acknowledge the sensitivity of the topic and to admit that it may be hard for some members of the class to feel free to contribute their ideas. Explain why the topic is relevant to the goals of the course. Comparing alternative approaches, perhaps by using the two-column method described in Chapter 5, may help students see the complexity of the issue. In conducting the discussion it is important to stress that each student should listen to other students with respect and try to understand their positions. You might ask a student to put into his or her own words what other students have said. Having students write a short essay advocating a position opposed to their own is effective in opening their minds (Miller et al., 1997).

IN CONCLUSION

1. Don't duck controversy.
2. Listen, and get students to listen to one another.
3. Keep your cool.
4. Remember that your problem students are human beings who have problems and need your sympathy and help—no matter how much you would like to strangle them.

Supplementary Reading

An excellent review of the attributional retraining research dealing with motivation of discouraged students is R. P. Perry, F. J. Hechter, V. H. Menec, and L. Weinberg, *A Review of Attributional Motivation and*

Performance in College Students from an Attributional Retraining Perspective, Occasional Papers in Higher Education, Centre for Higher Education Research and Development, The University of Manitoba, Winnipeg, Manitoba, Canada R3T 2N2.

A helpful source is Mary Deane Sorcinelli's chapter, Dealing with Troublesome Behaviors in the Classroom, in K. W. Prichard and R. M. Sawyer (eds.), *Handbook of College Teaching: Theory and Applications* (Westport, CT: Greenwood, 1994).

Barbara Hofer and Paul Pintrich review the various theories about epistemological beliefs and learning in "The Development of Epistemological Theories: Beliefs About Knowledge and Knowing and Their Relation to Learning," *Review of Educational Research,* 1997, 67, 88–140.

22 Counseling and Advising

COUNSELING*

Some of your most effective teaching may occur during office hours. As my hair has been turning to white, I have felt that students were more reluctant to impose upon me and come to my office. Thus, when I have a class of no more than 30 students, I pass around a signup sheet and ask every student to sign up for a half-hour "get acquainted" office visit either alone or with other students who have signed up for the same time. This at least breaks the ice so that they know where my office is and presumably find it not to be forbiddingly uncomfortable. My hope is that they will then feel freer to use my office hours and to make appointments to see me.

In this chapter I will first deal with the most common reason students come to talk to you—problems with the course. Next we move to academic advising (helping students plan their

---

* I use the word *counseling* as a generic term covering helping students with problems with your course, advising students about academic programs, and psychological counseling about personal problems.

programs), then to serious problems that may need the help of professional psychological counselors, and finally to individualized teaching.

I should warn you that a student's ostensible reasons for coming to you may be quite different from the real reasons. Often students ask about a study problem when their real desire is to know the instructor better. They complain of inadequate study habits when underneath there may be difficulties with their home life. I do not mean that you should disregard the problems the students actually present, but if you are aware of possible underlying factors, you may be more understanding and more effective as a counselor.

Counseling need not be restricted to the office. Arriving early and talking to students after class can meet some needs. Out of the classroom you may be able to get to the real problem more easily over a Coke in the student union than in a more formal office visit.

The most common student problem is worded something like this: "I study harder for this course than for all my other courses, but I just can't seem to pass the tests." In handling this problem I usually encourage the students to express their own ideas about their difficulties. Sometimes their diagnosis and plans for improvement will be much more accurate than any I can give them. If the student has no idea what to do, ask the student to describe in detail how he or she has spent time during the previous week and studied for your course. Frequently, simple information on budgeting time, on how the students can ask themselves questions about the assignment, or on getting an overview of a chapter before reading it can be of much help.

In general, the key is to get the students away from reading passively or trying to memorize and instead to question, relate, and think more actively about the assignment and lectures.* Sometimes you can help by getting the students to use the

* For further help you might suggest Paul Hettich, *Learning Skills for College and Career* (Pacific Grove, CA: Brooks-Cole, 1992), or Walter Pauk, *How to Study in College,* 6th ed. (Boston: Houghton Mifflin, 1997).

study guide often published as an ancillary to the textbook or by referring the student for reading and study skills to an agency providing training. Even better may be to encourage peer teaching. In Chapter 14 I noted that even poor students can learn by trying to explain something to a peer.

ADVISING AND PROGRAM PLANNING

The modern university is a complex organization. The student's path through this organization is supposedly mapped by handbooks and catalogues. Unfortunately, most of these documents are, at best, forbiddingly dull and confusingly written. In too many instances they are less than adequate road guides because almost every curriculum has its unwritten requirements. These are preferences for certain sequences of courses or for the choice of one of several alternatives that are so strongly adhered to by the department or college that they become, in effect, requirements for graduation. At the same time, because they are not formal requirements, they exist as part of the folklore rather than as part of the written law.

This state of affairs means that, where students are left on their own to select courses, there is great danger of having to extend the normal four-year program because of mistakes in curricular planning. This has given rise to the faculty counselor who is given the responsibility for guiding the students through the intricacies of their chosen curriculum.

The university usually places on this faculty counselor the responsibility for the enforcement of various other regulations governing the students' curricular activities—for example, the number of credits students may elect in a given period, the fulfillment of prerequisites, and the meeting of general requirements for graduation where they exist. The result is that relations between students and faculty are often strained, for the students going to see the faculty members become part of a bureaucratic, impersonal processing that they are impatient to pare down to its irreducible essentials.

DEALING WITH PSYCHOLOGICAL PROBLEMS

At some point you will suspect that a student needs psychological counseling. Some of the signs are belligerence, moodiness, excessive worry, suspiciousness, helplessness, emotional outbursts, or depression. Sometimes you will spot symptoms of drug or alcohol abuse. How do you get the student to the help needed?

The first step may be to get the student to talk to you. Usually this can be handled by asking the student to come in, perhaps to discuss a paper or test. Typically the student will be aware that things aren't going well, and you can simply ask, "How are things going?" or "What do you think is the reason for your problems?" Listen rather than intervening. After listening and questioning, you might then say, "What do you think you can do?" One alternative, probably the best, is to seek professional help. If the student agrees that this might be a good idea, I've found that it helps to pick up the phone and say, "I'll call to see when they can see you." In fact, most such agencies will at least carry out an initial interview with any student who walks in. But the sense of commitment involved when a faculty member has called seems to make students more likely to follow through than if they simply agree that they'll go in. Even if the student does not immediately get professional help, your concern and support will be helpful, and awareness of the availability of professional help may be valuable later.

POTENTIAL SUICIDES

The increasing concern with suicide risk among college students prompts a few words on the early recognition of the kinds of depressed states that accompany such risks. If you were to notice a sudden falling off of a particular student's faithfulness in attending class, you might want to inquire further, especially if you noted signs of neglect of personal grooming and hygiene, lethargy, and any marked weight changes. Your interest in the student should include concern with any other

changes he or she has been experiencing, including major sep-
arations or losses and mood states. You should listen for talk
of death or references to suicide or to getting one's personal
and legal affairs in order. Your major concern should not be to
reach an accurate assessment of suicide risk. A student manifest-
ing any of these characteristics is surely troubled and should be
urged to seek whatever professional counseling is available. Once
I walked with a student to the clinic to be sure that he got there.
On a couple of occasions when the student seemed unlikely to
seek help, I have asked the university health service to call the
student in.

INDIVIDUALIZED TEACHING

We dealt with one-on-one teaching in Chapter 15. Here I want to
discuss interactions with students dealing with larger issues of
their educational and personal development. The potentially
most fruitful and most appropriate interpretation of educational
counseling is the one least often defined explicitly and most
neglected. Even in classes of 40 to 60 students, it is difficult for the
learning process to include the meeting of a maturing and a
mature intellect. Too frequently students must be content to listen
to lectures and pursue readings aimed at some abstracted image
of a student.

In out-of-class interactions with students or as a student's academic advisor, you can supplement their course-related learning
with personalized learning that facilitates their adjustment to college. This is particularly necessary for first-year students, to
whom new intellectual spheres are being opened, usually at a
time when they have taken a big step away from their family and
community roots. This is likely to be a time when a great many
new assumptions and new ways of dealing with important ideas
need to be digested. Educational counselors, because they have
no commitment to covering a specific subject matter, can provide
students with an opportunity to digest and integrate the intellectual experiences they have been having. Far from being a chore to
be assigned to the least successful faculty member, such a

demanding responsibility is best undertaken by persons of broad intellectual interests and foundations who, at the same time, have strong pedagogical commitments.

This time, when students are making big strides toward greater independence from family and are trying to seek out models who can represent innovations of the adult role to which they aspire, is a time when there should be opportunities for close relationships with faculty members. The very characteristics of the large university throw obstacles in the way of such an experience. Educational counseling is one of the important means for achieving it. It seems probable that the most effective pattern for doing this would be for counselors to plan small-group meetings with the students assigned to them for counseling to provide an opportunity for the groups of new students coming from different parts of the state and country to exchange with each other and with a person of some intellectual maturity the impacts of their initial university experiences. A number of colleges and universities group first-year students into interest groups that meet regularly during the first term to help establish both academic and social support systems.

The problems of the older student entering college are in some ways similar despite the obvious differences in life experience. While both younger and older students often feel some anxiety about their ability to carry out academic work successfully, the older students may have even greater concerns than younger students about their ability to adapt to the college environment and to form helpful relationships with peers (most of whom are much younger and experiencing quite different social and recreational lives).

IN CONCLUSION

1. Listen carefully.
2. Try to empathize.
3. Paraphrase, question, and summarize but delay suggesting alternatives until you are confident that you understand.

Supplementary Reading

In Chickering, *The New American College* (San Francisco: Jossey-Bass, 1988), the chapter by Jane Shipton and Elizabeth Steltenpohl provides a useful perspective on the broad issues faced by academic advisors. The typical schedule of 15 minutes per advisee is clearly insufficient for planning an academic program in relationship to lifelong goals.

Recognizing and Assisting the Troubled Students is an excellent three-page list of ways to recognize and help troubled students. It is Volume 18, Number 5 (January 1997) of *Teaching at UNL,* the newsletter of the University of Nebraska-Lincoln Teaching and Learning Center, 121 Benton Hall, P. O. Box 880623, Lincoln, NE 68588-0623.

In *Tools for Teaching* (San Francisco: Jossey-Bass, 1993), Barbara Davis offers good practical advice in Chapter 44, Holding Office Hours, and Chapter 45, Academic Advising and Monitoring Undergraduates.

Also see A. G. Reinarz, and E. R. White, (eds.), *Teaching Through Academic Advising: New Directions for Teaching and Learning,* no. 62 (San Francisco: Jossey-Bass, 1995).

D. B. Ellis, *Becoming a Master Student,* 8th ed. (Boston: Houghton Mifflin, 1997).

Lifelong Learning
for You as Well
as Your Students

23 Appraising and Improving Your Teaching: Using Students, Peers, Experts, and Classroom Research

Teachers typically set high standards for their teaching as well as for their students' learning and feel obligated to improve their efforts. Improvements in teaching may arise from any number of sources, including experiences in the classroom, reading about teaching, attending workshops and seminars, and conversations with colleagues and students. This chapter discusses ways to determine how well teaching is going, to identify desirable changes, and to get those changes under way.

CHALLENGES OF CHANGE: INTELLECTUAL, MOTIVATIONAL, SOCIAL

Change is the constant companion of professors. In graduate school, academics learn how scholarly fields change over time, and graduate study culminates with a dissertation intended as yet one more contribution to advancing the discipline. Academics devise multiyear plans that chart intended changes in scholarly

This chapter was written by Robert J. Menges of Northwestern University. Professor Menges died on April 14, 1998. He was a good friend and a good scholar. I shall miss him greatly.

and creative activities. These habits of continuous improvement carry naturally into teaching.

The inclination toward change is in part intellectual. Exceptional curiosity and creativity contributed to professors' success as students, and these intellectual qualities sustain subsequent work in academia. Rather than being put off by problems, professors seek them out, and after solving one problem proceed to deconstruct another.

Teaching offers no end of problems that challenge the intellect—how to engage students at different levels of maturity with the fundamental concepts of a field, how to link those concepts with the world of experience that students bring to class, how to connect the content of one course with content of other courses, and how to bring coherence to the immense array of fragmentary information potentially relevant to a curriculum.

Second, change has a motivational component. Like other professionals, college teachers are motivated to seek feedback. As teachers we want to know how well we are doing, and we change what we do on the basis of information about our performance. Higher education is information-rich, but that information is rarely fed back to teachers in constructive and systematic ways. Many teaching objectives are vague, and teachers get little information about how well objectives have been met. Important consequences of teaching may be long delayed, perhaps never becoming visible to the teacher. The paucity of pertinent feedback about teaching creates considerable stress for academics (Gmelch, Lovrich, & Wilke, 1984). When useful feedback is available, it enhances motivation by increasing feelings of control and efficacy.

Third, the inclination toward change has a social component. Academics as a group are no less likely than other professionals to want to be highly regarded. Professors are alert for clues about what is expected by colleagues and students. How we present ourselves to others depends in part on what we think they expect and on the value we place on meeting their expectations.

The institutional teaching culture is critical for change. In departments and schools where the teaching culture is strong, newcomers quickly discern social norms that promote inquiry and innovation. Where high priority is given to student learning and involvement, student-centered teaching is more likely. Where teaching consultants and other teaching support services are easily available to faculty, instructional experimentation is more frequent. Of course, not all norms are supportive of teaching. Norms carried from graduate training may emphasize research at the expense of teaching. Thus, graduate school socialization into the discipline is sometimes dissonant with the institution's socialization into the workplace.

Teaching improvement can be facilitated by each of these professorial characteristics: the desire to solve intellectual problems, the motivation to seek feedback, and sensitivity to social norms.

LOOKING FOR NEW IDEAS: READING, WORKSHOPS, CONVERSATIONS, CLASSROOM RESEARCH

Changes in teaching often begin with new ideas. Here are some ways to find them.

Reading About Teaching

One might assume from the abundance of books, periodicals, and newsletters on college teaching that professors voraciously consume writings about pedagogy. Yet reading about teaching and learning lags far behind reading about one's field of specialization and may be as little as an hour a week according to one survey (Quinn, 1993).

Nevertheless, the variety of available reading materials is impressive. Books like *Teaching Tips* are used in courses on college teaching and at orientation programs. Most disciplines and professional fields have journals devoted to college teaching. Cross-disciplinary periodicals, such as *College Teaching* and *New Directions for Teaching and Learning,* are available through college libraries and teaching centers. *The Teaching Professor, The National Teaching and Learning Forum,* and other newsletters are distributed nationally, and many individual campuses circulate their own teaching-oriented publications. (For a list of several dozen periodicals on college teaching, see Weimer, 1993.)

Whether reading about teaching leads to actual improvements in teaching is difficult to say. I am not aware of studies on that precise topic, but there is some interesting research from the related field of psychotherapy. Authors of therapeutic self-help books claim that their text helps one understand problems and change behavior. Treating problems of living by prescribing a book, as some therapists do, is known as "bibliotherapy," and research on its effectiveness has produced mixed results. There is some evidence that books oriented toward specific behavior changes are effective, but less support exists for books of fiction, poetry, or inspirational reading (Riordan & Wilson, 1989) despite claims by their authors and publishers.

If we generalize this research to teaching, it implies that change is more likely when readings include detailed discussions and concrete examples at the level of specific behavior. Further, I believe that details and examples are most effective when they are placed in the context of a conceptual framework that makes apparent the rationale underlying their use.

Workshops and Seminars

Workshops and seminars are common activities at most campus teaching centers. Their topics range from theories of learning to skills of teaching to techniques for managing time and for writing grants. When workshops and seminars are carefully planned in response to needs expressed by faculty and when they are skillfully conducted by informed leaders, they can be highly rewarding. At the very least, they occasion interactions among colleagues on topics related to teaching, interactions that might not otherwise occur. The box on page 260 has advice for choosing workshops.

Conversations About Teaching

Faculty tell us that new ideas about teaching come more frequently from colleagues than from readings or workshops. I suspect this is because conversations with departmental colleagues are likely to cover content as well as method. Conversations with students can be highly informative if they are kept to areas where student reactions are credible and thoughtful. Students cannot accurately judge the quality or currency of course content, but they are

On Choosing Workshops

Here are some consumer tips for deciding which workshops are likely to be most worthwhile.

- Clear objectives. Know in advance what the session claims to accomplish so you can judge whether your own work will benefit.
- Qualified leadership. The leader should be expert about the topic of the meeting, and the presentation should model relevant skills of teaching and learning.
- Interactive format. Passive listening is insufficient. One might as well read independently about the topic. Further, sessions that center on the presenter fail to draw out the considerable expertise present in a group. Be sure the format is interactive.
- Opportunity to practice and demonstrate. For skill objectives in particular, learning cannot be assumed unless there are opportunities to practice skills and to receive feedback. Check that practice is part of the workshop design.
- Explicit behavioral intentions. If a workshop is to make a difference in subsequent weeks and months, specific goals about new behaviors and attitudes should be explicated by each participant before the session ends. The workshop should devote time to develop goals. Persons who do not want to commit themselves to specific changes should avoid the workshop.
- Obligatory followup. The greatest weakness of workshops is the lack of followup. A savvy leader will work out a contract with each participant and subsequently check about progress toward individual goals. How has teaching changed? Which goals have been realized and which have not? What additional support is needed?

reliable reporters about such matters as attentiveness during class, the teacher's clarity, and the value of various components of the course, including readings, examinations, and projects.

If conversations about teaching are to be productive, they must have some structure. At a brown-bag discussion, for example, a skillful convener can play devil's advocate, ask for evidence to support speculative comments, and insist that participants pursue implications of their suggestions. Elsewhere I outlined a four-step discussion process for such meetings: (1) articulate a belief about teaching; (2) identify a situation that is problematic with regard to that belief; (3) describe a behavior intended to resolve the problem; and (4) articulate a rationale that links the belief with the behavior (Menges, 1990).

Here is an example of how that discussion process might work. Assume that the belief in question is stated as "Students never come to class prepared." A problematic situation occurs when silence follows questions posed by the teacher. Suppose that the teacher suggests daily quizzes as a way of dealing with this problem. Her colleagues will challenge her to find a rationale that links the behavior (giving quizzes) and the belief. They will offer their own advice, and the group then discusses various actions that the teacher might take. The convener ensures that all relevant views are aired, introduces information from research which might illuminate the discussion, and ultimately helps the teacher develop a feasible and defensible plan for change. Results can be reported at the next meeting.

Conversations with students also benefit from structure. Structure protects against undue attention to a vocal, opinionated student whose views are unrepresentative. Structure can also rule out comments that are disparaging and unconstructive. Students might be asked under what circumstances they learn best, are most attentive, are most inclined to contribute to discussion, and so on.

Teaching improvements derived from readings, workshops, and conversations are not implemented automatically, of course. Later in the chapter, steps in a deliberate implementation process are described.

New Ideas Prepare the Way for Change

New ideas from reading, workshops, and conversations affect the teacher in ways that create conditions favorable for change.

New Knowledge and Concepts Modify Cognitive Structures

Reading about attribution theory, for example, provides a wealth of knowledge and concepts. Attribution theory deals with how we explain the causes of events. When students think about a test on which they did not do as well as expected, they may attribute their performance to circumstances that are outside their control, thereby escaping responsibility for improving performance next time. A teacher who wants to encourage students to attribute exam performance to controllable causes, such as effort, should avoid sympathizing about the difficult material or the inconvenient test schedule. Instead, emphasis should be on things that are under the control of students, such as "effort, note-taking skill, diligence, preparation" (McMillan & Forsyth, 1991, p. 59). A teacher who becomes well versed in attribution theory has acquired a new cognitive structure through which to view instruction.

New Skills Modify Practices   A likely topic at a workshop on the skills of questioning is "wait time," the skill of pausing for an appropriate interval after posing a question. Wait time in college classes tends to be shorter than students require, especially if the question is one that calls for a complex response. Once the teacher's "question-posing schema" has been altered by practicing the skill, it is more likely that longer pauses will be used during class discussion.

New Beliefs Modify Personal Theories   Conversations as sources of new ideas are likely to influence the teacher's beliefs. Students often say that they are disappointed to be in so many classes where faculty merely expect them to memorize information and then to regurgitate it for tests. Faculty, on the other hand, complain about students' lack of motivation, saying that students simply *want* to memorize and regurgitate information for tests. These mirrored views by faculty and students were documented in a report of focus group discussions held at 18 colleges in New Jersey. More than 400 faculty and students discussed the "major challenges" in facilitating student learning. Faculty focused on students and commented that they are academically unprepared, distracted by outside commitments, and generally unmotivated. Students focused on faculty whom they saw as unreasonable in their expectations, unavailable due to outside commitments, and uninterested in motivating students (New Jersey Institute for Collegiate Teaching and Learning, 1990).

Teachers' beliefs are put to the test by such student views. Articulating beliefs about students and how they learn makes explicit one's previously implicit theory of teaching. If information from students fails to fit the theory, dissonance occurs, and that dissonance creates pressure for change.

Classroom Research

Classroom research and classroom assessment are very practical ways to appraise and improve teaching—ways that are under the control of teachers themselves.

What Is Classroom Research?   Classroom research was inspired in part because educational researchers often address issues that are important to other researchers but do not have obvious implications for teaching. K. Patricia Cross and Thomas Angelo proposed classroom research as a way to bring faculty into the investigatory process.

Classroom research is action oriented. Rather than seeking general principles that apply across diverse settings, as formal educational research tries to do, classroom research is quite specific. How do these students in this course learn differently or more effectively when I use a new approach?

> The purpose of Classroom Research is to contribute to the professionalization of teaching, to provide the knowledge, understanding, and insights that will sensitize teachers to the struggles of students to learn. Classroom Research consists of any systematic inquiry designed and conducted for the purpose of increasing insight and understanding of the relationships between teaching and learning. (Cross, 1990, p. 136).

For examples of classroom research, see two volumes of *New Directions for Teaching and Learning* (46, 1991, and 75, 1998) and the book by Cross and Steadman (1996).

To help teachers begin inquiries into their own teaching, Cross and Angelo suggest the process of classroom assessment. Classroom assessment techniques (CATs) are frequent, small-scale efforts, conducted by teachers themselves. "The primary purpose of Classroom Assessment . . . is to improve learning directly by providing teachers with the kind of feedback they need to inform their instructional decisions" (Angelo, 1991, p. 9). Angelo and Cross (1993) have compiled a useful compendium of techniques to assess students' attitudes, values, and self-awareness as well as their course-related skills and knowledge. Other CATs address learner reactions to the teacher and to teaching methods. Step-by-step guidelines are also provided. Before we can make much progress with classroom research, we must think about the criteria by which our efforts will be judged. The obvious criteria for a teaching improvement project are changes in students.

Student Learning as the Criterion   The ultimate criterion for evaluating teaching is student learning. John Dewey said, "Teaching is like selling; you can't have a sale unless someone buys. You haven't taught unless someone has learned." Not that student learning is simply a function of the teacher. You may face classes in which students lack the necessary prerequisites; you may be assigned to a classroom in the deepest cell in a dungeon; you may encounter a group of anxious, hostile students; or you may have a class full of eager, highly motivated, well-prepared students who will learn well regardless of the teacher.

Nonetheless, we teachers all too often evaluate student papers, examinations, clinical work, or other performance thinking only of grading the student without looking at the implications of common student difficulties for our own teaching. After grading an examination, look back to see what errors were common and think about how you can do a better job of teaching those topics next time.

But using student learning as a method of appraising teaching has limitations. We may need to use criteria in addition to student learning as we attempt to assess our attempts to improve teaching. These criteria may include student satisfaction with instruction, motivation to take additional courses, and more general categories of student development such as the Perry scheme. (See Chapter 21.)

Frameworks for Change   Attempts to change teaching through Classroom Research or other methods are sometimes prompted by a particular problem, by a desire to experiment, or by readings or workshops or conversations, as described above.

The Teaching Goals Inventory (Cross & Angelo, 1993), is a 52-item instrument to assess one's teaching goals. The inventory yields scores for six clusters of goals which I believe nicely cover the range of goals that most instructors pursue: higher-order thinking skills, basic academic success skills, discipline-specific knowledge and skills, liberal arts and academic values, work and career preparation, and personal development. The inventory can help to analyze whether teaching methods are appropriate and whether students are learning what the instructor intends.

Another framework for thinking about areas for improving teaching is called the Seven Principles for Good Practice in Undergraduate Education. While the veracity of the principles, such as promoting student time on task and providing prompt feedback, may seem obvious, no research-based list as comprehensive as this one had previously been developed. The popularity of the principles prompted preparation of inventories by which faculty could rate their use of the seven principles. For example, inventory items for time on task include the following: "I underscore the importance of regular work, steady application, sound self-pacing, and scheduling" and "If students miss my classes, I require them to make up lost work." An institutional inventory was also developed with items about institutional climate, academic practice, curriculum, faculty, academic and student support services, and facilities. For example, items in the faculty category include the following: "Explicit criteria are used for evaluating teaching performance" and "Faculty evaluate administrators' contributions to the educational climate of this institution." (Both inventories are reprinted in Chickering & Gamson, 1991, along with accounts of how the principles were developed and research findings on which they are based.)

Here are all seven principles, briefly stated:

1. Encourage student-faculty contact.

2. Encourage cooperation among students (sharing backgrounds, use of study groups, peer tutoring).

3. Encourage active learning (students may summarize to the class, use role playing or simulations, use field trips or internships).

4. Give prompt feedback (prompt, detailed evaluations on performance).

5. Emphasize time on task (clarify class preparation expectations, emphasize the need for studying).

6. Communicate high expectations.

7. Respect different learning styles and talents (create a safe environment where students can ask questions; discourage uncivil remarks; use diverse teaching activities to encompass different learning styles).

These inventories can be completed by students as well as faculty. Discrepancies between student and those teacher responses may well indicate areas where classroom research would be useful.

Choose Clear and Specific Goals   In one of my courses, I asked students to apply psychological principles of change to their own behavior. The first step was to choose what they wished to change. Here is what several students chose:

- To spend more time with those I care about
- To reward myself more when I complete a task
- To return phone calls as soon as I get them
- To research and identify three new job leads each week, mail a cover letter and resume, and follow up with a phone call the next week
- To participate at least twice in every discussion class

Each of these is more specific than the one before. It will not surprise you to learn that students with clearer and more specific goals were relatively more successful in their change projects. So it is with teaching: Success is more likely when the end is clearly identified and the means are well defined. Yet many plans to improve teaching founder for lack of clear goals or because progress toward success cannot be measured.

Consider some goals that teachers have expressed.

1. I want to motivate my students.

2. I want to explain things more clearly in my lectures.

3. I want more students to participate in the discussion.

4. I want to pause longer after asking a question in class.

5. I want students to come to class prepared for discussion.

6. I want to raise student achievement in my course.

7. I want to create a new interdisciplinary course.

These goals vary in numerous ways. Some refer to what the teacher does, some refer to what students do, and at least one (creating an interdisciplinary course) refers to what happens in committees and departments. For some goals it is fairly clear what should happen, but others (motivating students, raising achievement) imply little about what the teacher should do differently. Criteria of success can be specified for some of these goals (the length of a pause, the number of students participating), but vague goals (such as wanting to motivate students) typically elude measurement. Goals for instructional improvement should be just as clear as the objectives for student learning that appear on the course syllabus (see Chapter 2).

Identify Particular Changes and Create Conditions That Encourage Those Changes   Ask if the goal is related to the person or to the environment. Longer pauses after questions, for example, are probably well within the teacher's capacity, but it may be difficult to monitor that behavior in a busy classroom. Explaining things more clearly in lectures may require the teacher to develop a new capacity, perhaps the skill of creating appropriate analogies and metaphors. Students may not prepare by doing assigned readings because they cannot understand course material or because they feel anxious about speaking in class (characteristics of the person). Or students may think that they have no incentive to prepare. They may reason that participating in discussion will not help their performance in the course because test questions are drawn only from lecture material (a characteristic of the incentive structure of the course).

Once changes are clearly envisioned, new behaviors should be rehearsed. Rehearsing new skills is most productive in a safe setting, perhaps using a mirror or video camera or working with a colleague or teaching consultant. The new behaviors should feel natural and comfortable. Persistent discomfort probably means that something is wrong with either the goal or the plan.

Expectations should be significant but modest. A few long pauses will demonstrate to the teacher that the new behavior is possible and will convey to students that the teacher's expectations have changed. A small increase in student participation may be reward enough to continue the new behavior. The general principle is to start with manageable changes that can be further increased or elaborated as appropriate.

Monitor progress regularly. To decide how well the change is going, consider using a short survey at the end of class. It might include one or two questions about content and one or two questions about teaching method. Collect representative student notes. Make an audiotape for later review, or invite a colleague to visit the class or to interview students. Since end-of-course evaluations and final examinations are too general and too long delayed to be very useful as sources of information, consider gathering early feedback from students.

Evaluate Your Efforts Although classroom research is usually informal, you may sometimes want to try a more formal approach, perhaps with an eye toward contributing to the pedagogical literature in your discipline. In that case, a number of evaluation challenges should be anticipated and addressed.

Suppose, for example, that a group of students is given an opportunity to take a class taught by a method quite unusual in their college. The very fact that the method is different gives it excitement. Sometimes the reaction may be one of enthusiasm; in other cases it may be one of outraged hostility. The latter reaction seems to be particularly likely when students taught by a new method know that they are competing on examinations with students taught by the tried-and-true traditional methods. In any case it is difficult to know how much of student improvement (or loss) in learning may be accounted for by the emotional reaction to a new and different method and how much can be expected when the new method is routine. How many new curricula, courses, or teaching methods have flowered briefly and then faded as the innovators' enthusiasm waned or as new staff members replaced the originators? Relatively few studies have made comparisons over a period longer than one semester. Students who experience a semester of instruction by a new method may be more likely to choose a section taught by this method than are students without previous experience.

A second methodological problem is establishing a suitable control group. In some experiments a single instructor uses both teaching methods. Here the obvious problem is the difficulty of determining how much the instructor's own personality and skills have influenced the outcome. It is impossible to know whether or not other teachers would obtain similar results.

Another problem in establishing controls is that the conditions of the experiment may introduce special factors that interfere with normal results. For example, the experiment may require extensive testing, the presence of observers in the class, or other interferences with normal classroom routine. A class in which a "live" professor is talking to television cameras is probably not a suitable comparison group for classes watching the lesson at a distant location.

A fourth problem is biased sampling. According to many studies (Russell, 1997) students taking the course at a distant location learn as much as those on campus. But those using distance learning may well be more strongly motivated than those who choose the campus course.

A fifth problem arises in the statistical methods used to analyze the results of teaching methods experiments. Ordinarily experimenters are concerned about avoiding the type of error involved in concluding that one method is more effective than another when in reality they do not differ significantly. However, they are less likely to be sensitive to another type of error that may be just as damaging—the error of concluding that there is no difference in effectiveness when two methods are not found to differ significantly. With "weak" statistics, a difference is less likely to be detected than with "strong" statistics. The true effect of a variable may be clouded if no effort is made to remove other sources of variance. Multivariate statistics might, by taking out other sources of variance, reveal more clearly the true effects of varying methods. Further, when several tests of the same hypothesis are made with different groups, experimenters might well use combined tests of significance. For example, if ten groups come out in the same direction, it is extremely unlikely that the methods are not differentially effective even though no one difference would be statistically significant.

A sixth problem is the interaction among teaching methods, student characteristics, teacher characteristics, and other variables. What is effective for some students may not be for others.

Even with better statistical methods, large, consistent effects are not likely. Education is a tremendously complex effort affected by many variables. No one thing, or group of variables, is likely to stand out clearly amidst the presence of the other variables not under study.

Qualitative methods of collecting data often provide insights that go beyond those of statistical tests. In our own research we use

- Interviews of instructors and students
- Videotapes of classes or cooperative learning groups
- "Stimulated recall" (playing audiotapes or videotapes of classes and asking the students involved what they were thinking at certain points in the episode)
- Having students think aloud while studying or solving problems

All of these have given us useful information.

INFORMATION FROM STUDENTS

Nearly all colleges and universities conduct end-of-term evaluations in their courses. Most of them use surveys that gather quantifiable information; hence the phrase "student ratings of instruction." This section begins with that topic and then discusses some alternatives to end-of-course student ratings.

Uses of Student Ratings

Student ratings can be used for decisions about salary and promotion, and for decisions about developing and improving teaching. In all, we can discern four constructive purposes for student ratings:

1. Improving teaching
2. Providing data relevant to judgment about teaching effectiveness
3. Aiding student choice of course and instructor
4. Stimulating students to think about their education

Student ratings are not automatically valid and useful for any of these purposes. We need to understand what student ratings can and cannot do before embarking on large-scale institutional programs of student ratings. No matter how technically sophisticated our questionnaire and our evaluation system, they are worthless if their use generates such conflict, anxiety, or confusion that education is affected adversely.

Student ratings should not be used as the single measure of teaching. Rather we should think of them as data valuable for problem solving. Their impact on the climate for teaching is more important than the technical excellence of the form to be used.

If students are to provide careful ratings and if faculty members are to make good use of the information, both need to have confidence in the methods used. Even a good form should be reexamined and revised frequently by student-faculty committees if new generations are to have a sense that the system is theirs rather than one imposed on them.

Are Student Ratings Valid?

Literally thousands of studies about student evaluations of teachers and of teaching have been conducted. So many separate studies and research reviews had appeared by the mid-1980s that many issues seemed to be resolved. I wrote then, "Well-designed programs for evaluating courses and teachers, when used for personnel review, are much more beneficial than they are harmful. Further, programs of student ratings can contribute to significant improvements in teaching, at least when faculty can consult with someone about their evaluations" (Menges & Mathis, 1988, p. 18). Those conclusions still stand; nevertheless, research interest in this topic continues. Recent literature focuses on the proper place of student evaluations in an overall faculty development program as well as on more specific topics, including validity.

How can we demonstrate that student ratings are valid; that is, that they measure what they are intended to measure? Strictly speaking, student ratings are measures of student satisfaction with teachers and with teaching, and it is within that definition that they should be interpreted. But satisfaction is a hypothetical construct, and any collection of questionnaire items will be an imperfect representation of satisfaction. At best, student ratings can be validated against criteria with which we reasonably expect them to correlate, including measures of learning, ratings by former students, faculty self-evaluations, and instructor classroom behaviors. It would be surprising if student evaluations had no relationship or a negative relationship with any of these criteria.

In fact, research is clear: consistently positive relationships have been found between student evaluations and (1) student learning, most notably in multisection sources; (2) ratings by former students; and (3) faculty self-evaluations of teaching, although faculty tend to rate themselves more positively than students do. Student evaluations have also been validated against the instructor's classroom behaviors. In a series of studies, trained observers rated classroom behaviors of teachers (for example, "talks with students before or after class" and "signals the transition from one topic and the next"). In these studies, more positive student evaluations and more learning were associated with several instructor behavior factors, especially clarity, expressiveness, and interaction. These results suggest that when students complete evaluation forms they are responding to what teachers do rather than to something extraneous and general, such as "popularity." Related studies show that instructors can increase these behaviors, and consequently their ratings, through appropriate feedback and training programs. (For details of studies, see the excellent review chapters in Perry & Smart, 1997.)

These correlations are less than perfect, as they should be. Measurement imprecision and conceptual complications will always constrain the magnitude of these statistical relationships. Exam scores, for instance, are quite imperfect measures of all the learning that students (or instructors) might consider important for a course. Nevertheless, these correlations clearly support the validity of student evaluations. In fact, the body of research supporting student ratings is far more substantial than for any other component of faculty evaluation, including methods used to assess research productivity.

As noted in a recent review of this literature (Menges & Austin, in press), skepticism about student evaluations is often based on failure to acknowledge the worth of this research; for example, see the case study reported by Williams and Ceci (1997). Sometimes quantitative data are overinterpreted, as in assuming that there are meaningful distinctions in teaching effectiveness when statistical differences in ratings are very small. And sometimes people inflate the importance of student evaluations by considering them to be a proxy for other measures of teaching effectiveness. When interpreting results of student ratings, the context of teaching must always be considered, including such matters as the teacher's previous performance and present goals, expectations that are held by the teachers' department, and so on. Many of these issues are addressed in a code of practice about how students can contribute to summative evaluation of teaching, published by the Association of University Staff of New Zealand (Hall & Fitzgerald, 1995).

Another threat to validity of ratings is bias, that is, influence from circumstances over which the teacher has little or no control, circumstances such as class size and prescribed course content. For bias to be established it is necessary to demonstrate that the variable in question (class size, for example) is uncorrelated with teaching effectiveness. But it seems reasonable that better teaching may well occur in smaller classes. If that is the case, ratings differences are not attributable to bias. The error is not in student evaluations, but in comparing things that should not be directly compared, namely large and small classes. Humanities courses typically receive more positive ratings than do natural science courses, but it is difficult to know whether the difference is due to the disciplinary course content or to the true quality of instruction. Instructor expressiveness was once seen as a biasing characteristic, but later research found that more expressive instructors are acting in ways that positively influence learning. (For relevant citations see Menges & Austin, in press.)

More research is needed about several sources of possible bias, including student motivation to take the course, grading leniency, gender of students and teachers, workload (where the general finding is that courses with heavier workloads are actually rated more favorably), and the kinds of study strategies that are used by students. None of these is likely to be serious, however, especially if student evaluations are kept in their proper place as only *one* indicator of instructional effectiveness.

What to Ask: The Dimensions of Teaching

Teaching is a complex activity, and determining its underlying dimensions or component parts is no easy matter. One of the most thorough research programs about the dimensions of teaching uses the Students' Evaluation of Educational Quality (SEEQ). This instrument was derived from research and theory about adult learning and has been subjected to more than 30 published factor analyses, drawing on an archive of 50,000 classes (Marsh & Dunkin, 1997). Studies using the SEEQ put the number of teaching dimensions at nine: learning, enthusiasm, breadth, organization, group interaction, rapport, exams, assignments, and workload. These categories can comprise a profile of teaching in each course and help to identify teaching strengths and areas for improvements.

Other researchers (Abrami, d'Apollonia, & Rosenfield, 1997) have argued for a single underlying trait for teaching effectiveness (analogous to a general factor for intelligence). In their analysis, "an overall skill factor" is most important by far. They also note three less important components; namely, viewing the teacher as instructor (including clarity, preparation, stimulation of interest, relevance); as a person (including general attitudes, respect for others, enthusiasm for subject); and as regulator including evaluation and feedback).

I believe it is misleading to think of teaching as having only one factor or dimension. This happens when evaluation is based on a single overall rating or an average across several items. Using only one or two numbers per course surely oversimplifies the complexities of teaching and loses a great deal of information. The purposes of instruction differ from course to course and from instructor to instructor, and reviewers should be able to consider separate ratings for such factors as clarity, group interaction, and workload. These distinctions are lost in a single, overall rating. At minimum, scores should be available for two areas which most factor analyses find distinguishable: (1) clarity and organization and (2) rapport and enthusiasm.

Choosing Items

Whether one plans to use one of the ready-made scales or to construct one's own, a necessary prerequisite is to examine one's goals in gathering student impressions, for different goals imply different items. If the goal is to assist in personnel decisions, a relatively small core may be sufficient; if the purpose is to improve instruction, a more detailed, behaviorally oriented set of items relevant to particular kinds of courses is probably more appropriate.

As an alternative to developing your own scales, you might wish to consider the use of a scale developed elsewhere, such as those described by Braskamp and Ony (1994) and Centra (1993).

In choosing items appropriate for different goals, you may be helped by differentiating five types of items.

1. Items in which students report classroom events or teacher behaviors
2. Items reporting the student's perception of his or her achievement of course goals
3. Items reporting the student's own evaluation of the effectiveness of different aspects of the course
4. Items reporting the student's own behavior or thinking in the course
5. Items reporting student satisfaction

Items for Improving Instruction The use of student ratings is likely to result in improvement when (1) the ratings provide new information; (2) the teacher is motivated to improve; or (3) the teacher can use alternative methods of teaching effectively.

Items chosen by the instructor because he or she wants the information are more likely to be informative than items on scales written for more general purposes. Aside from an item or two to indicate general feelings of satisfaction, more specific items reporting perceptions or evaluations of teacher behaviors or specific aspects of the course are likely to be more helpful than very general items.

Moreover, one would guess that items worded in evaluative fashion would elicit more defensiveness than those that are worded descriptively. Thus one might prefer "The instructor writes key points on the blackboard" to "Lectures are well organized."

The "low-inference" items used by Murray (1983) may be helpful to get at behaviors about which an instructor desires feedback; for example, states teaching objectives, sticks to point when answering, avoids eye contact with students, praises students for good ideas, and so on.

Items for Personnel Decisions A uniform standard scale is not likely to be very helpful for improving teaching—nor is a lengthy standard scale likely to be helpful for personnel decisions, since it may not be equally well suited for different disciplines or different courses within a discipline. Since comparisons between instructors in different courses can at best be only very general, one should probably not attempt much more than to determine whether students rate an instructor as excellent, adequate, or poor.

Items covering the major dimensions of teaching should be sufficient for most personnel purposes. Some instructors achieve excellence through skillful presentations; others achieve excellence through stimulating high student involvement. It is all too easy for faculty committees to develop stereotypes of faculty teaching on the basis of hearsay, and having scores on somewhat differentiated dimensions of teaching should help break down the simple good-bad classification that we all too often fall into.

Certain items have proved to relate to teacher effectiveness as measured by mean student performance on an examination. Frey, Leonard, and Beatty's (1975) validity studies included both calculus and psychology courses and are particularly worthy of consideration:

"Each class period was carefully planned in advance."

"The instructor presented the material clearly."

"This course has increased my knowledge and competence."

Other validated items include:

"Does the professor make students feel free to ask questions, disagree, express their ideas, etc.?"

"Does the professor use examples from his/her own research or experience?"

I like to use items that ask students about themselves rather than focusing on evaluation of the teacher. Examples of such items are:

"I learned a great deal in this course."

"I became more interested in this subject matter."

"I tried to relate material in the course to my own experience."

"I developed an overall framework for learning and understanding this topic."

Items Designed to Be Educational for Students   Learning should be a joint responsibility of students and instructor. Before blaming the instructor for failure to achieve educational goals, students should consider whether they have done all they should have done to make the course a valuable experience.

On my own student rating form I often include a section on student responsibility for learning. My purpose is to increase students' sense of responsibility for their own learning and to encourage them to think about their own educational goals. I include such items as:

"I attend class regularly."
"I have created learning experiences for myself in connection with the course."
"I have helped classmates learn."

Measuring Gains in Motivation and Learning Strategies   It is useful to know how well students are progressing in achieving educational goals. Thus student rating forms might include items such as:

"I learned a great deal in this course."
"I am learning to think more clearly about the area of this course."
"I became more interested in the subject matter of this course."

In courses I am studying or teaching, I like to get detailed information on the students' gains, or losses, in motivation and learning strategies, using a measure such as the LASSI (Learning and Study Strategies Inventory) (Weinstein et al., 1987) or the MSLQ (Motivated Strategies for Learning Questionnaire) (Pintrich et al., 1991).

When to Ask: The Value of Early Feedback

A major shortcoming of end-of-course student ratings is that they occur too late to benefit currently enrolled students. More and more teachers are gathering feedback early in the term so that it can be put to immediate use. Teachers who gather information through early feedback show that they care about the quality of their teaching and about the views of their students. "Early-term student feedback," as it is called, happens in time to allow instructors to build on the things that are working well in a course and to rethink those that are not.

A sourcebook about this method (Rando & Lenze, 1994) includes reports from teachers who have used early-term student feedback. They describe how early feedback has helped make teaching and learning more effective in their courses. The sourcebook organizes sample items that might be asked on early feedback surveys under six topics:

1. Learning Objectives: Are Students Learning What I Set out to Teach?
2. Course Structure: How Much Content and in What Order?
3. Content Delivery: Am I Making Myself Clear?
4. Student Participation: Are My Students Actively Involved?
5. Evaluation: How Does My Grading Affect Students?
6. Classroom Climate: Is My Classroom Comfortable for Learning?

Some campus teaching centers offer computer banks of items that can easily be incorporated into an early-feedback questionnaire and quickly scored.

Alternatives to Student Questionnaires

Despite the value of feedback from written student surveys, questionnaires quickly wear out their welcome if students are asked to fill them out in each class several times a term. Other options for gathering information include asking students pertinent questions in interviews, requesting short reaction essays or learning journals, and inviting a letter to the instructor about the student's experience in the course. Many classroom assessment techniques (Angelo & Cross, 1993) are appropriate for this purpose, and other methods are described by Rando and Lenze (1994).

Group interviews are used on several campuses to appraise teaching. In this approach, a consultant visits a class and asks groups of students to comment on strengths and to recommend changes. Using this technique, the consultant can probe more deeply into sources of difficulty, uncovering critical incidents or examples that clarify problems. This method also has the advantage of demonstrating to students the extent to which complaints of some students are shared by their classmates. Abbott and colleagues (1990) compared eight methods of collecting student opinions of instruction and found that students preferred interviews at midterm. Satisfaction was greatly increased if the instructor talked about the consultants' summary of student opinion and discussed what changes could be made as well as what could not be changed.

General Comments About Procedures for Student Evaluations

1. Allow space for comments. Students need the chance to express feelings that do not quite fit the prestructured questionnaire format. Frequently comments give examples or incidents that clarify the meaning of ratings or indicate what changes need to be made.

2. Indicate in the instructions who will read the comments. Students will be more focused if they understand to whom they are writing.

3. I prefer items worded in terms of the individual student's perception or evaluation to more general statements. I think a faculty member is likely to resent global evaluations more than those worded in terms of the impression made on a particular student, and I think a student is generally better able to report how he or she felt than to make global judgments.

4. Faculty members should have the right to participate in selecting items or forms to be used in evaluating teaching so that the form is appropriate for the goals of their class.

5. If ratings are to be used in personnel decisions, some control should be exercised over conditions of administration. Rumors circulate about instructors who roam up and down the aisles, lose

poor evaluations, or introduce the ratings by announcing that the students will be determining not only the instructor's fate but those of spouse and children.

6. Reports of student ratings should be in a format that encourages good feelings rather than discouragement. Thus a report emphasizing percentile ranks in relation to norms may be less helpful than a report emphasizing the distribution of student responses (since typical classes like their instructor). It probably is not very helpful to tell teachers rated as "good" by their students that this is only "average."

7. If teaching ratings are to be published for students and made available to colleagues, faculty motivation is enhanced when reports include teacher strengths as well as weaknesses.

8. Effective teaching is a skill that can be learned and that develops over time. Basing career decisions on ratings in a single course early in a teaching career is neither wise nor fair. Basing decisions on a single visit by a peer or superior is even more unwise. Institutions should pair their evaluation programs with development services.

9. If student ratings are used in personnel decisions, the instructor should have an opportunity to present his or her interpretation of the data as well as whatever additional evidence seems relevant.

10. Student ratings tend to focus on classroom teaching. Evidence with respect to out-of-class educational functions, such as course planning, advising, and so on, is also needed.

11. When student ratings are used in personnel decisions, they should be evaluated by peers who are familiar with the courses in which the ratings were gathered, know the teaching methods used, and can take into account the circumstances under which the course was taught.

Using Feedback to Improve

So you've given out student rating forms and now you have them back. Naturally you'll use this feedback to improve—maybe! What can you do to use the information effectively?

1. Don't become obsessed with the criticisms and negative ratings of a few students. The biggest barrier to improvement is discouragement. No matter how well I'm rated, the negative comments still feel like stabs. Focus on the positive comments, and keep them in sight while you look at the criticisms. Then see if there are some things you could do to reduce the number of criticisms without losing your supporters.

2. Ask a colleague or consultant to go over the ratings with you to help interpret them and make suggestions of alternative strategies you might try.

3. Summarize your impressions and plans for change or continuity and discuss them with the class to get their reactions. Regardless of the effectiveness of your planned changes, your students will give you credit for listening and trying.

CONSULTING COLLEAGUES AND EXPERTS

One of the most frequently used methods of appraising teaching is classroom visitation by administrators or fellow teachers. Such visits can be helpful for improving teaching; however, their value as evidence for promotion decisions is probably overestimated.

To take this last point first—the problem is reliability. Centra (1975) showed that peer ratings based on classroom visitation failed to discriminate between teachers consistently. The problem is that it is difficult to get a good estimate of teachers' abilities from a few visits, especially when the teachers are under the special pressure of knowing that their performance on these days may affect their salary or future. Thus using peer visitation as a primary source of data for personnel decisions is probably not cost-effective.

Examining teaching materials—syllabi, assignments, examinations—is probably a better use of colleagues' time. A special issue of *Innovative Higher Education* (1996, 20, 4) is devoted to peer review of teaching. Authors describe various ways to conduct peer reviews, noting that reviewers as well as those reviewed gain from participating and discussing potential conflicts between peer reviews used to improve teaching or to judge effectiveness.

For improving teaching, consultation can add greatly to the value of feedback. Talking to colleagues about teaching is an important strategy for improvement, and talking to a colleague who has visited your class is especially useful. You can increase the value of such a visitation if you brief your colleague before class about what you are hoping to accomplish. If there are particular things that you would like observed, mention them.

In training university teachers I have frequently asked them to form pairs for mutual observation. One learns both by observing how one's partner handles problems as well as by getting advice on the basis of the partner's observations.

While peers have the advantage of knowing the particularities of teaching your discipline, experts from a faculty development center can also be useful in having a broader knowledge of a range of teaching strategies and the ability to look at teaching characteristics independent of subject matter issues. We sometimes videotape classes and refer to the videotapes to allow the teacher to see particular incidents illustrating points that need attention.

Expert consultants from a faculty development center also have the advantage of not being involved in personnel decisions—an important consideration. Robert Wilson at the University of California at Berkeley handled the problem of the conflict between the two purposes of helping and personnel evaluation by arranging for retired professors to act as mentors for new faculty members.

Expert consultants do more than meet one on one with faculty. A sourcebook on instructional consultation describes, in addition to individual meetings, training faculty to become peer consultants, giving professional leadership to faculty groups where members consider teaching problems, and setting up self-directed teaching supporting groups (Brinko & Menges, 1997). One very important role is to assist faculty as they review their student ratings. A University of Michigan study (McKeachie et al., 1980) had consultants counsel faculty to provide encouragement and suggest alternative teaching strategies. This proved superior to simply receiving a printed report of student ratings. Marsh and Roche (1993) reviewed previous research showing the positive effects of consultation and carried out a carefully controlled study demonstrating significant improvement in teaching after feedback with consultation. A meta-analysis (Menges & Brinko, 1986) found an increase in subsequent student ratings that was four times larger when consultation was provided than with written feedback alone.

Thus student ratings feedback by itself has a small effect on subsequent ratings, but adding personal consultation or other feedback (such as notes provided to the instructor from student discussion groups) to written reports of student ratings is associated with stronger positive effects on subsequent ratings. This finding applies to faculty in various fields and in various countries. Of course, the teacher must be an active and sympathetic participant in the process, since instructors' subjective theories about teaching affect how they use student evaluations and what aspects of their teaching they are willing to consider changing. Improvements are typically greatest in areas where the teacher expresses a desire to change.

THE TEACHING PORTFOLIO

Appraisal of faculty work requires full documentation of teaching; information must be accurate and complete. The teaching portfolio is designed to provide a portrait of oneself as a teacher or, to put it differently, it provides an opportunity to portray one's teaching self. Portfolios typically contain materials like the following: a statement of one's beliefs, goals, and development as a teacher; sample teaching materials; videotapes of interactions with students; examples of student work evaluated by the teacher; evaluations of the teaching and learning experience by students, colleagues, and others; documentation of noncourse teaching activities; and evidence of efforts to improve one's teaching (Edgerton, Hutchings, & Quinlan, 1991; Seldin, 1993). The portfolio should display the teacher's strengths and reveal what one especially values in teaching.

The teaching portfolio can help improve teaching as well as judge teaching effectiveness. For improving teaching, the portfolio brings together materials that would not otherwise be assembled. Reflecting on that information, the teacher can check the consistency between stated learning objectives and the actual activities of teaching and learning, and can consider whether there is convincing evidence that students are learning what was intended. Any discrepancies indicate areas for investigation and possible improvement.

To judge teaching effectiveness, the portfolio should be prepared according to guidelines developed by the department or institution and judged according to collaboratively derived criteria. At Northwestern University, a committee recommended that one course each year be documented with sufficient thoroughness that an outside reviewer could ascertain from the portfolio what the course goals were, what activities were completed by teacher and students, what the student outcomes were, and how those outcomes matched the goals and objectives. With regard to student work, for example, it was recommended that the portfolio include representative samples of the work of two students: one with grades in the top third of the class, the other from the lower third. For most courses, these work samples would probably be the final exam, a major paper, or a major project, but the professor could submit any sample that fairly communicated work of the students and illustrated the kind of feedback that the teacher provided to students.

When the portfolio is used for performance reviews, faculty should regard it as a "persuasive" document. From the teacher's perspective, the portfolio is intended to persuade reviewers that a positive decision about salary, retention, promotion, or tenure is warranted. The portfolio should convey the activities of the faculty member as a teacher, discuss the rationale for those activities, and provide evidence for the quality of teaching and learning.

ENSURING THAT CHANGES LAST

Improving teaching is hard work, and it often requires uncomfortable adjustments. While the suggestions in this section will not make change any easier, they can make it more likely that hard-won changes will endure.

Estimating Costs and Benefits

Especially at the beginning, when success is not certain, regressing to the comfortable patterns of the past can be appealing. Do not ignore the costs of change, but also acknowledge and anticipate the benefits.

A teacher experimenting with new, unpracticed roles naturally feels vulnerable. Students, uncertain of what is expected of them, may become resentful or withdrawn. It is only fair to explain to students what is expected and to invite their endorsement of a new classroom compact.

These reactions are natural emotional correlates of change. No one wants to fail, and everyone wants to appear to be in control. If the attempt fails, remember that even failure can be instructive, particularly if the experience is reviewed and analyzed with students and other interested parties. With each success, even a small success, there are great benefits—increased confidence, a sense of learning, and a feeling of growth—all of which help to renew professional vitality.

Anticipating Relapse

Maintaining new behaviors is difficult, and it is important to have procedures in place that reduce the risk of relapsing into old patterns (Walton, 1989). Effective strategies for anticipating and preventing relapse include how to deal with slips and how to enlist support from others.

Impending relapse may be signaled by a slip. For a dieter, a slip is a small, but clear, violation of the eating plan. For a teacher trying to increase class discussion, a slip would be lapsing into a lecture when confronted with unprepared students. A slip should be dealt with immediately, according to plans developed in advance. Perhaps a discussion should be held with the class about what happened and why it happened. In any case, the slip should be regarded as nothing more than a mistake that need not be repeated rather than as a failure of the entire improvement project. If circumstances that led to the slip are carefully analyzed, the experience becomes one of learning rather than of failure.

Enlisting support from others is a relapse prevention strategy that is social in nature. A trusted colleague or someone from the campus teaching center might be asked to provide regular feedback by directly observing the target behaviors or by phoning the teacher at regular intervals for a progress report. Or the teacher's log of events, reactions, and feelings about the improvement might be shared on a regular schedule with a friend or consultant. These procedures themselves influence improvement, since one naturally wishes to avoid failure in the eyes of friends and since close monitoring of behavior may itself enhance change.

Predicting Whether Improvements Will Succeed

A particular improvement is less likely to succeed if it seriously clashes with the teacher's personal theories of teaching and learning. Or the improvement may be something that the teacher feels little control over. Or its consequences, though generally positive, may be viewed as unlikely or unimportant. Or social and institutional structures may be unsupportive.

Here are some questions worth asking before deciding whether or not to pursue an improvement project. These questions are derived from the theory of reasoned action (Ajzen & Madden, 1986). Each of these questions should be asked with reference to a particular goal. As an example, I have chosen the goal of "increasing student discussion in class."

First, ask about your *beliefs*. How do you regard increased student discussion? To what extent is it useful, good, wise, important? Answers that are not strongly positive probably reveal dissonance between the goal and your personal theories.

Second, ask about the *control* you have in the situation. To what extent are *you* able to bring about increased student discussion? What aspects of this change can you control? What aspects are outside of your control?

Third, consider the *consequences*. Possible consequences of increased discussion include more animated students, noisier classrooms, less content coverage, better critical thinking, and so on. How positive do you find each of these consequences? How likely is it that each consequence will occur?

Finally, ask *what views others hold* about the change. People whose views you regard as important might include colleagues, students, dean, research collaborators, spouse, and so on. How positive is each of them regarding this change? How important to you is each one's view, and how much do you wish to conform to it?

Depending on how these questions are answered prior to the start of a planned improvement, you may modify the plan and make success more likely. The time and effort invested in answering questions like these pay good dividends, enhancing both the intellectual and the emotional satisfactions that accompany successful improvements in teaching.

IN CONCLUSION

As you appraise and improve your teaching, here are several important points to bear in mind:

1. The pursuit of improvement is challenging. Like other challenges, it can also be rewarding—intellectually, motivationally, and socially.

2. New ideas for teaching are easy to find, if we are alert for them. They appear in the things we read and in conversations with colleagues and students, as well as in more formal activities such as workshops, seminars, and classroom research.

3. Changes in teaching (and learning) are most likely to be successful when goals for change are clear and specific, when changes are deliberately implemented, and when the change process is monitored with care.

4. Information from students, including midterm and end-of-term surveys, is essential for identifying areas for change and for assessing results.

5. Student ratings are a necessary component in a faculty personnel review system. For this purpose, they should be carefully collected and interpreted, accompanied by commentary from the teacher, and part of a system that includes sample instructional materials, comments from peers, information about noncourse teaching activities, and documentation about

efforts to disseminate one's teaching successes and remedy one's teaching deficiencies. All this material might be gathered and displayed in a teaching portfolio.

6. Improving teaching requires an investment of time and energy. Improvements are most likely to persist when costs and benefits are thoughtfully estimated in advance, when other people are enlisted to support the changes, and when changes are consonant with one's beliefs, and personal theories about teaching and learning.

Supplementary Reading

To learn more about research on effective teaching and learning, see chapters in R. J. Menges, M. Weimer, et al., *Teaching on Solid Ground: Using Scholarship to Improve Practice* (San Francisco: Jossey-Bass, 1996), especially the chapter by Dinham, on what college teachers need to know, and Menges and Rando, on using feedback to improve teaching.

Information about assessing teaching, including useful surveys and observation checklists, is given in the following:

T. A. Angelo, and K. P. Cross, *Classroom Assessment Techniques: A Handbook for College Teachers*, 2nd ed. (San Francisco: Jossey-Bass; 1993).

R. A. Arreola, *Developing a Comprehensive Faculty Evaluation System: A Handbook for College Faculty and Administrators on Designing and Operating a Comprehensive Faculty Evaluation System.* (Bolton, MA: Anker, 1995).

L. A. Braskamp and J. C. Ory, *Assessing Faculty Work: Enhancing Individual and Institutional Performance.* (San Francisco: Jossey-Bass, 1994).

Seldin, P. (1997). *The Teaching Portfolio: A Practical Guide to Improved Performance and Promotion/Tenure Decisions,* 2nd ed. (Bolton, MA: Anker, 1997), describes how the teaching portfolio is being used for assessing and improving teaching.

When evaluation results suggest that changes in teaching are needed, a wealth of ideas about alternative approaches can be gleaned from the following: B. G. Davis, *Tools for Teaching.* (San Francisco: Jossey-Bass, 1993); G. Brown and M. Atkins, *Effective Teaching in Higher Education* (New York: Methuen, 1988); and J. Lowman, *Mastering the Techniques of Teaching,* (San Francisco: Jossey-Bass, 1995).

Ethics in College Teaching

24

. . . .

Imagine you're teaching a course at the introductory level, which is required of all students who want to major in your department. And let's suppose that a student whose performance was much below standard approaches you after the first exam. That person offers you a considerable sum of money if you'll change a grade on the exam so he or she can pass. What is the ethical thing to do in this situation?

Now suppose that it's the same situation, but instead of offering you money, the student pleads for an opportunity to retake the exam because of extenuating circumstances during the first test administration. Now what is the ethical choice?

Now it's the same situation, but this time you are the one who notices that a student who has been working hard in your class and whom you expected to do very well has instead failed the exam miserably. How does this situation compare with the others from an ethical standpoint?

The first of these scenarios seems fairly straightforward: it would be a definite violation of ethics if you were to accept the money to change the grade. The second example is not as

This chapter was written by Marilla D. Svinicki of the University of Texas at Austin.

straightforward; to what extent should the student be allowed an opportunity that is not available to all the other students? Does providing that opportunity constitute unethical behavior? Or is it just unfair? Or is there a difference? And in the third instance, to what extent should your assessment of a student's abilities counter actual performance? Where do you draw the line in helping students?

The most difficult questions that teachers face often have nothing to do with the content of the course or the way it is presented. They focus instead on the ethical issues of teaching and how we relate to our students, our institution, our discipline, and society at large. What are our responsibilities to each constituency, and what do we do when they conflict? Unfortunately, there are no easy answers to these questions. I raise them here as food for thought because you *will* face them sometime in your teaching career.

This chapter addresses the issue of ethics in teaching. What do we mean by "ethics in teaching"? In recent years, more and more is being written about the topic as the teaching mission of the university comes under increasing scrutiny (Cahn, 1986; Fisch, 1996; Matthews, 1991; Strike, 1988). It seems only proper that those who currently teach and those who aspire to a faculty career be introduced to the concept.

What is an ethical question in teaching? Ethical questions are sometimes defined in terms of right and wrong (Strike, 1988); in terms of cultural norms such as honesty, promise keeping, and so on (Smith, 1996); or as "general guidelines, ideals, or expectations that need to be taken into account, along with other relevant conditions and circumstances, in the design and analysis of teaching" (Murray et al., 1996, p. 57).

In general, *ethical standards are intended to guide us in carrying out the responsibilities we have to the different groups with whom we interact.* Ethics violations can occur when we are tempted to act contrary to those standards. Ethical dilemmas occur when multiple responsibilities conflict or have more than one right answer (Strike, 1988). It is often surprising to consider all the different things that can cause ethical problems for instructors. They range from the obvious bribe attempt described above, to failure to present all legitimate sides of an issue adequately, to accepting remuneration for extra tutoring for a class with which one is already connected.

In a 1991 research study of psychologists teaching at academic institutions, Tabachnick, Keith-Spiegel, and Pope report reactions to various ethical questions involved in teaching at the college level. Respondents were asked to report how frequently they engaged in a wide range of various activities and the extent to which those activities were ethical or unethical. The activities included those as drastic as sexual harassment to more mundane activities such as teaching materials that the instructor had not yet fully mastered.

The behavior *most often* engaged in was teaching when not adequately prepared, although it was not a consistent pattern for most people. The authors attribute this more to busy workloads and rapid advances in the field than to the shirking of responsibilities. The rarest of behaviors were those related to sexual harassment. Whether this is an accurate reflection of behavior or a reluctance to report such behavior is impossible to tell. Also rare were actual sexual encounters with students.

Perhaps the most interesting sources of ethical conflicts for this group were a result of the conflicting roles of mentor/sponsor and evaluator. For example, over two-thirds believed that allowing a student's likeability to influence a grade was unethical, but over two-thirds reported doing it at some point anyway. The same sort of dilemma is seen when instructors interact socially with students. On the one hand, the interaction with faculty is reported as vital to student growth by Pascarella and Terenzini (1991); on the other, it raises the possibility of conflict.

In a more recent study attempting to identify norms of ethical conduct, a national sample of faculty in higher education was asked to rate the acceptability of a range of violations of teaching standards, such as "The instructor insists that the student take one particular perspective on course content" or "The instructor does not introduce new teaching methods or procedures." Of the norm categories (encouragement of faculty student contact, systematic advising, feedback on student performance, learning about students, fostering an egalitarian, tolerant classroom, and demonstrating a concern for teaching) only "feedback on student performance" was broadly accepted as an area in which poor performance would be violating a norm (Braxton, Eimers, & Bayer, 1996).

How can an instructor decide what is an appropriate set of norms to follow? The American Association of University Professors has provided a statement of professional ethics dealing with the responsibilities of faculty members which highlights what it considers to be the special responsibilities of one in an academic position (AAUP, 1987). A similar set of principles was developed by the Society for Teaching and Learning in Higher Education (STLHE) and distributed to faculty in Canadian institutions (Murray et al., 1996). Perhaps these standards can help highlight what a faculty member should consider in making personal choices.

RESPONSIBILITIES TO STUDENTS

Both the AAUP and the STLHE guidelines recognize that one of a faculty member's first responsibilities is to the students. The specifics that follow illustrate the broad range of impact that faculty can have on student lives.

1. To Encourage the Free Pursuit of Learning

The primary purpose of teaching is to encourage learning; therefore, the first ethical responsibility of an instructor is to that goal. All that we do to prepare and conduct well-designed instruction is part of that responsibility. The ethical instructor knows the content to be learned, the students who will do the learning, and the methods that could be used to foster the learning. The STLHE guidelines state this explicitly in their first and second principles: content competence and pedagogical competence (Murray et al., 1996). In a discussion of the ethics of teaching psychology, Matthews (1991) interprets the American Psychological Association's professional standards as they apply to teaching and cites the issues of responsibility and competence as two key contributors to encouraging learning. In her interpretation, faculty are responsible for remaining current and presenting accurate and balanced views of the field, an idea also related to the concept of scholarly behavior discussed later in this chapter.

There are many ways an instructor might violate these standards. Here are two examples:

- Most obvious is to fail in our duties in class preparation. One can't always be in top form, but just as we expect students to come to class prepared, we must make the same effort. This is one of the most commonly occurring violations reported by the sample (Tabachnick et al., 1991).

- A second, less obvious way is failing to remain current both in the content area and in instructional methods that foster learning. While it is unlikely that faculty will not be current in the content, it is very likely that faculty will not have kept up with research into better instructional methods.

A second part of this responsibility is to protect and encourage the autonomy of our students so that eventually they no longer need our constant guidance. The STLHE guidelines list this as the fourth of their eight principles: "to contribute to the intellectual development of the student" (Murray et al., 1996). If students are to develop into thinking individuals, we must structure our interactions with them in such a way as to both model and support independent thinking, even when this means they might end up disagreeing with us.

2. To Demonstrate Respect for Students

Ethical instructors also respect the "otherness of students" (Churchill, 1982); that is, the individual and independent nature of the students and the fact that students are at different stages of their lives than are the instructors. For example, instructors need to be aware of the special needs of their students, whether those be cultural, physical, or based on background (Matthews, 1991). This also means respecting students' goals, their choices, and their value as individuals (Strike, 1988).

The most obvious venue for this particular principle is in the interactions we have with students in and out of class. During class the way in which we respond to students' questions and comments should convey the idea that everyone's participation is welcome and respected. How we respond to a student's question affects more than just the student who asked it. And outside of class, the way we greet students who come to office hours or see us in the halls speaks volumes about the level of respect we have for them. We show respect by being available when we say we will be, by keeping promised appointments, by being willing to listen to students' concerns, by giving as much thought and preparation to our interactions with undergraduates as we do to graduate students and colleagues.

An example of a not-so-obvious need to respect students as individuals is discussed in an article by Grauerholz and Copenhaver (1994) about the use of experiential teaching methods, especially those that involve a great deal of self-disclosure on the part of students. The choice of instructional strategies such as journaling and small-group problem sharing may violate your students' rights and be harmful as well as unethical, unless done with a great deal of care and concern for the students' well-being. To guard against the possibility of harm here are some suggestions on how to structure the experience. For example, you should choose strategies carefully and make their purpose clear to your students. It might also be appropriate to allow alternative ways of satisfying the learning requirement for those who do not feel comfortable with these methods. Use of such teaching methods raises the issue of trust, because when students trust an instructor, they are more willing to engage in self-examination. Making self-examination safe for students is reason enough to be sure that one's relationship with students is one of trust and respect.

Similar issues of trust arise during the discussion of sensitive topics, such as race, sexual preference, and religion. When faced with a potentially sensitive situation, you can:

- Provide early disclosure of the potentially sensitive nature of the topics

- Make sure that students understand what is being presented as fact and what as opinion

- Offer extra time outside of class to those students who need to discuss the topics and their reactions to them (Keith-Spiegel & Koocher, 1985)

In my own case, I have advised faculty to draw up a set of "rules of engagement" for sensitive topics that could spark heated debate in class. These rules specify how these debates will be conducted and feature cooling-down activities, the obligation to be able to state the other person's position before attacking it, the avoidance of personalizing arguments, and so on. If such guidelines are provided early in the course, students can feel more comfortable when sensitive topics are raised.

This does not mean that the topics will be avoided, since that would be a violation of the first of our guidelines: open inquiry. One can see how this conflict would raise ethical dilemmas for teachers, especially in disciplines where sensitive topics are the norm rather than the exception.

3. To Respect Confidentiality

The issue of self-disclosure leads to another large component of respect, the belief that students have a right to privacy in their dealings with us. Not only does this principle have the weight of ethics behind it, in many cases it also carries the weight of law. Here, however, we are speaking of less egregious violations of privacy, such as discussing a single student's situation with someone who does not have a legitimate interest in that student's case. Practices such as leaving student papers out so that they can be retrieved at the students' convenience might be a violation of this principle since that means students have access to their peers' work (Murray et al., 1996). At my institution, the posting of grades in a public place in any way that would allow an individual's grade to be identified by others is prohibited.

4. To Model the Best Scholarly and Ethical Standards

A teacher, whether by accident or by design, is more to students than a content expert. The teacher is a model of all that it means to be a scholar, a thinking person. We teach not only what we know but what we are. Part of the ethics of teaching is to realize this responsibility and to become the best models we can be, which requires some serious self-reflection on our personal standards of scholarship and living. Clark Kerr (1994), in a discussion of ethics in the academic culture, supported this struggle when he said that we are obliged to present a variety of perspectives, our own as well as others', so that the facts can be judged for themselves. This does not imply that you must always take a dispassionate stance; but even, or perhaps especially, when you feel strongly about an issue, it is necessary to demonstrate by your actions that intelligent people can disagree and still remain rational. Giving students the ability to differentiate emotion from reason is an especially important responsibility of instructors, according to Hanson (1996). As she says, "Teachers who can nimbly convey the strengths of a position they in fact oppose, who can clearly display the weaknesses in a position they in fact embrace, are *modeling* a critical engagement from which students may learn their most important lessons" (p. 35).

5. To Foster Honest Academic Conduct and to Ensure Fair Evaluation

Perhaps the most obvious ethical problems arise in the area of evaluation of student learning, a point echoed in both the AAUP guidelines and those from the STLHE. Instructors are the arbiters of entrance into the profession and are therefore responsible for seeing to it that standards are upheld. However, we are also responsible for guaranteeing that all are given a fair chance of demonstrating their abilities. When we allow academic dishonesty to go unheeded, we violate the rights of all the other students who are abiding by the rules. If we fail to establish an evaluation system that accurately assesses the students' progress, we are abdicating our responsibilities to both the students and the profession.

The most important type of fairness for students is interactional fairness (how individuals are treated), followed by procedural fairness (the degree to which there is impartiality in how grades are determined and performance evaluated), and finally, outcome fairness (the degree to which grades and other outcomes reflect performance) (Rodabaugh, 1996). This concern for fair evaluations is echoed in research by Braxton, Eimers and Bayer (1996), who report that for faculty the importance of feedback to students was the set of items that came closest to representing a universally accepted norm of teaching.

The conflicts most often occur when this standard of fairness is pitted against the first responsibility of respecting the individual and fostering independence. The examples that opened this chapter speak to this issue. How important is it that all students be evaluated in the same way? Are we being fairer if we maintain standards and vary conditions of evaluation or if we use individual standards according to the special situation of each student? Which factors are legitimate considerations? There is no agreement on these issues. The best we can do is to continue to discuss and deliberate, alone and in groups, because the conditions under which we operate today will not be the same as those in the future.

6. To Avoid Exploitation, Harassment, or Discrimination

One of the variables that should be at the forefront of our thinking about the ethics of teaching is the great power discrepancy between teacher and students. Whether we like it or not, whether we seek it or not, by virtue of our position alone, we are invested with a great deal of power over the lives of our students. To make matters worse, many students invest us with even more power than we are entitled to. For this reason, both the AAUP and the STLHE guidelines list one or more principles concerning exploitation, harassment, and discrimination.

Abuse of this power is at the base of many of the ethical traps that lie strewn across our paths as teachers. The very special nature of the relationship between teacher and student is all too easy to abuse (Smith, 1996). The most blatant examples of unethical behavior, those most frequently mentioned in written codes of ethics, deal with exploitation or harassment of various types: sexual, racial, religious, even intellectual. The most egregious of these (and possibly the most debated) is sexual harassment in the form of improper relationships between instructors and students. The area of proper relationships between teachers and students is particularly difficult for graduate students, who are both teachers and students, since because of their age they occupy a place between their own students and their own professors. Thus they can be either the harasser or the harassed. Intimate relationships between teachers and students are generally considered inappropriate, at best. The best decision for an instructor or a student is to keep the relationship on a professional level as long as the power imbalance exists.

But there are plenty of other forms of exploitation that occur in academia. For example, requiring students to engage in class activities that are unrelated to the educational purposes of the course but that serve our personal ends is an abuse of power. Making derogatory comments about population subgroups is an obvious example of harassment.

Another area of ethical problems involves receiving special considerations or benefits as a result of being in a position of authority. For example, is it a violation of ethics to adopt a less-than-adequate book simply because of an incentive made available by the publisher? How legitimate is it to accept an invitation to a party or other event as the guest of a student in your class? Does it matter if that student is no longer in your class? Does it matter if the event is somehow connected with the student's academic program—for example, a dinner honoring that student's work? We must be aware that by our position alone we will sometimes be put in a compromised situation in all innocence on our part and the student's.

RESPONSIBILITIES TO COLLEAGUES, THE INSTITUTION, AND THE DISCIPLINE

The AAUP and STLHE guidelines go beyond those just focused on our role as teacher; they deal with all aspects of faculty life, including relations with colleagues and responsibilities to the institution for which we work and to the discipline we represent. Taken as a whole, however, the same ideas apply. The standards cluster around the issues of promoting and defending free and honest inquiry, showing respect for others, meeting institutional and professional responsibilities, and continuing to grow as scholars throughout professional life.

Ethical failures in this area include falsification of research results, failure to give due credit to the work of colleagues or students, unwillingness to participate in institutional governance, and unfair or unfounded evaluation of colleagues. More difficult choices might be things like continuing to teach in a situation that does not meet the needs of the students, such as overcrowded or understaffed classes, ignoring the inadequate teaching of colleagues, taking on so much outside work that work with students suffers, or refusing to teach a sufficient number of "service" courses to help students graduate in a timely manner (Hogan & Kimmel, 1992; Keith-Spiegel et al., 1996; Kerr, 1994; Matthews, 1991; Tabachnick et al., 1991).

MAKING ETHICAL CHOICES

The array of possibilities for ethical decisions seems endless. How, then, can we avoid stumbling somewhere along the line? While there are no easy answers, there may be some ways of thinking about our actions as professionals that will maximize the possibility of acting ethically. Some very interesting strategies are suggested by several authors in a book on ethical dimensions of teaching edited by Fisch (1996). I recommend it to you for further study.

Here, however, I draw the following principles for evaluating one's actions from two sources, the first five from Brown and Krager (1985) and the last from Schoen (1983):

1. *Autonomy.* Am I acting in ways that respect freedom and treat others as autonomous?

2. *Nonmaleficence.* Am I causing harm through either commission or omission?

3. *Beneficence.* Do my actions benefit the other person rather than myself?

4. *Justice.* Do I treat those for whom I am responsible equitably?

5. *Fidelity.* Do I uphold my part of any relationship?

6. *Act consciously.* Do I understand the assumptions on which I base my actions, and are they valid?

IN CONCLUSION

It is a great privilege to be a teacher. But all great privileges carry great responsibilities as well. Many of those responsibilities are subtle, thrust on us by the expectations of others rather than sought by us. Keeping these six principles in mind won't solve all the ethical dilemmas you face as a teacher, but they might give you a way to reflect on them alone and with other teachers. That reflection should never stop, because conscious reflection on values is perhaps the cornerstone of the ethics of teaching.

Supplementary Reading

American Association of University Professors, Statement on Professional Ethics, *Academe,* 1987, 73(4), 49.

S. M. Cahn, *Saints and Scamps: Ethics in Academia* (Totowa, NH: Rowman & Littlefield, 1986).

L. Fisch (ed.), Ethical Dimensions of College and University Teaching: Understanding and Honoring the Special Relationship Between Teachers and Students. *New Directions for Teaching and Learning, No. 66* (San Francisco: Jossey-Bass, 1996).

C. Kerr, Knowledge Ethics and the New Academic Culture, *Change,* 1994, 26(1), 8–16.

D. Schoen, *The Reflective Practitioner* (San Francisco: Jossey-Bass, 1983).

Teaching for Higher-Level Goals

25 Motivating Students for Your Course and for Lifelong Learning

Most beginning teachers have so many immediate problems that they don't worry very much about general questions of educational theory or higher-level goals. It is only after you have mastered some of the day-to-day problems that you are able to sit back and reflect on long-term goals. The next four chapters deal with psychological material relevant to a better understanding of students and of the "higher-level" goals of education.

MOTIVATION THEORY

Instructors know that student learning and memory are closely tied to *motivation*. Students are not unmotivated for learning. They are learning all the time—the status hierarchy on campus, football strategy, and many other more or less complex things— but the sort of learning for which students are motivated is not always that which contributes to attaining the goals of our courses. Too often, teachers think of learning only in terms of formal instruction. It might be more realistic for teachers to think of themselves as individuals who facilitate the kinds of learning that are called "education." They can neither learn for their students nor stop them from learning.

A primary problem, then, is motivating students toward course goals. Basically one can affect motivation for learning in two ways: by increasing the *value* of learning or by affecting the students' *expectancy* that investment in course activities will lead to success in achieving their *goals* (values).

One way to increase the value of learning is to link the course to the motives students bring to class—motives that have developed through years of socialization at home and in school. Teachers know, for example, that many of their students are taught by their parents to want to do well in school. Thus we can count motivation for *achievement* as important for many students. There are other motives that are also important.

Intrinsic Motivation

Psychology has a good deal more to contribute on the subject of motivation for learning than it did a few years ago. A few decades ago, psychologists would have talked about reward and punishment and would have asked you to look at the rewards for learning in the classroom. This is still worth considering. Rewards and punishments often influence learning. But the revolution in research and theory lies in evidence that people are naturally curious. They seek new experiences; they enjoy learning new things; they find satisfaction in solving puzzles, perfecting skills, and developing competence. Psychologists differentiate between *extrinsic motivation*—motivation for grades, money, or other rewards that are a consequence of learning—and *intrinsic motivation*—enjoying an activity regardless of the consequences. Curiosity, interest, enjoying problem solving and achievable challenge—these are examples of intrinsic motivation.

Thus one of the major tasks in teaching is not how to scare students into doing their homework, but rather how to nurture intrinsic motivation for learning. In fact, your goals should be not only to motivate students to learn in your course but also to develop motivation for continued learning throughout their lives.

Fortunately, I can do more than point to curiosity as an important motive for learning. A good deal of research suggests that people seek and enjoy stimuli that are different from those they are used to—but that these stimuli must not be too different.

When stimuli are totally incongruous or very strange, students develop anxiety instead of curiosity.

How does this generalization apply to learning in college? It is tempting to answer this question in vague phrases like "varied teaching methods," "posing new, but soluble problems," or "setting realistic standards of achievement." But it is possible to go beyond this. One hint comes from studies by Berlyne (1954a, 1954b). He found that asking students questions, rather than presenting statements of fact, not only improved learning but also increased interest in learning more about the topic. Questions were particularly effective in arousing curiosity about things that were already familiar. The most successful questions were those that were most unexpected. The interplay between familiar and novel may be very significant in the development of curiosity.

How do instructors bring students into contact with novelty? Meaningful field or laboratory experience may be one answer. For example, outstanding scientists report that their motivation for science resulted from early participation in research. This has implications for other disciplines. Perhaps instructors offer too few opportunities for students to experience the thrill of discovery.

Complexity can also arouse curiosity. Chapter 11 reviewed evidence that study questions requiring thought produce greater learning from reading. This is not only because of greater meaningfulness but also because questions requiring "deep processing" make studying more interesting (Svensson, 1976).

Choices and a sense of personal control foster the development of motivation for understanding and self-evaluation of learning (Hagen & Weinstein, 1995; Zimmerman, 1994).

Competence

Another intrinsic motive for learning is competence or self-efficacy. Human beings receive pleasure from doing things well. Students report that their motivation for learning is maintained or increased if they receive feedback that they are improving (Van Etten et al., in press). To the degree that teachers can help students develop a sense of standards that will enable them to see that they are developing increasing skill, teachers can also contribute to the goal of continued learning after the class has been completed.

Bandura (1997) has developed in some depth a theory of self-efficacy. This theory suggests that, while teachers are important sources of information about self-efficacy, students will interpret the same information in differing ways depending on the context of the information and their previous experience. Thus seeing the teacher or other students perform a task will encourage students who see themselves as similar to the successful students, but will not help students who see themselves as so different that another's success bears no relationship to their own chances of success. Even their own success may be misinterpreted as luck. For such students, teachers need to link success with the perception that the success was due to the student's own ability and effort. Success alone is not enough. For students who lack a sense of efficacy teachers must not only provide situations where success occurs but also give students opportunities to undertake challenging tasks on their own to prove to themselves that they can achieve (McKeachie, 1990).

Motives That Sometimes Conflict: Affiliation, Achievement, and Autonomy

Most students want to be liked. In general, warm, friendly teachers are more effective than cold, distant ones. As we saw in Chapter 21 on diversity, feeling that the teacher welcomes them and is committed to their learning is particularly important for minority students. But affiliation motivation, and the need to be liked, may work against instructors as well as for them. In some colleges, students who want acceptance by their classmates may avoid any conspicuous display of academic achievement. Because human beings are motivated by other human beings, cooperative groups and other peer learning methods enhance motivation for learning (as we saw in Chapter 14, on peer learning.)

Most of our students have developed strong motivation for achievement and for autonomy, but their need for achievement and autonomy does not prevent them from being anxious when they are not sure what they need to do in order to achieve their goals. As a result, there is often a conflict between independence and dependence. Some students are likely to resent the teacher who directs their activities too closely, but students are likely to be anxious when given independence; so the teachers have the neat trick of finding ways of simultaneously satisfying those desiring autonomy and those who become anxious without teacher direction. Student apathy in a required course may be an irrational expression of resentment about being required to do anything. If you are striving to enhance lifelong learning, you need to help students become autonomous learners. Research suggests that teachers who support student autonomy help students feel more competent and become more independent (Williams & Deci, 1996).

Achievement Motivation and Expectancy

Atkinson's theory of achievement motivation suggested that students with high achievement motivation would be more highly motivated in situations where they perceived their chances of success as about 50-50 or higher. From Berlyne we have the suggestion that motivation is highest in situations of moderate novelty. Both of these findings point to the value of pacing learning so that each step offers some newness and only a moderate risk of failure—a motivational principle also found by Lepper and Malone (1985) in their analysis of motivational elements in computer games.

Your feedback on student papers or comments is important in enhancing motivation. For students performing poorly, you need to provide encouragement and guidance for improvement; for others, you need to present new challenges.

Grades as Incentives

Let's consider the case of grades. Whatever students' motivations for being in college, grades are important to them. If students are really interested in learning, grades represent an expert's appraisal of their success; if they're interested in getting into professional school, good grades are the key that unlock graduate school doors; if they want to play basketball, grades are necessary for maintaining eligibility. Most students are motivated to get at least passing grades, and much as instructors resent record keeping, the grades they are responsible for are a powerful motivational tool. Unfortunately, grades motivate studying to get a good grade rather than studying for learning that will be retained and used.

Because grades are important to them, many students will learn whatever is necessary to get the grades they desire. If instructors base grades on memorization of details, students will memorize the text. If they believe grades are based on their ability to integrate and apply principles, they'll attempt to do this.

Grades can be used to induce students to get through some of the drudgery of initial learning to the point where the student feels a sense of mastery and can enjoy learning. A good deal of evidence has accumulated to suggest that negative (fear) and positive (hope) motives affect behavior differently. When students are motivated by the threat of low grades, they may work hard, but only if this is the only way to avoid undesirable consequences. If there are other ways out of the situation, they'll take them. The result frequently is that students do the least they can get away with or spend their time devising elaborate methods of cheating.

Negative motives are not as effective outside the learning situation as are positive motives, because fear is a more effective motivational device if the threatened danger is close than if it is distant. Students who are afraid are likely to want to avoid being reminded of the possibility of failure. Hence they may avoid study until the pressures are so great that they simply have no alternative. Thus teachers who motivate their students by fear of bad grades need to use frequent tests if their threats are to be effective.

The striking difference in behavior between students motivated by fear and students motivated by hope is illustrated in their behavior during examinations. A study by Atkinson and Litwin (1960) showed that male students who were high in anxiety about tests were among the first to leave the examination room and tended to do more poorly on the examination than in their work during the course. Students with positive motivation to succeed tended to stay in the examination room longer. (Note that this illustrates the tendency of the fearful person to avoid the situation that arouses anxiety.)

Attributions

Such students can be helped. Heckhausen (1974) showed that students who fear failure improved in performance when they were helped to attribute failure to lack of effort rather than to lack of ability and to set reasonable standards for themselves. But many students work hard and still do poorly. Is there hope for them? Yes! I currently teach a course, "Learning to Learn," that has both cognitive and motivational goals. Motivationally I aim at teaching students that they can achieve better success by practicing skills for effective learning, such as peer learning, and by using these skills strategically. A study by Anderson and Jennings (1980) showed that attributing failure to ineffective strategies improved motivation for success.

To sum up my argument thus far, motivation is important in learning. Curiosity and competence motivation are important motives for learning. We can use student motivation for success, approval, and so on to produce learning. Grades are important incentives for many kinds of motivation. Thus it's important to make sure that grades are not separate from the kind of learning desired. Using grades chiefly as a threat may produce avoidance rather than interest.

THE TEACHER AS MODEL

One of the major sources of stimulation of motivation is the teacher. Your own enthusiasm and values have much to do with your students' interest in the subject matter. Probably nonverbal as well as verbal methods communicate such attitudes; facial expression, animation, and vocal intensity may be as important as the words you use. Simply feeling that you care about their learning is an important motivator for student learning.

COMPETITION VERSUS COOPERATION

Teachers sometimes attempt to stimulate motivation by engendering competition. In American society competition is valued, and if carried out in gamelike situations, competition can be a stimulating motivational device. For example, my teaching assistants frequently hold a "quiz bowl" as a review session before a major test or examination. Students and teachers prepare questions in advance for the quiz bowl. (The teacher may screen out inappropriate questions.) The class is divided into two or more groups. The teacher draws the first question for the first team; the teams are given one minute to consult (more for some questions), and then the first team presents its answer, which is then given 0 to 2 points by the teacher. If the question is not answered adequately, other groups may gain the remaining points by giving a better answer. Another question is then drawn and given to the second group, and the game continues in this fashion.

In an atmosphere of fun and group support, such competition can be a useful motivational device, but intense individual competition is detrimental to learning for most students. When there are few winners and many losers, it may be easier to protect one's sense of self-worth by not trying, than to try and still not succeed. Thus grading on a curve, in which students are competing with one another for grades, is likely to produce anxiety and poorer learning.

WHAT CAN YOU DO TO HELP STUDENTS IMPROVE THEIR MOTIVATIONAL STRATEGIES?

We have seen that motivation is a function of one's goals and expectations about what will lead to those goals (self-efficacy). Can we help students develop strategies that will not only increase their motivation for learning in our course but also be useful for motivating other learning? The answer is "yes." In fact, these are strategies that we can use for ourselves as well.

1. Establish specific, challenging goals. Having students write specific goals for learning in your course should increase their motivation. If your course is one in which student motivation is particularly low, as may be the case in some required courses, you may need to start on a less direct level. For example, you might suggest that they begin by answering questions such as:

a. "What do I want out of my life?"
b. "What do I hope to get out of college?"
c. "Why did anyone think this course should be required? What did they expect students to learn from it?"
d. "What would I like to get out of this course?" (other than a decent grade!)

2. Have students develop a plan of actions necessary for achieving their goals.

3. Have students record progress toward their goals. For example, you might have them write goals for this month, this week, today, and tomorrow and check off those they achieve. Writing short-term and intermediate goals does two things. First, it brings long-term goals into focus, increasing the sense that the goals are achievable. Second, it provides a way of monitoring progress. If most short-term goals are achieved, the students' self-efficacy is likely to be enhanced.

IN CONCLUSION

Grades are an important source of motivation for student learning, but a heavy emphasis on grades may be detrimental to memory of what was learned, as well as to motivation for learning when grades no longer provide a goad. Thus, to develop intrinsic motivation for learning, teachers need to stimulate curiosity, provide choices, and give students a sense of increasing competence. Teachers cannot only motivate students for learning their classes but also help students develop motivational strategies for learning in other situations as well.

Supplementary Reading

Two paperback books dealing with motivation for learning at all levels of education are very useful for thinking about motivating students in colleges and universities. Both are well written and practical:

M. Covington, *Making the Grade* (Cambridge: Cambridge University Press, 1992).

J. Brophy, *Motivating Students to Learn* (Boston: McGraw-Hill, 1998).

The ultimate word on self-efficacy is A. Bandura, *Self-Efficacy: The Exercise of Control* (New York: Freeman, 1997).

My colleagues and I developed a questionnaire to assess student motivation and learning strategies. We used it in our own courses and for research, but it is now used by many teachers, not only in the United States but also in Europe, Asia, Africa, and New Zealand: P. R. Pintrich, D. A. F. Smith, T. Garcia, and W. J. McKeachie, *A Manual for the Use of the Motivated Strategies for Learning Questionnaire (MSLQ)* (Ann Arbor: National Center for Research to Improve Postsecondary Learning and Teaching, School of Education, University of Michigan, 1991).

A group of experts in training college teachers developed a manual for faculty members to use in improving student motivation and learning: G. R. Johnson, J. A. Eison, R. Abbott, G. T. Meiss, K. Moran, J. A. Morgan, T. L. Pasternack, and E. Zaremba, *Teaching Tips for Users of the Motivated Strategies for Learning Questionnaire* (Ann Arbor: National Center for Research to Improve Postsecondary Learning and Teaching, School of Education, University of Michigan, 1991).

26 Teaching Students How to Learn

For many years, the study of student learning was divorced from the study of teaching. Good teaching practices were assumed to be universals that did not depend on individual differences among students or on teaching students to think and learn. Recent developments in educational and cognitive psychology have changed our views of the teaching/learning process and now provide both conceptual and practical information about the ways that students learn and how instructors can use this information to inform their teaching practices. We now know that it is the interaction of good instructional practices with students' strategic learning strategies and skills that results in positive learning outcomes. However, many college students do not know what to do to learn the content in all the different content domain areas that they study. All instructors have some implicit or explicit conceptions or theories about what it means to learn and think in their own discipline. Helping students become aware of these conceptions is an important aspect of teaching. As students

This chapter was written by Claire Ellen Weinstein, University of Texas; Debra K. Meyer, Elmhurst College; Jenefer Husman, University of Texas; Gretchen Van Mater Stone, Shenandoah University; and Wilbert J. McKeachie, University of Michigan.

learn subject matter they also need to learn something about the skills involved in learning that subject matter. For example, students need to know how to reason through problems in engineering, how to read math texts, and how to identify important information about a piece of literature. Therefore, it is important that you use effective instructional practices for presenting content information, as well as effective instructional practices for fostering the development and elaboration of both general learning strategies (such as previewing a textbook chapter) and content-specific learning strategies (such as how to learn mathematical formulas). Active learning is one of the seven principles of good practice in undergraduate education (Gamson, 1991).

THE IMPORTANCE OF GOALS AND SELF-REFLECTION

How can you help students to become more effective learners? We know that strategic learners need to be able to set and use meaningful goals to help them learn and to help them generate and maintain their motivation for studying (Schunk, 1989). As we saw in Chapter 25, we can help students become clearer about their goals by encouraging them to set useful goals for our classes. Unfortunately, many students are clear about neither their educational goals in general nor about their goals for specific courses. Not every course will hold the same interest value for every student, but usually there are at least some aspects of the course that can be perceived as useful for each person. Providing your students with opportunities to identify how the material presented in your courses might be useful to them as they strive to reach their own educational, personal, social, or occupational goals can enhance motivation and cognitive effort (Husman, in preparation). Even a brief class discussion about upcoming topics and how these topics might relate to students' present or future interests can help. Asking students to write a brief paragraph or two about a topic and why it might be relevant to them now or in the future is another way to establish perceived relevance.

It is important to remember that we cannot give students goals—they must own their goals. However, with goal ownership comes responsibility. Students need to learn how to negotiate goals and how to respond to goal achievement and failure. In teaching students multiple learning strategies, you should stress the need to balance goals (for example, adjusting goals for grades with goals for learning; Hagen & Weinstein, 1995). Students should also learn how to implement strategies that will help them negotiate emotional responses to achieving or not achieving their goals (Boekaerts, 1995; Garcia, 1995). In the following sections, we address several ways of learning how to learn in the college classroom through the instructor's role in increasing students' self-awareness, connecting new ideas with existing knowledge, teaching domain-specific strategies, modeling and teaching learning strategies, and providing feedback on these learning strategies.

INCREASING STUDENTS' SELF-AWARENESS

Students who are aware of their learning goals tend to reflect on what it takes to learn. Thinking about thinking, or knowing about knowing, has come to be known as *metacognition* (Flavell, 1979; Pintrich et al., in press; Zimmerman, 1995). Metacognitive processes include knowledge about oneself as a learner, knowledge about academic tasks, and knowledge about strategies to use in order to accomplish academic tasks. Awareness about oneself as a learner helps students to allocate their personal resources, or the resources that are available in their academic institution, such as group study sessions, tutoring programs, or learning centers. If students do not anticipate needing help with a potentially difficult course, it is unlikely that they will take advantage of resources. It also will be difficult for them to judge the personal resources they will need, such as extra study time, or more opportunities for review and consolidation of the material before a test (Entwistle, 1992).

Increasing student self-awareness is imperative for effective strategy instruction. If students attribute their successes or failures to luck, an easy test, or innate ability, then there is no need for effort, time management, or learning strategies (for a review see Pintrich & Schunk, 1996). Therefore, college instructors should provide opportunities for students to reflect on the general characteristics of their approaches to learning (see suggestions in Chapter 25) and on their specific actions toward academic tasks. You may want to survey students to promote self-awareness of strategies by asking questions on the first major assignment or test, such as:

1. How many hours do you spend a week studying for this course?
2. Are you up to date on course assignments and readings?
3. How do you take notes or study while reading the text?
4. How do you take notes in class? Do you review your notes? When? How?

Self-reflection is important for self-regulation, which Zimmerman (1989) defines as "the degree that [students] are metacognitively, motivationally, and behaviorally active participants in their own learning" (p. 4). As college faculty, we should increase student self-awareness of learning strategies and teach them when and how to use strategies (Svinicki, Hagen, & Meyer, 1995).

USING EXISTING KNOWLEDGE

College professors have long known that teaching an introductory course is often more difficult than teaching an advanced course in the same area. While many explanations for this finding have been offered, most of them involve the students' lack of prior knowledge. It is all but impossible to think or solve problems in an area without relevant knowledge. In addition, thinking about relevant knowledge also strengthens new learning by generating meaningful relations to new information. For example, thinking about the economic causes of World War I can help a student understand the economic causes of the second world war. Strategic learners understand the role of relevant prior knowledge and can use this knowledge to help learn new things (Alexander & Judy, 1988). We tend to use prior knowledge in one of two main ways: to create direct relations and to create analogical relations. When we create direct relations, we directly relate our prior knowledge to what we are trying to learn. For example, comparing and contrasting the causes of the two world wars involves direct relations. However, there are times when we do not have directly applicable prior knowledge, but we do have knowledge in an area that is somehow similar and may help us to understand the new information, ideas, or skills we are trying to learn. For example, we use analogies to help us relate familiar and new things that share some key characteristics but are very different in other ways. Using a post office to explain aspects of computer storage, referring to social disagreements to explain conflicts in organizations, and using the structure of a bird to explain design elements of an airplane are all ways we use analogies to help students build meaning for new concepts which may at first seem totally unfamiliar.

TEACHING DOMAIN-SPECIFIC AND COURSE-SPECIFIC STRATEGIES

College faculty teach students not only content about history, biology, or psychology but also modes of thought and strategies for learning (Decyk, 1994; Donald, 1995). Different instructional means may result in students having the same knowledge but not the same broader understanding needed for different applications using this new knowledge. Comparisons of college teaching methods typically find no significant differences in tests of knowledge. There are, however, differences between teaching methods in retention, application, and transfer (Donald, 1995).

Greeno (1991) suggests that general ways of thinking about the material need to be taught along with content because they are prerequisites to understanding content. Students who have no general modes of thinking for understanding science may be as lost in a biological science course as a student attempting to use conventional English narrative structures to understand it. Thus instructors have to consider ways of thinking not only as results of instruction but also as prerequisites for instruction. In addition, you must find ways of helping students transition from existing knowledge structures in their minds to more accurate or advanced knowledge structures.

In addition to thinking about how to provide students with instruction concerning the ways of thinking within their domains, you should also provide direct instruction concerning strategic approaches to the tasks that are specific to their content area. You can have an impact on your students' strategic learning by helping them understand the nature and requirements of academic tasks in the course. As we assign a variety of academic tasks throughout the course, we should define clearly how each assignment relates to course learning goals, so that students can approach them strategically.

There are two levels at which we should address strategies: the domain of the course (e.g., how to think and write like a psychologist) and the course-specific materials and pedagogy (e.g., how lectures and labs are organized, how collaborative problem solving is structured). Many college students approach all their courses in the same way, so we must explicitly teach learning strategies that are domain-specific to our courses. For example, different disciplines have different discourse structures, different forms of argument, and different ways of approaching and solving problems. The domain differences between our course and our students' other courses should be clearly established. To be self-regulated, students must learn strategies that are appropriate for the domain (Alexander, 1995; Boekaerts, 1995). College faculty have found that cognitive modeling, thinking out loud, and demonstrating the use of texts in a self-regulated manner are ways to provide opportunities for students to learn about domain-specific strategies (Coppola, 1995). Most students cannot write like scientists unless they are taught scientific writing. Domain-specific approaches to learning are especially critical in introductory courses. Therefore, you should consider activities like

1. Previewing the textbook and its text structure.
2. Providing anonymous examples of student work to illustrate both do's and don't's.
3. Giving sample items from previous tests as practice.
4. Being clear about terminology that has domain-specific meaning.

In addition to learning strategies that are applicable to the domain of the course, students must learn strategies that are effective with the instructor's methodological and material choices. When modeling the use of the course textbook as a domain-specific strategy, the instructor also can explicitly outline how the text complements or supplements the lecture or lab materials. As we introduce students to new approaches (such as problem-based learning or writing-across-the-curriculum techniques), it is important also to introduce them to the skills needed to successfully participate in our methods and enhance their confidence in applying these skills (Bridges & Hallinger, 1996). Therefore, faculty should help students approach their courses strategically by outlining their individual instructional approaches and materials. For example,

1. As you deliver your first lecture, take notes on the overhead to emphasize the important points.
2. Before you begin a specific pedagogical approach, such as the case study method, take time to explain the method and the skills necessary to use it successfully.

We must remember that faculty can be models of self-regulated learning (Pintrich, 1994). Therefore, we should strive to model discipline-specific thinking processes and course-specific strategies for learning in our classrooms. If an instructor models self-regulation and provides feedback and guidance concerning the students' self-regulation, the instructor can have a significant effect on students' self-regulation (Zimmerman & Schunk, 1997).

We have said that strategic learners can take much of the responsibility for helping themselves study effectively and reach their learning goals. For these students, a core component of strategic learning is their repertoire of cognitive learning strategies (Weinstein & Mayer, 1986). Cognitive learning strategies are goal-directed approaches and methods of thought that help students to build bridges between what they already know or have experienced and what they are trying to learn. These strategies are used to help build meaning in such a way that new information becomes part of an organized knowledge base that can be accessed in the future for recall, application, or problem solving. Research has shown that one of the hallmarks of expertise in an area is an organized knowledge base and a set of strategies for acquiring and integrating new knowledge (Chi, Glaser, & Farr, 1988).

The simplest forms of learning strategies involve repetition or review, such as reading over a difficult section of text or repeating an equation or rule. A bit more complexity is added when students try to paraphrase or summarize in their own words the material they are studying. Other strategies focus on organizing the information they are trying to learn by creating some type of scheme for the material. For example, creating an outline of the main events and characters in a story, making a timeline for historical occurrences, classifying scientific phenomena, or separating foreign vocabulary into parts of speech are all organizational strategies. Some learning strategies involve elaborating on or analyzing what one is trying to learn, to make it more meaningful and memorable. For example, using analogies to access relevant prior knowledge, comparing and contrasting the explanations offered by two competing scientific theories, and thinking about the implications of a policy proposal are examples of elaboration strategies.

We can have a tremendous impact on helping students to develop a useful repertoire of learning strategies. One of the most powerful ways to teach these strategies is modeling. By using different types of strategies in our teaching, we can expose students to a wide variety of strategies in different content areas. However, it is not enough simply to use strategies in our teaching. It is also necessary to teach students how to do this on their own when they are studying. For example, after paraphrasing a discussion in class, point out what you did and why. Briefly explain to the students what paraphrasing is and why it helps people to learn. You also could explain that it helps people to identify areas that they might not understand. If students have trouble paraphrasing something they are studying, it probably means they have not yet really learned it.

Finally, you should provide students with opportunities over time to practice and reflect on their uses of different learning strategies. As Pintrich (1994) noted, modeling ways to learn strategically in our courses is necessary, but not sufficient. We must structure opportunities for students to practice using these strategies. We also need to ask students not only *what* they think, but *how* they think, and *if* this was the most effective process for them. Guided practice with feedback is a powerful way to teach students how to learn because it provides students with opportunities to practice strategies and evaluate them.

Testing practices also influence students' use of learning strategies. Rote memory questions such as "According to the author, the shortage of teachers depends on three factors. Which three?" produce surface-level processing, whereas deep-level processing can be induced by questions such as "Explain the meaning of the following quotation: 'Too many poor teachers will drive good ones out of the market.'" According to Pressley and McCormick (1995), one of the most powerful ways to influence the degree to which students use deep rather than surface strategies is through test demands. Students are more willing to learn to use deep processing strategies when it is evident to them that these types of strategies will help them to meet the demands of the test.

METHODS FOR CHECKING UNDERSTANDING

Strategic learners periodically check on the usefulness of their learning methods by monitoring their progress toward learning goals and subgoals (Brown, 1987). Without checking actively on their progress, many students may think that they understand when, in fact, they do not. Often students do not realize there are holes in their understanding until they receive their grade on a test. This is because the test is the first time they were asked to check on their new knowledge in a way that would identify gaps or misunderstandings. Strategic learners know that the time to check on their understanding is long before taking a test or other formal assessment measure. Checking on understanding and looking for gaps in knowledge integration should be an ongoing activity in every studying and learning context.

Checking understanding can be as simple as having students try to paraphrase or apply what they have been trying to learn. In fact, many homework or project assignments are designed to help students identify gaps in their knowledge or areas of misunderstanding so that they can be corrected. Getting past these problems helps students to deepen their understanding of a topic. Many of the learning strategies we discussed earlier can also be used to test understanding. For example, trying to paraphrase in one's own words what one reads in a textbook is a good way to help build meaning, but it also helps identify gaps or errors in understanding. If students try to apply their knowledge and have difficulty using it, or if they try to explain it to someone else and cannot do it, they would also know that they have some comprehension problems. Monitoring comprehension is an important part of strategic learning that fosters self-regulation. Only when students know they have a problem in their understanding or a gap in their knowledge can they do something about it. Involving students in the evaluation of their college work is another general approach to helping them think about their learning and check their understanding (see MacGregor, 1993).

A very useful method for checking on understanding and helping to teach a variety of learning strategies is the use of cooperative learning. Cooperative learning is a method that builds on peer tutoring. We have long known that, in many traditional tutoring situations, it is the tutor, and not the student receiving the tutoring, who benefits the most. While processing the content for presentation, the tutor is consolidating and integrating his or her content knowledge. At the same time, the tutor is also learning a great deal about how to learn. The tutor needs to diagnose the tutee's learning problem or knowledge gap in order to help overcome it. Refer to Chapter 14, on peer learning, for a more complete discussion of the benefits of cooperative learning within "learning cells."

KNOWING HOW TO LEARN IS NOT ENOUGH— STUDENTS MUST ALSO WANT TO LEARN

Strategic learners know a great deal about learning and the types of strategies that will help them meet their learning goals. However, knowing what to do is not enough. Knowing how to do it is still not enough. Students must *want* to learn if they are to use the knowledge, strategies, and skills we have addressed so far. It is the interaction of what Scott Paris and his colleagues have called "skill and will" that results in self-regulated learning (Paris, Lipson, & Wixson, 1983; Pintrich & De Groot, 1990). Many students know much more about effective study practices than they use. Just like the overweight person who is an expert in weight loss techniques, knowledge is not always sufficient for action. We all have many different potential goals and actions competing for our attention and resources at any point in time. Which goals we select and how much effort we put toward the goals we have selected are at least partially determined by our motivations. Strategic learners know how to learn, but they also want to be effective learners. It is the interaction of skill and will that gives direction to their actions and helps them to persist at tasks, even in the face of obstacles.

One way to enhance students' perceptions of their competence is by giving performance feedback that focuses on strategic effort and skill development. Simply telling students that they did well does not really focus on their role in the performance. Telling a student, "This is great! I can really see the effort you put into this," says a lot more. Talking directly about students' strategic efforts and the skills they are developing helps them to focus on their role in the learning process. Remember that a key component of strategic learning is believing that you can play an active role. If students do not believe they can make a difference, they will not use many of the effective strategies we have been discussing. Many students listen to strategy instruction and believe the strategies are very useful—but not for them! Our task is to help students understand that they can take more responsibility for their own learning.

Remember that motivation results from a number of interacting factors (McCombs & Marzano, 1990; Pintrich & De Groot, 1990; Schunk, 1989). As we discussed under goal setting, establishing the potential usefulness of new learning helps to generate interest and direction for students' learning activities. Chapter 25, on motivating students, includes a more complete discussion of the effects of motivation on learning.

PUTTING IT ALL TOGETHER: EXECUTIVE CONTROL PROCESSES IN STRATEGIC LEARNING

We have discussed both skill and will as important components of strategic learning. A third essential component is the use of executive control processes. These control processes are used to manage the learning process from the beginning (setting the learning goal) to the end result. Strategic learners use executive control processes to (1) organize and manage their approach to reaching a learning goal, (2) keep them on target and warn them if they are not making sufficient progress toward meeting the goal in a timely and effective manner, and (3) build up a repertoire of effective strategies they can call on in the future to complete similar tasks, thereby increasing their learning efficiency and productivity (Weinstein, 1988). When students are facing new and unfamiliar tasks, they must do a lot of planning to help identify potentially effective methods to achieve their goals for task performance. Unfortunately, many students simply adopt a trial-and-error approach to learning, or try to adapt other familiar strategies they have used for different tasks to the current one. Students do not realize that this approach is often neither effective nor efficient. The time invested in generating, following, monitoring, and perhaps modifying a plan is a good investment in reaching learning goals now and in the future. As students develop expertise, they do not need to dwell on developing a plan for each task they face. Generating and evaluating plans for reaching learning goals helps build up an effective repertoire that they can call on in the future when similar learning needs arise.

Several instructional approaches emphasize how college instructors can help students generate, maintain, and evaluate their learning—self-regulating their learning within college coursework. For example, Zimmerman and Paulson (1995) reported a four-phase sequence to teach self-monitoring skills. Such skills are essential for checking understanding and assessing the effectiveness of strategies. When self-monitoring is successful, the student not only learns more but also develops better strategies. In addition, students' successes increase their self-efficacy in the course and their motivation to learn. As college instructors, we must be careful not to emphasize one stage of learning, such as planning, over implementation. Thus another important aspect of learning is the use of volitional strategies. For example, Trawick and Corno (1995) have outlined a volitional training plan that includes specific instructional activities, modeling, role playing, record keeping, and instructor and peer feedback. They emphasize that faculty need to teach volitional skills in addition to cognitive and motivational strategies. Finally, in addition to learning how to learn course content and learning how to control motivation and volition, Boekaerts (1995) emphasized that students must also learn "emotion control." Emotion control refers to the management of emotions and levels of arousal while learning.

College faculty can help facilitate self-regulated learning by encouraging students to share with each other examples of successful approaches to learning. Guided discussions about what is and is not working helps students refine their own methods and get ideas for other potential approaches. They also focus students' attention on the importance of not simply working hard, but also working strategically to meet their goals. Discussions of self-regulated learning should emphasize the need to change strategies in different contexts and for different purposes. Working strategically should be addressed as a challenging endeavor, cognitively, motivationally, and affectively. Students' successes in meeting these challenges are the intrinsic rewards of learning and teaching.

IN CONCLUSION

Teaching strategic learning is more than an investment in your students' future learning; it is also an investment in the present. Strategic learners are better able to take advantage of your instruction and their studying activities. The time you invest will come back to you in enhanced student understanding and performance, as well as in increased motivation. It is also important to remember that all of us have goals for what we hope the students in our classes will learn. In today's rapidly changing world, the ability to acquire or use knowledge and skills is more important than compiling a static knowledge base. There is an old Talmudic expression that loosely translates as "If you feed a person a fish, you have fed them for a day, but if you teach them how to fish, you have fed them for a lifetime!" As college instructors our task is to provide edible fish (content knowledge), but our task is also to teach our students how to fish (learn how to become strategic learners in our field).

Supplementary Readings

P. R. Pintrich, D. R. Brown, and C. E. Weinstein, *Student Motivation, Cognition, and Learning: Essays in Honor of Wilbert J. McKeachie.* (Hillsdale, NJ: Lawrence Erlbaum, 1994).

M. Pressley and C. B. McCormick, *Cognition, Teaching and Assessment* (New York: HarperCollins, 1995).

C. E. Weinstein and B. L. McCombs, *Strategic Learning: The Merging of Skill, Will and Self-Regulation in Academic Environments* (Hillsdale, NJ: Lawrence Erlbaum, in press).

27 Teaching Thinking

Everyone agrees that students learn in college, but whether they learn to think is more controversial.

Thinking is defined in so many ways that the boundary between learning and thinking is fuzzy and perhaps nonexistent. The two processes are inextricably entwined—even a simple learning task, such as reading a textbook assignment, requires thinking.

Thus the preceding chapter, "Teaching Students How to Learn," is actually about teaching students to think. Setting goals, thinking about what strategy to use in tackling an assignment, accessing relevant previous knowledge, and monitoring one's progress—these are all important components of critical thinking and problem solving.

CAN WE TEACH THINKING?

Can we teach thinking? The preceding chapters indicate that my answer is "Yes." Yet some would argue that we can only give students the knowledge necessary for thinking—that the intellectual ability required for thinking is inborn and thus not teachable.

It is true that human beings evolved as thinkers; we all are natural problem solvers. We enjoy solving puzzles and problems. But this does not mean that thinking cannot be improved. College education usually results in higher scores on intelligence tests, but we can do better if we use methods that encourage and train students to think more effectively.

HOW DO WE TEACH THINKING?

So we do teach thinking, but how can we do better?

Almost every chapter of this book has dealt with methods of teaching thinking. Discussions, lecturing, and testing are critical elements in a program for teaching students to think more effectively. Writing, laboratory work, field work, peer learning, project methods, case method, instructional games, journals, role playing, and computers can all contribute to teaching thinking. This chapter would be excessively long if we reviewed, or even summarized, all of the foregoing material on thinking. Therefore I will simply highlight a few general points.

Practice

Knowledge is not enough. Our ever-present pressure to "cover" the content may, in fact, militate against effectiveness in teaching thinking because we fail to allow time for thinking. Thinking, like other skills, requires practice, particularly practice that brings our thinking into the open where it can be challenged, corrected, or encouraged. Thus we teachers need to give students opportunities to talk, write, do laboratory or field projects, or carry out other activities that stimulate and reveal their thinking. One doesn't become a skillful musician or basketball player by listening to an expert three hours a week. Developing skills in thinking requires no less practice. Just as a pianist practices more challenging pieces as skill develops, so, too, a developing thinker needs practice with varied problems—problems that at first are relatively simple but become more and more difficult as the learner becomes more expert, problems that deal with different content, applications, and situations.

Even though knowledge is not sufficient, thinking does require knowledge. Our own research has shown that measures of thinking relate to how well students have achieved an organized structure of concepts. (Naveh-Benjamin, Lin, & McKeachie, 1989).

Do Courses Help?

Surprisingly, standard courses in logic do not seem to improve practical reasoning skills unless the abstract concepts are coupled with concrete examples. Training in statistics, however, can be generalized—even brief training (by giving either rules or examples) in the law of large numbers results in generalization, probably because students have intuitive ideas approximating statistical abstraction (Nisbett et al., 1987). Typical laboratory courses in science have a poor track record in teaching thinking. Yet they, too, can have a positive effect when taught with specific emphasis upon thinking (Bainter, 1955).

If knowledge of subject matter, knowledge of logic, and knowledge of laboratory procedures fail to produce more effective thinkers, what can we do?

Strategies for Teaching

Learning to think usually begins by (1) bringing order out of chaos, (2) discovering uncovered ideas, and (3) developing strategies while avoiding jumping to conclusions. Teaching students to describe the elements of a problem or to create a schematic or graphic representation may help them bring order out of chaos. Verbalizing the reason for taking a step before the step is actually taken also can lead to improved thinking. Good thinkers ask for the reasons for a particular phenomenon or outcome. You can help students develop this skill by frequent use of "Why?" and by continued emphasis on the importance of evidence. You can ask buzz groups (described in Chapter 5, on discussion) to develop alternative theories to explain an unexpected outcome—an exercise in creativity. Or you could have groups develop possible applications of a theory. Students can bring to class examples of faulty thinking found in speeches, newspaper articles, or the Internet. The problem-based and case methods discussed in Chapter 16 are particularly useful for teaching thinking.

A Useful Mnemonic for Teaching Problem Solving: IDEAL

I = Identifying the existence of problem(s)
D = Defining the nature of the problem.
E = Exploring possible strategies for solving the problem.
A = Acting on the basis of the strategy chosen.
L = Looking at the effects. Did the strategy work?

Bransford & Stein, 1993.

Bloom and Broder (1950) asked good students to think aloud while answering mock exam questions requiring problem solving. Other students were asked to compare their own thought processes with those used by the good students and to practice thinking procedures that were successful. Although this procedure was not effective for all students, thinking aloud has often been used since, both in research and in training in thinking, and is an additional strategy for you to use in teaching thinking.

Alverno College has made measurable progress in teaching critical thinking by stressing explicitness, multiple opportunities to practice in differing contexts, and emphasis on developing student self-awareness and self-assessment (Loacker et al., 1984). Students need to think about their own thinking; they need language to describe their thinking, words like *hypothesis*, *evidence*, and *inference* need to be part of their working vocabulary.

Research on teaching problem solving in particular courses suggests explicitly focusing on the specific methods and strategies to be used in solving particular types of problems. Noting different approaches also helps. Many mathematics, science, and engineering courses now assign problems that are open ended; that is, there may be more than one appropriate approach to the problem and more than one satisfactory solution. In such courses students should become more aware of the processes used in problem solving and should develop greater skill in monitoring and evaluating their own progress.

Student participation, teacher encouragement, and student-to-student interaction positively relate to improved critical thinking. These three activities confirm other research and theory stressing the importance of active practice on varied problems, motivation, and feedback using concepts that facilitate transfer of skills to other kinds of problems. As we saw earlier, discussions are superior to lectures in improving thinking and problem solving. As I pointed out in Chapter 7, on testing, student learning is affected as much by your testing as by your teaching. So if you want to teach thinking, be sure that your tests assess thinking.

Many studies point to the importance of developing understanding rather than simply teaching routine steps for problem solving. Increasing understanding and skill lead in turn to increased intrinsic motivation for thinking.

IN CONCLUSION

Learning thinking skills is not easy. Students do not make much progress without specific training. And skill training in itself is not enough. Students need to develop habits of reflection—of thinking about their experience, their successes and failures, their plans and purposes, their choices, and their consequences.

At least four elements of teaching seem to make a difference in student gains in thinking: (1) student writing and discussion; (2) explicit emphasis on problem-solving procedures and methods using varied examples; (3) verbalization of methods and strategies to encourage development of metacognition; and (4) *time* to think and reflect.

Supplementary Reading

There are a number of good books for courses in thinking. These books are also useful references for teachers who want to improve thinking in their own subject matter courses.

J. D. Bransford and B. S. Stein, *The Ideal Problem Solver,* 2nd ed. (San Francisco: Freeman, 1993).

D. F. Halpern, *Thought and Knowledge,* 3rd ed. (Hillsdale, NJ: Erlbaum, 1995).

Among the best sources on teaching thinking are:

J. B. Baron, R. J. Sternberg (eds.), *Teaching Thinking Skills: Theory and Practice.* (New York: Freeman, 1987).

Chet Myers, *Teaching Students to Think Critically: A Guide for Faculty in All Disciplines.* (San Francisco: Jossey-Bass, 1986).

P. Robert-Jan Simon, From Romanticism to Practice in Learning, *LLINE: Lifelong Learning in Europe,* 1997, 1 8-15.

R. J. Sternberg and L. Spear-Swirling, *Teaching for Thinking* (Washington, DC: American Psychological Association, 1996).

Just as I was writing this edition of *Teaching Tips,* a new edition of John Dewey's classic *How We Think* (Boston: Houghton Mifflin, 1998) arrived in my mail. Dewey's ideas, written over a half-century ago, underlie much of the work since his time and are still fresh and helpful today.

David Levy's book *Tools of Critical Thinking* (Boston: Allyn and Bacon, 1997) deals with many of the biases and errors in everyday thinking and includes excellent exercises to help students become better thinkers.

In two and a half pages, Bette Ericksen and Diane Strommer give seven good suggestions for teaching thinking. See pages 74–76 in their book *Teaching College Freshmen* (San Francisco: Jossey-Bass, 1991).

I suggested that one aspect of good thinking is reflection. Jean McGregor has edited a useful book, *Student Self-Evaluation: Fostering Reflective Thinking, New Directions for Teaching and Learning, No. 56* (San Francisco: Jossey-Bass, 1993).

28 Teaching Values: Should We? Can We?*

As you may suspect, this chapter would not be in this book if the answer to either question in its title were "no." So, after answering "yes," I will try to engage you in thinking with me about the more difficult questions: What should we teach? And how should we teach?

Valuing is as natural as thinking or breathing. We automatically make value judgments about our experiences. "This was good, that was bad; this is beautiful, that's ugly." You have already made judgments about the value of this book. Our students are continually valuing. It would be strange if their college

In thinking about our role in teaching values, I owe much to Brewster Smith, both for his writing about psychology and values and for my interactions with him through the years. We served together for many years on the Board of Directors of the American Psychological Association, and I always admired the consistency with which he exemplified his own values in his behavior and comments on various controversial issues. We haven't always agreed, but I think we both tried to represent out values when issues came before us. I have benefited from Brewster's comments on an earlier draft of this chapter as well as from thoughtful reactions by Larry Greenfield and George Lambrides, but none of the above should be held responsible for the final version, which was influenced by some, but not all, of their ideas.

experiences had no impact on that valuing process. And, we as teachers are continually guided in our behavior by our values. I write on this topic because of my own basic values. They influence this choice of topic; they strongly influence what I'm going to write; and they influenced me in thinking that it was important to get you thinking with me about our role in teaching values. And because my major point is that we ought to be more open in our discussion of values, I should begin by giving you a brief statement of my own values—the perspective from which this chapter is written.

I'm a strongly religious person, a humanist active in my local American Baptist church. I believe strongly that love and respect for other human beings is not a *relative* value—simply a current norm taught in our society—but rather a universal value that should guide the behavior of all human beings at all times. As a Baptist I have a passionate commitment to talking with people about theology, philosophy of religion, ethics, and values issues. I believe that no one has the ultimate answer to the question human beings have wrestled with since the beginning of human self-consciousness—What is Good? Each of us must make a commitment to the best we can conceive of, to give our insights to fellow human beings, and to welcome their thoughts in order that we may come closer to ultimate truth.

SHOULD WE?

That, of course, implies that I think we *should* teach values. In fact, I argue that we can't avoid teaching values. Value neutrality, so-called value-free teaching, is simply advocacy by default. It's using our influence covertly, rather than openly. Our choices of content, our choices of teaching methods, our very ways of conducting classes reveal our values and influence our students' reactions.

My own subject matter, psychology, is particularly value laden. Concepts such as "mental health," "adjustment," "maturity," "personality integration," and "effective leadership" all involve value terms that we sometimes teach to our students as if they were scientific constructs developed in an empirical way on the basis of research without any value implications. The practice of psychology and the research that psychologists have done have clear implications for political and ethical behavior.

I was a mathematics major as an undergraduate, and even in this purest of disciplines there were values. Some proofs were more beautiful than others; the examples and illustrations intended to maintain our interest carried certain implicit values. So, even though some disciplines probably face value questions less directly than others, we teachers cannot escape values. We can't avoid teaching values.

"But," you say, "isn't it a misuse of our position if we indoctrinate students with our values?" True. Probably our avoidance of explicit attention to values results from our concern about the evil of indoctrination. But there are two aspects to my answer.

The *first* is that I would have no compunction about indoctrination with respect to such values as honesty and respect for other individuals as human beings. We cannot teach our students well if they plagiarize papers, fake laboratory results, or cheat on examinations. We cannot carry out effective classroom discussions without an atmosphere of respect for others' feelings or a sense of shared humanity. In a multicultural society like ours there is a special need for thinking seriously about values—how we differ and what we share.

The *second* is that we can help students to become more sensitive to values issues, to recognize value implications, to understand others' values, without indoctrination. Even with respect to fundamental values such as honesty, discussion, exploration, and debate about their implications are more useful than simple advocacy. Open consideration of the complexity of value issues is probably less subversive than disregarding values altogether.

CAN WE?

This leaves us with this chapter's second question: Can we? Do we have an impact? There is research evidence that we do. Students do change during their college years. There have been a number of studies of college graduates versus noncollege graduates (with reasonable controls for socioeconomic status and other factors) that show differences. In general these are supported by longitudinal studies showing similar differences between student values at the beginning of their college years as compared with their values toward the end of their senior year (Pascarella & Terenzini, 1991).

Among the sometimes modest *average* changes, there are great *individual* changes, as well as changes of particular groups according to the curricula chosen, social groupings, or other elements of the college culture. So students change; the issue for us is: Does our teaching make a difference?

Certainly teaching is one element of the culture that supports or opposes other elements of the culture, some of which may be pulling in different directions. The social culture, the fraternity/sorority culture, the athletic culture, the bar and tavern culture, the administrative, institutional culture—even the culture of religious groups—these and others are also influencing the students.

Here again we have some research evidence. Teaching can make a difference. A number of studies, in fact, have found changes in values and attitudes in individual courses in which different teaching methods were compared. In general, courses with more emphasis on discussion or active learning methods have more influence than those in which students are passive (McKeachie et al., 1990). Thus we can answer the question—Can we?—affirmatively. The questions now become: What should we be teaching? How should we teach values?

WHAT VALUES SHOULD WE TEACH?

Those who say we should be taking a neutral stance on values typically are restricting their definition of values to sociopolitical ones. Very few would dispute the fact that we are concerned about honesty, respect for others, and rationality. A major goal of education presumably is to increase students' skills in critical, rational thinking. We want students to value rational thought, but not at the exclusion of other ways of knowing and thinking. In considering problems in society or in their everyday lives, our graduates will, I hope, look for evidence rather than react on the basis of unreasoning prejudice; they will be aware of the implications of their values but not let their values close their minds. Particularly in social science courses we ask our students to ask "What is the evidence?" before jumping to conclusions. Even those who point out that "rationality" has sometimes been defined in ways that confirm power and status relationships present rational arguments and evidence for their position. Our greater sensitivity to the issues raised by feminist and other critics is itself a tribute to rationality.

In psychology courses we expect our students to learn respect for individuality and freedom of choice, particularly as this involves treatment of human beings in research studies. We train our graduate students not to exploit their status or power over students or clients for participation in research or for sexual or other activities that are outside the bounds of the normal college course requirements.

Through the years my own thinking has changed. The first research project I coordinated was a study in which we compared three methods of teaching: discussion, tutorial, and recitation-drill. We worked very hard to be sure that the teachers in our sample conformed to those methods in their three classes. I now feel that it is not ethical for me to require a teacher, as part of an experiment, to teach in a way that the teacher thinks is not the best way that he or she can teach. So I no longer attempt to constrain my experiments in the same way. When I run an experiment in a real class, I try to add something beyond what the teacher would ordinarily do—something that both the teacher and I believe will enhance the students' educational experience, rather than constraining the teacher in ways that might be detrimental to the students.

The big question in teaching is what to do about controversial social and political values. Here it seems to me that we are not privileged to demand acceptance of our own values, as I think we are privileged to do with respect to requiring academic honesty. But this does not imply avoiding values issues. Too often we communicate—by the way we handle touchy material—that you don't rock the boat by taking a position.

In avoiding controversial issues we communicate the notion that it may be all right to talk about these things in dormitories or in other places, but not in educational settings where rational arguments and the complexities of the issue are more likely to be salient.

The apple of temptation for us as teachers is that we may too easily accept affirmation of values that we share, letting students get away with simply stating a position with which we agree, without asking for rational support, as we might for a position that conflicts with our own.

On the other side, however, is the problem of dealing with those with whom we disagree. There is the danger that we will yield to the temptation of demolishing the student with the force of our logic, but arguing can also be a way of showing respect. Remember that the power you have in your role as teacher may make it difficult for the student to muster a strong defense. Take it easy until students trust you enough to argue without fear of retribution. It is all too easy to intentionally, or unintentionally, coerce students into overt agreement.

Perry (1970, 1981) has described the development of Harvard students as progressing from the dualistic belief that things are either true or false, good or evil, through a stage of relativism in which they feel all beliefs are equally valid, to a stage of commitment to values and beliefs that are recognized to be incomplete and imperfect but are open to correction and further development. We may not all reach Perry's highest stage, or we may reach it in some areas but not in others, but Perry suggests that as teachers and members of the community of learners, we have the responsibility not only to model commitment and open-mindedness but also to share our own doubts and uncertainties. He says:

> We need to teach dialectically—that is, to introduce our students, as our greatest teachers have introduced us, not only to the orderly certainties of our subject matter, but to its unresolved dilemmas. This is an art that requires timing, learned only by paying close attention to students' ways of making meaning. (Perry, 1981, p. 109)

We need to teach students to begin to become aware of the complexities of their positions, of the fact that there are always costs and gains—tradeoffs between competing values. Just as teachers in music are not satisfied when their students simply like a particular symphony or a particular kind of music, but insist that the students develop a disciplined appreciation of the complexity underlying their preferences, so, too, in other disciplines we need to help students value and understand the pros and cons, the arguments and evidence that are involved in critical judgments and decisions. In the social sciences we need to communicate that liking people or liking certain kinds of people or institutions and their values is not enough. Our ethical judgments in human affairs need to have at least as much complexity in their analysis and exposition as we would give to analyzing the strengths and weaknesses of our favorite baseball team or our judgments of restaurants.

My major concern is not that we teach values such as honesty, which we agree are essential to the academic enterprise, but that we be open and explicit in helping our students to become *sensitive* to values issues. Whichever side they come out on, they should be aware that large numbers of things that we take for granted in this world involve serious moral and ethical values. Much of the evil that I see is not just the result of lack of values but rather a lack of sensitivity to value implications of actions or policies that are more or less taken for granted or are accepted as part of one's role in an institution—governmental, business, or academic.

In college I hope that students will develop firm enough commitments and have enough practice in considering values issues that in most situations they automatically act in accordance with their values. But I also hope that they will be more likely and able to think about values implications in the many areas in which values are not salient or where values are in conflict.

The Dutch psychologist Jan Elshout (1987) suggests that there are three levels of problems. I believe that his metaphor can be extended to values issues and decision making as well.

Elshout says that the first zone is one in which no thinking is needed. The problem solver can solve the problem automatically on the basis of previous knowledge and expertise. Similarly, there are situations in which we don't have to think about values issues because we automatically do the right thing. (This is not to imply that such values are immune from examination!)

But there is a second, problematic zone where the solution is not obvious, and the problem solver has to think about alternative ways of approaching the problem because there is no obvious solution. Nonetheless, the problem solver tackles the problem because he or she has skills and strategies that may lead to a solution. Similarly, there are ethical issues that we recognize as ethical problems and can resolve with appropriate consideration of the pros and cons.

Elshout then suggests that there is a top zone where the situation is so complicated, so remote from our experience, that we don't know what approach to use and our usual strategies of problem solving are no longer likely to be very effective. So, too, in ethics there are problems that we fail to recognize, or if recognized, simply avoid thinking about.

In the area of ethics and values we hope that as teachers we can expand the area in which humane values are carried out as the normal pattern of behavior; we hope to increase our students' ability to consider and weigh conflicting values in the middle zone, to consult others when in doubt, and we also hope to cut down the big area where our students avoid considering values because the whole area seems so complicated that they don't want to think.

HOW CAN WE TEACH VALUES?

We exemplify and communicate our values in what we teach and in the way we teach. Teaching values does not mean neglecting knowledge. Knowledge is a powerful sword to protect students from biased, emotional appeals.

Probably every teacher, whether in the arts, the sciences, or the professions, tries to teach students that it is not enough simply to respond to material or performance as good or bad, but rather to be able to back up one's judgment with evidence that is reasonable in terms of the standards of that discipline. We communicate that value by our comments on papers, our reactions to student comments or performance, and ultimately by our grades. So we have a group of values that we accept and either explicitly or implicitly communicate to our students through our behavior as teachers.

Our values also affect our course planning. We begin with the goals we take for the course. Who should determine those goals? Is this something to be determined by the university, by the department, by the instructor, or should students be involved? Personally, I have faith that in a situation in which students and faculty members participate jointly, our decisions will come out with reasonable values, reasonable content, and reasonable coverage—all the things that we worry about when we're thinking about how to set up a course. A cooperative approach exemplifies the value of respect for others.

Modeling Values

We demonstrate our values and those of our discipline in almost every class. Yesterday I spent a good part of the class period having students introduce one another. I indicated that this represented the value to me of knowing students as individuals rather than as faces in a crowd. Even in classes of 500 I have used seating charts so that I could call students by name.

Perhaps most important is the model of ethical behavior we provide (see Chapter 24). Clearly, sarcasm, favoritism, and failure to respect diversity of students' cultures, values, and attitudes represent a negative model. But avoiding unethical behavior is not enough. How do we handle legitimate requests for exceptions from a policy printed in our syllabus? Do we weigh individual needs or are we rule-bound? How do we handle students with handicaps or learning disabilities? When a student comment is wrong or inappropriate, do we make it clear that we are criticizing the idea and not the person?

What about the ethical decisions we face in preparing and conducting the course? Do we give proper credit to the sources we use? Are our assignments and learning assessments dictated by student learning or by our own need to save time? Are we conscientious about preparation and attendance at class? Are we ethical in our use of licensed software? Each of the ethical situations discussed in Chapter 24 is an opportunity for you to model your values.

Service Learning

Idealism isn't dead among students. The annual nationwide surveys of American college freshmen carried out by UCLA Higher

Education Research Institute show that goals such as helping other people and developing a philosophy of life, which had been dropping in relation to more materialistic goals, are now resurgent. In fact, 72 percent of 1996–1997 freshmen reported that they do volunteer services.

Evaluations of our University of Michigan service courses, Project Outreach and Project Community, suggest that these courses have had some success in affecting student values. Such courses tend to confirm and reinforce altruistic values and probably help make students' altruistic impulses become more realistic when faced with the complexities of helping other people. Additional research supporting the value of service learning is discussed in Chapter 13.

Dealing with Alternative Views

One major values issue in teaching is whether to present a single view or multiple positions in areas where theories differ. Certainly our students prefer that we tell them the "truth." And I suppose that if you really believe strongly that a particular position is true, you should teach that position. But I don't think that relieves you of the obligation to let students know that there is a competing theory.

As teachers and scholars we must hold to the faith that even though there is little, if any, unchanging absolute "truth," the positions we hold to be closer to truth than the alternatives can be supported by evidence and reason. Our task is to help students develop the habits of thinking that are used in our disciplines, to determine what is more or less valid.

We don't develop these habits of thinking by avoiding areas where there are conflicting theories or values. Be up front about the differences. Use the two-column method described in Chapter 5 or set up a debate, perhaps asking participants to take the side opposite to their own.

A classic values clarification exercise is to place the signs "Strongly agree," "Agree," "Disagree," and "Strongly Disagree" on the four walls of the classroom. Read a controversial statement and ask students to stand by the wall that represents their position. Ask students to defend their positions and to move to another wall if their opinion changes during the discussion. At the end of the discussion you might have students write a minute paper on what they learned.

In the social sciences we can use cross-cultural research that indicates to our students that there are different ways of viewing the world and differing value positions on a number of things that we take for granted.

What Kinds of Teaching Methods Should We Use?

There is some relevant research evidence here. One of the classic studies was done by Stern and Cope (1956; also Stern, 1962) at Syracuse some years ago. They selected authoritarian students with stereotyped conceptions of race, minorities, and others different from themselves. These students were assigned to a special discussion section. Their achievement in this homogeneous section proved to be superior to that of similar students in conventional sections of the course.

What did the teacher do with these students who were unusually difficult to teach? At the beginning of the term the instructor of the homogeneous section was distressed by the students' lack of responsiveness and negativism, but he adopted a strategy of frequently taking a devil's advocate position, in which he would present strong positions that would arouse the students so much that they simply had to respond. The ensuing debate resulted in changes that didn't occur in the classes where similar students were able to sit back and not participate. The students in the experimental class not only performed better academically but also became less ethnocentric and authoritarian than similar students in the conventional classes. This finding fits with research comparing discussions versus lectures, suggesting that more attitude change occurs in discussion sections.

Cooperative peer learning often has a positive effect on attitudes and values. Cooperation is itself an important value in our culture, and success in learning how to work cooperatively with other students in a project or other learning experience is likely to have a positive impact on students' value for cooperation.

The results of the studies of discussion methods, cooperative learning, and experiential learning fit with our theories of change. If we want students to change, they have to have a chance to express their ideas and values in words or actions and see how they work. They need reactions not only from teachers but also from peers and others who share or oppose their positions.

Students also need opportunities to make choices—topics for papers, alternative assignments, even (as in my classes) choice of textbooks. We espouse freedom as a value in our culture, yet our own behavior as teachers may exemplify authoritarian power.

We know that students remember the content of our courses better if they elaborate the content by relating it to other knowledge—if they question, explain, or summarize. Such elaboration is important in the values area as well. And, it's important that the discussion and experiences be in places where there is mutual respect and support. Values are not likely to be changed much simply by passively listening and observing a lecturer. Change is more likely in situations in which the teacher, as well as students, listen and learn from one another.

THE TEACHER AS A PERSON

The teaching methods one uses may be less important than aspects of teaching that cut across methods. The degree to which students feel we know them as individuals and care about their learning, the extent to which they feel they know us as individuals (not simply as experts or authorities), the openness we have to questions and opposing points of view, our willingness to risk change in ourselves—these have much to do with the students' willingness to open their values to examination and change.

Teaching does not end at the classroom door. Wilson et al. (1975) found that professors who were perceived by students and colleagues as having significant impact on student development demanded high standards of performance and interacted a great deal with students both in and *out* of the classroom. When students see that you are willing to sacrifice time from your own endeavors in order to help them, you communicate your values.

IN CONCLUSION

We develop values by observing and modeling ourselves after others and testing out our values in thought and words and action. Teachers are significant models, and teacher behavior is important, both as it models values and as teachers create situations in which the expression of values becomes salient.

The process of value development and value change is very much like the process of scientific theory development or of self-development in general. For example, we have experiences; we develop ways of trying to think about those experiences to make sense of them; we test our theories (in this case our values) by consciously thinking about them, by studying what others have said or done, by talking to other people, and by behaving and seeing what happens. My basic faith is that everyone has within himself or herself the capacity to discriminate good from evil and to act to achieve the good. William James said, "The significance of religious belief is not in affirmation, but in its consequences for behavior." And so it is with values in general.

St. Augustine wrote, "Hope has two lovely daughters, anger and courage. Anger at the way things are, and courage to see that they need not remain as they are." Let us have hope.

Supplementary Reading

A thoughtful discussion of these as well as ethical issues in teaching may be found in:

W. L. Humphreys, Values in Teaching and the Teaching of Values, *Teaching-Learning Issues No. 58* (Knoxville: Learning Research Center, The University of Tennessee, 1986).

Self-reflective learning involves much consideration of values. See J. MacGregor, ed., *Student Self-evaluation: Fostering Reflective Learning, New Directions for Teaching and Learning, No. 56* (San Francisco: Jossey-Bass, 1993).

Joseph Lowman has a brief but helpful discussion of how to handle controversial issues in his book, *Mastering the Techniques of Teaching* (San Francisco: Jossey-Bass, 1984).

REFERENCES

Abbott, R. D., et al. (1990). Satisfaction with processes of collecting student opinions about instruction: A student perspective. *Journal of Educational Psychology, 82,* 201–206.

Abrami, P. C., d'Apollonia, S., & Rosenfield, S. (1997). The dimensionality of student ratings of instruction: What we know and what we do not. In R. P. Perry & J. C. Smart (Eds)., *Effective teaching in higher education: Research and practice* (pp. 321–367). New York: Agathon.

Adams, M. (1992). Cultural inclusion in the American college classroom. In L. Border & N. Chism (Eds.), Teaching for diversity, *New Directions in Teaching and Learning, 49,* pp. 5–17. San Francisco: Jossey-Bass.

Ajzen, I., & Madden, T. J. (1986). Prediction of goal directed behavior: Attitudes, intentions, and perceived behavioral control. *Journal of Experimental Social Psychology, 22,* 453–474.

Alexander, P. A. (1995). Superimposing a situation-specific and domain-specific perspective on an account of self-regulated learning. *Educational Psychologist, 30,* 189–193.

Alexander, P. A., & Judy, J. E. (1988). The interaction of domain-specific and strategic knowledge in academic performance. *Review of Educational Research, 58*(4), 375–404.

Allen, B. P., & Niss, J. F. (1990). A chill in the college classroom? *Phi Delta Kappan, 71,* 607–609.

Alverno College Faculty. (1994). *Student Assessment Learning at Alverno College,* Milwaukee, WI: Alverno Productions.

American Council on Education and University of California at Los Angeles Higher Education Research Council. (1996). *The American freshman: National norms for fall 1996.* Washington, DC: American Council on Education.

Anderson, C. A., & Jennings, D. L. (1980). When experiences of failure promote expectations of success: The impact of attributing failure to ineffective strategies. *Journal of Personality, 48,* 393–407.

Anderson, J. A., & Adams, M. (1992). Acknowledging the learning styles of diverse populations: Implications for instructional design. In L. Border & N. Chism (Eds.), Teaching for diversity. *New Directions in Teaching and Learning, 49,* pp. 19–33. San Francisco: Jossey-Bass.

Andre, T. (1987). Questions and learning from reading. *Questioning Exchange, 1*(1), 47–86.

Angelo, T. A. (Ed.), (1991). Classroom research: Early lessons from success. *New Directions for Teaching and Learning, 46,* San Francisco: Jossey-Bass.

Angelo, T. A., & Cross, K. P. (1993). *Classroom assessment techniques: A handbook for college faculty* (2nd ed.). San Francisco: Jossey-Bass.

Annis, L. F. (1981). Effect of preference for assigned lecture notes on student achievement. *Journal of Educational Research, 74,* 179–181.

———. (1983a). The processes and effects of peer tutoring. *Human Learning, 2,* 39–47.

———. (1983b). *Study techniques.* Dubuque: Wm. C. Brown.

Asante, M. K. (1987). *The Afrocentric idea.* Philadelphia: Temple University Press.

———. (1988). *Afrocentricity.* Trenton, NJ: Africa World Press.

Astin, A. (1975). *Preventing students from dropping out.* San Francisco: Jossey-Bass.

Atkinson, J. W., & Litwin, G. H. (1960). Achievement motive and test anxiety conceived as motive to approach success and motive to avoid failure. *Journal of Abnormal and Social Psychology, 60,* 52–63.

Attiyeh, R., & Lumsden, K. G. (1972). Some modern myths in teaching economics: The U. K. experience. *American Economics Review, 62,* 429–433.

Bainter, M. E. (1955). A study of the outcomes of two types of laboratory techniques used in a course in general college physics for students planning to be teachers in the elementary grades. *Dissertation Abstracts, 15,* 2485–2486.

Bandura, A. (1997). *Self-Efficacy: The exercise of control,* New York: W. H. Freeman.

Bargh, J. A., & Schul, Y. (1980). On the cognitive benefits of teaching. *Journal of Educational Psychology, 72*(5), 593–604.

Barnard, W. H. (1936) Note on the comparative efficacy of lecture and socialized recitation method vs. group study method. *Journal of Educational Psychology, 27,* 388–390.

Barr, R. B., & Tagg, J. (1995). From teaching to learning—A new paradigm for undergraduate education. *Change, 27,* 12–25.

Baxter Magolda, M. B. (1992). *Knowing and reasoning in college: Gender-related patterns in students' intellectual development.* San Francisco: Jossey-Bass.

Beach, L. R. (1960). Sociability and academic achievement in various types of learning situations. *Journal of Educational Psychology, 51,* 208–212.

———. (1968). *Student interaction and learning in small self-directed college groups.* Final Report. Washington, DC: Department of Health, Education and Welfare.

Beach, R. & Bridwell, L. (1984). Learning through writing: a rationale for writing across the curriculum. In A. Pellegrini and T. Yawkey (Eds.), *The development of oral and written language in social contexts.* Norwood, NJ: Abbey.

Belenky, M. F., Clinchy, B. M., Goldberger, N. R., & Tarule, J. M. (1986). *Women's ways of knowing: The development of self, voice, and mind.* New York: Basic Books.

Benjamin, L. (1991). Personalization and active learning in the large introductory psychology class. *Teaching of Psychology, 18*(2), 68–74.

Berlyne, D. E. (1954a). A theory of human curiosity. *British Journal of Psychology, 45,* 180–181.

———. (1954b). An experimental study of human curiosity. *British Journal of Psychology, 45,* 256–265.

———. (1960). *Conflict, arousal, and curiosity.* New York: McGraw-Hill.

Blackwell, J. E. (1990). Operationalizing faculty diversity. *AAHE Bulletin, 42*(10), 8–9.

Bligh, D. (1971). *What's the use of lectures?* Exeter: Bligh and Bligh.

Bloom, B. S. (1953). Thought processes in lectures and discussions. *Journal of General Education, 7,* 160–169.

———. (Ed.). *Taxonomy of educational objectives, handbook I: Cognitive domain.* New York: Longmans, Green.

Bloom, B. S. & Broder, L. J. (1950). *Problem solving processes of college students.* Chicago: University of Chicago Press.

Boekaerts, M. (1995). Self-regulated learning: Bridging the gap between metacognitive and metamotivational theories. *Educational Psychologist, 30,* 195–200.

Border, L. B., & Chism, N. V. N. (Eds.). (1992). Teaching for diversity, *New Directions in Teaching and Learning, 49.* San Francisco: Jossey-Bass.

Boris, E. Z. (1983). Classroom minutes: a valuable teaching device. *Improving College and University Teaching, 31*(2), 70–73.

Boss, J. (1994). The effect of community service on the moral development of college ethics students. *Journal of Moral Education, 23,* 183–198.

Boud, D., Dunn, J., & Hegarty-Hazel, E. (1986). *Teaching in laboratories.* Guildford, Surrey, U. K.: Society for Research into Higher Education and NFER-Nelson.

Bowser, B. P., Jones, T., & Young, G. A. (Eds.). (1995). *Toward the multicultural university.* Westport, CT: Praeger.

Boyer, E. (1990). *Scholarship reconsidered: Priorities of the professoriate.* Princeton, NJ: Carnegie Foundation for the Advancement of Teaching.

Boyer, E. L. (1990). Campus life: In search of community. Princeton, NJ: Carnegie Foundation for the Advancement of Teaching.

Braskamp, L. A., & Ory, J. C. (1994). *Assessing faculty work: Enhancing individual and institutional performance.* San Francisco: Jossey-Bass.

Braxton, J. M., Eimers, M. T. & Bayer, A. E. (1996). The implications of teaching norms for the improvement of undergraduate education. *Journal of Higher Education, 67*(6), 603–626.

Bridges, E. M., & Hallinger, P. (1996). In L. Wilkerson & W. H. Gijselaers (Eds.), Bringing problem-based learning to higher education: Theory and practice. *New Directions for Teaching and Learning, 68,* (pp. 53–61). San Francisco: Jossey-Bass.

Brinko, K. T., & Menges, R. J. (Eds.). (1997). *Practically speaking: Sourcebook for instructional consultants in higher education.* Stillwater, OK: New Forums Press.

Brittingham, B. E. (1988). Undergraduate students' use of time: A classroom investigation. *To Improve the Academy, 7,* 45–52.

Brown, A. L. (1987). Metacognition, executive control, self-regulation, and other more mysterious mechanisms. In F. E. Weinert & R. H. Kluwe (Eds.), *Metacognition, motivation, and understanding* (pp. 65–116). Hillsdale, NJ: Erlbaum.

Brown, G., & Atkins, M. (1988). *Effective teaching in higher education.* London: Methuen.

Brown, R. D., & Krager, L. (1985). Ethical issues in graduate education: Faculty and student responsibilities. *Journal of Higher Education, 56,* 403–418.

Cahn, S. M. (1986). *Saints and scamps: Ethics in academia.* Totowa, NJ: Rowman & Littlefield.

Cambridge, B. (1996). Looking ahead. *AAHE Bulletin,* 10–11.

Caron, M. D., Whitbourne, S. K., & Halgin, R. P. (1992). Fraudulent excuse making among college students. *Teaching of Psychology, 19*(2), 90–93.

Centra, J. A. (1975). Colleagues as raters of classroom instruction. *Journal of Higher Education, 46,* 327–337.

————. (1993). *Reflective faculty evaluation: Enhancing teaching and determining faculty effectiveness.* San Francisco: Jossey-Bass.

Chang, T. M., Crombag, H. F., van der Drift, K. D. J. M., & Moonen, J. M. (1983). *Distance learning: on the design of an open university.* Boston: Kluwer-Nijhoff.

Chi, M. T. H., Glaser, R., & Farr, M. J., (Eds.). (1988). *The nature of expertise.* Hillsdale, NJ: Erlbaum.

Chickering, A. W., & Gamson, Z. F. (1987). Seven principles for good practice in undergraduate education. *American Association for Higher Education Bulletin, 39,* 3–7.

————. (Eds.). (1991). Applying the seven principles for good practice in undergraduate education. *New Directions for Teaching and Learning, 47.* San Francisco: Jossey-Bass.

Chronicle of Higher Education (1997). *The Chronicle of Higher Education 1997–98 Almanac Issue, 44,* 1.

Churchill, L. R. (1982). The teaching of ethics and moral values in teaching. *Journal of Higher Education, 53*(3), 296–306.

Cohen, P., Kulik, J., & Kulik, C.-L. (1982). Educational outcomes of tutoring: A meta-analysis of findings. *American Educational Research Journal, 19*(2), 237–248.

Collett, J., & Serrano, B. (1992). Stirring it up: The inclusive classroom. In L. Border & N. Chism (Eds.), Teaching for diversity, *New Directions in Teaching and Learning, 49* (pp. 35–48). San Francisco: Jossey-Bass.

Collins, A. (1977). Processes in acquiring knowledge. In R. C. Anderson, R. J. Spiro, & W. E. Montague, (Eds.), *Schooling and the acquisition of knowledge.* Hillsdale, NJ: Erlbaum.

———. (1982). Goals and strategies of inquiry teaching. In R. Glaser (Ed.), *Advances in instructional psychology.* Hillsdale, NJ: Erlbaum.

Coppola, B. P. (1995). Progress in practice: Using concepts from motivation and self-regulated learning research to improve chemistry instruction. In P. Pintrich (Ed.), Understanding self-regulated learning. *New Directions for Teaching and Learning, 63* (pp. 87–96). San Francisco: Jossey-Bass.

Costin, F. (1972). Three-choice versus four-choice items: Implications for reliability and validity of objective achievement tests. *Educational and Psychological Measurement, 32,* 1035–1038.

Covington, M. V., & Wiedenhaupt, S. (1997). Turning work into play: The nature and nurturing of intrinsic task engagement. In R. P. Perry & J. C. Smart (Eds.), *Effective teaching in higher education: research and practice.* New York: Agathon Press.

Cronbach, L. J., & Snow, R. E. (1977). *Aptitudes and instructional methods: A handbook for research on interaction.* New York: Irvington.

Cross, K. P. Classroom research: Helping professors learn more about teaching and learning. In P. Seldin & Associates (Eds.), *How administrators can improve teaching* (pp. 122–142). San Francisco: Jossey-Bass.

Cross, K. P., & Steadman, M. H. (1996). *Classroom research: Implementing the scholarship of teaching.* San Francisco: Jossey-Bass.

Davis, S. F. (1992, Spring). Students and faculty: A beneficial interface. *Psi Chi Newsletter,* 3–4.

Day, R. S. (1980). Teaching from notes: Some cognitive consequences. In W. J. McKeachie (Ed.), Learning, cognition, and college teaching. *New directions for teaching and learning, 2,* San Francisco: Jossey-Bass.

Deutsch, M. (1949). An experimental study of the effects of cooperation and competition upon group processes. *Human Relations, 2,* 199–232.

Dewey, R. (1995, March). Finding the right introductory psychology textbook. *APS Observer,* 32–35.

Dillon, J. T. (1982). The effect of questions in education and other enterprises. *Journal of Curriculum Studies, 14,* 127–152.

Donald, J. G. (1995). Disciplinary differences in knowledge validation. Understanding self-regulated learning. *New Directions for Teaching and Learning, 64* (pp. 7–17). San Francisco: Jossey-Bass.

Duchastel, P. C., & Merrill, P. F. (1973). The effects of behavioral objectives on learning: A review of empirical studies. *Review of Educational Research, 43,* 53–69.

D'Ydewalle, G., Swerts, A., & de Corte, E. (1983). Study time and test performance as a function of test expectations. *Contemporary Educational Psychology, 8*(1), 55–67.

Edgerton, R., Hutchings, P., & Quinlan, K. (1991). *The teaching portfolio: Capturing the scholarship of teaching.* Washington, DC: American Association for Higher Education.

Edmondson, J. B., & Mulder, F. J. (1924). Size of class as a factor in university instruction. *Journal of Educational Research, 9,* 1–12.

Ege, S. N., Coppola, B. F., & Lawton, R. G. (1997). The University of Michigan undergraduate chemistry curriculum. *Journal of Chemical Education, 74,* 74–94.

Entwistle, N. J. (1992). Student learning and study strategies. In B. R. Clark & G. Neave (Eds.), *Encyclopedia of higher education.* Oxford: Pergamon.

Falk, D. (1995, Winter). Preflection. A strategy for enhancing reflection. *NSEE Quarterly,* 13.

Feldman, K. A., & Newcomb, T. M. (1969). *The Impact of College on Students,* (Vol. 2). San Francisco: Jossey-Bass.

Ferguson, M. (1990). The role of faculty in increasing student retention. *College and University, 65,* 127–134.

Fisch, L. (Ed.). (1996). Ethical dimensions of college and university teaching: Understanding and honoring the special relationship between teachers and students. *New directions for teaching and learning, No. 66.* San Francisco: Jossey Bass.

Flavell, J. H. (1979). Metacognition and cognitive mentoring: A new area of cognitive-developmental inquiry. *American Psychologist, 34,* 906–911.

Foos, P. W., & Fisher, R. P. (1988). Using tests as learning opportunities. *Journal of Educational Psychology, 88*(2), 179–183.

Forbes, D., & Spence, J. (1991). An experiment in assessment for a large class. In R. Smith (Ed.), *Innovations in engineering education.* London: Ellis Horwood.

Frey, P. W., Leonard, D. W., & Beatty, W. W. (1975). Students' ratings of instruction: Validation research. *American Educational Research Journal, 12,* 327–336.

Friedman, E. G., Kolmar, W. K., Flint, C. B., & Rothenberg, P. (1996). *Creating an inclusive curriculum.* New York: Teachers College Press.

Gamson, W. A. (1966). *SIMSOC: a manual for participants*. Ann Arbor, MI: Campus Publishers.

Gamson. Z. F. (1991). A brief history of the seven principles for good practice in undergraduate education. In A. W. Chickering & Z. F. Gamson (Eds.), Applying the seven principles for good practice in undergraduate education. *New Directions for Teaching and Learning, 47* (pp. 5–12). San Francisco: Jossey-Bass.

Garcia, T. (1995). The role of motivational strategies in self-regulated learning. In P. Pintrich (Ed.), Understanding self-regulated learning. *New Directions for Teaching and Learning, 63* (pp. 29–42). San Francisco: Jossey-Bass.

Gardiner, L. F. (1997). *Redesigning higher education: Producing dramatic gains in student learning.* ASHE-ERIC Higher Education Reports, *23*,(7). Washington, DC: Association for the Study of Higher Education.

Garrett, R. M., & Roberts, I. F. (1982). Demonstration versus small group practical work in science education: A critical review of studies since 1900. *Studies in Science Education, 9,* 109–146.

Gay, G. (1995). Curriculum theory and multicultural education. In J. A. Banks & C. A. Banks (Eds.), *Handbook of research on multicultural education.* (pp. 25–43). New York: Simon & Schuster Macmillan.

Gibbs, G. (1992). *Teaching more students 1: Problems and course design strategies.* Oxford: Oxford Centre for Staff Development.

Gibbs, G., & Jenkins, A. (1984). Break up your lectures. *Journal of Geography in Higher Education 8,*(1), 27–39.

Gmelch, W. H., Lovrich, N., & Wilkie, P. K. (1984). Sources of stress in academe: A national perspective. *Research in Higher Education, 20,* 477–490.

Goldschmid, M. L. (1971). The learning cell: An instructional innovation. *Learning and Development, 2*(5), 1–6.

———. (1975, May). When students teach students. Paper presented at the International Conference on Improving University Teaching, Heidelberg, Germany.

Goldschmid, M. L., & Shore, B. M. (1974). The learning cell: A field test of an educational innovation. In W. A. Verreck (Ed.), *Methodological problems in research and development in higher education* (pp. 218–236). Amsterdam: Swets and Zeitlinger.

Goldstein, A. (1956). A controlled comparison of the project method with standard laboratory teaching in pharmacology. *Journal of Medical Education, 31,* 365–375.

Grabe, M., and Grabe, C. (1998). *Integrating technology into meaningful learning.* (2nd ed.). Boston: Houghton Mifflin.

Grauerholz, E., & Copenhaver, S. (1994). When the personal becomes problematic: The ethics of using experiential teaching methods. *Teaching Sociology, 22*(4), 319–327.

Greeno, J. G. (1991). Number sense as situated knowing in a conceptual domain. *Research in Mathematical Education, 22,* 170–218.

Gruber, H. E., & Weitman, M. (1960, April). Cognitive processes in higher education: Curiosity and critical thinking. Paper read at Western Psychological Association, San Jose, CA.

————. (1962, April). *Self-directed study: Experiments in higher education,* Report No. 19. Boulder: University of Colorado, Behavior Research Laboratory.

Hagen, A. S., & Weinstein, C. E. (1995). Achievement goals, self-regulated learning, and the role of classroom context. In P. Pintrich (Ed.), Understanding self-regulated learning. *New Directions for Teaching and Learning, 63* (pp. 43–56). San Francisco: Jossey-Bass.

Haines, D. B., & McKeachie, W. J. (1967). Cooperative vs. competitive discussion methods in teaching introductory psychology. *Journal of Educational Psychology, 58,* 386–390.

Hall, C., & Fitzgerald, C. (1995). Student summative evaluation of teaching: Code of practice. *Assessment & Evaluation in Higher Education, 20,* 307–311.

Hall, R. H., et al. (1988). The role of individual differences in the cooperative learning of technical material. *Journal of Educational Psychology, 80,* 172–178.

Hall, R. M., & Sandler, B. R. (1982). *The classroom climate: A chilly one for women?* Project on the Status and Education of Women. Washington, DC: Association of American Colleges.

Hanson, K. (1996). Between apathy and advocacy: Teaching and modeling ethical reflection. In L. Fisch (Ed.), Ethical dimensions of college and university teaching: Understanding and honoring the special relationship between teachers and students. *New Directions for Teaching and Learning, 66* San Francisco: Jossey-Bass, 33–36.

Harter, S. (1978). Effective motivation reconsidered: Toward a developmental model. *Human Development, 21,* 34–64.

Hartley, J., & Davies, I. K. (1978). Note-taking: A critical review. *Programmed Learning and Educational Technology, 15,* 207–224.

Hartman, F. R. (1961). Recognition learning under multiple channel presentation and testing conditions. *Audio-Visual Communication Review, 9,* 24–43.

Hartman, H. J. (1990). Factors affecting the tutoring process. *Journal of Developmental Education, 14*(2), 2–6.

Hartman, N. (1989). Syndicate based peer group learning: an alternative process. *South African Journal of Higher Education, 3,* 98–106.

Heckhausen, H. (1974, August). How to improve poor motivation in students. Paper presented at the 18th International Congress of Applied Psychology, Montreal.

Hettich, P. (1990). Journal writing: Old fare or nouvelle cuisine? *Teaching of Psychology, 17,* 36–39.

Hillocks, G. (1982). The interaction of instruction, teacher comment, and revision in teaching the composing process. *Research in Teaching of English, 16,* 261–278.

Hodgkinson, H. L. (1995). Demographic imperatives for the future. In B. P. Bowser, T. Jones, & G. A. Young (Eds.), *Toward the multicultural university* (pp. 3–19). Westport, CT: Praeger.

Hofer, B. (1997). *The development of personal epistemology: Dimensions, disciplinary differences, and instructional practices.* Unpublished doctoral thesis, University of Michigan.

Hofstede, G. (1986). Cultural differences in teaching and learning. *International Journal of Intercultural Relations, 10,* 301–320.

Hogan, P., & Kimmel, A. (1992). Ethical teaching of psychology: One department's attempts at self-regulation. *Teaching of Psychology, 19*(4), 205–210.

Houston, J. P. (1983). Alternate test forms as a means of reducing multiple-choice answer copying in the classroom. *Journal of Educational Psychology, 75*(4), 572–575.

Hovland, C. I. (Ed.). (1957). *The order of presentation in persuasion.* New Haven, CT: Yale University Press.

Hudelson, E. (1928). *Class size at the college level.* Minneapolis: University of Minnesota Press.

Hutchings, P., Marchese, T., & Wright, B. (1991). *Using assessment to strengthen general education.* Washington, DC: American Association for Higher Education.

Innis, K. (1996). *Diary survey: How undergraduate full-time students spend their time.* Leeds: Leeds Metropolitan University.

Irvine, J. J., & York, D. E. (1995). Learning styles and culturally diverse learners: A literature review. In J. A. Banks & C. A. Banks (Eds.), *Handbook of research on multicultural education* (pp. 484–497). New York: Simon & Schuster Macmillan.

Johnson, D. W., & Johnson, R. T. (1975). *Learning together and alone: Cooperation, competition and individualization.* Englewood Cliffs, NJ: Prentice-Hall.

Johnson, D. W., Maruyama, G., Johnson, R., Nelson, D., & Skon, L. (1981). The effects of cooperative, competitive, and individualistic goal structures on achievement: A meta-analysis. *Psychological Bulletin, 89,* 47–62.

Karenga, M. (1995). Afrocentricity and multicultural education: Concept, challenge, and contribution. In B. P. Bowser, T. Jones, & G. A. Young (Eds.), *Toward the multicultural university* (pp. 41–64). Westport, CT: Praeger.

Katz, D. (1950). *Gestalt psychology.* New York: Ronald Press.

Keith-Spiegel, P., & Koocher, G. (1985). *Ethics in psychology: Professional standards and cases.* Hillsdale, NJ: Erlbaum.

Keith-Spiegel, P., Wittig, A., Perkins, D., Balogh, D. W., Whitley, B. (1996). Intervening with colleagues. In L. Fisch (Ed.), Ethical dimensions of college and university teaching: Understanding and honoring the special relationship between teachers and students. *New Directions for Teaching and Learning, 66.* San Francisco: Jossey-Bass, 75–78.

Keller, F. S. (1968). Goodbye teacher, . . . *Journal of Applied Behavior Analysis, 10,* 165–167.

Kember, D. (1991). *Writing study guides.* Bristol: Technical and Educational Services.

Kendrick, J. R. (1996). Outcomes of service learning in an introduction to sociology course. *Michigan Journal of Community Service Learning, 3,* 72–81.

Kerr, C. (1994). Knowledge ethics and the new academic culture. *Change, 26*(1), 8–16.

Kiewra, K. A. (1989). A review of notetaking: the encoding storage paradigm and beyond. *Educational Psychology Review, 1*(2), 147–172.

King, A. (1990). Enhancing peer interaction and learning in the classroom. *American Educational Research Journal, 27,* 664–687.

Kitano, M. K. (1997). What a course will look like after multicultural change. In A. I. Morey & M. K. Kitano (Eds.), *Multicultural course transformation in higher education: A broader truth* (pp. 18–34). Needham Heights, MA: Allyn and Bacon.

Kluger, A. N., & DeNisi, A. (1996). The effects of feedback intervention on performance: A historical review, a meta-analysis, and a preliminary feedback intervention theory. *Psychological Bulletin, 119,* 254–284.

Kozma, R. B. (1982). The design of instruction in a chemistry laboratory course. *Journal for Research in Science Teaching, 19,* 261–270.

Krathwohl, D., Bloom, B. S., & Masia, B. (Eds.) (1964). *Taxonomy of educational objectives, handbook II: Affective domain.* New York: David McKay.

Kulik, J. A., & Kulik, C. -L. C. (1989). Meta-analysis in education. *International Journal of Educational Research, 13,* 221–340.

Kulik, J. A., Kulik, C. -L. C., & Bangert-Drowns, R. L. (1988). *Effectiveness of mastery learning programs: A meta-analysis.* Ann Arbor: University of Michigan, Center for Research on Learning and Teaching.

Lahti, A. M. (1956). The inductive-deductive method and the physical science laboratory. *Journal of Experimental Education, 24,* 149–163.

LaPree, G. (1977). Establishing criteria for grading student papers: Moving beyond mysticism. *Teaching and Learning* (Indiana University), *3*(1).

Larson, C. O., et al. (1984). Verbal ability and cooperative learning: Transfer of effects. *Journal of Reading Behavior, 16,* 289–295.

Laurillard, D. (1993). *Rethinking university teaching: A framework for the effective use of educational technology.* London: Routledge.

LaVergne, T., & Corno, L. (1995). Expanding the volitional resources of urban community college students. In P. Pintrich (Ed.), Understanding self-regulated learning. *New Directions for Teaching and Learning, 63* (pp. 57–70). San Francisco: Jossey-Bass.

Lawrenz, F. (1985). Aptitude-treatment effects of laboratory grouping methods for students of differing reasoning ability. *Journal of Research in Science Teaching, 22,* 279–287.

Leith, G. O. M. (1974a). Individual differences in learning: Interactions of personality and teaching methods. In Association of Educational Psychologists, *Personality and Academic Progress,* London.

———. (1974b). Goals, methods and materials for a small-group, modular-instruction approach to teaching social psychology. Paper presented for the Institute of Social Psychology, University of Utrecht.

———. (1977). Implications of cognitive psychology for the improvement of teaching and learning in universities. In B. Massey (Ed.), *Proceedings of the Third International Conference, Improving University Teaching* (pp. 111–138). College Park: University of Maryland.

Lepper, M. R., & Malone, T. W. (1985). Intrinsic motivation and instructional effectiveness in computer-based education. In R. E. Snow & M. J. Farr (Eds.), *Aptitude, learning and instruction: III. Conative and affective process analyses.* Hillsdale, NJ: Erlbaum.

Lidren, D. M., Meier, S. E., & Brigham, T. A. (1991). The effects of minimal and maximal peer tutoring systems on the academic performance of college students. *Psychological Record, 41,* 69–77.

Lifson, N., Rempel, P., & Johnson, J. A. (1956). A comparison between lecture and conference methods of teaching psychology. *Journal of Medical Education, 31,* 376–382.

Loacker, G., Cromwell, L., Fey, J., & Rutherford, D. (1984). *Analysis and communication at Alverno: An approach to critical thinking.* Milwaukee, WI: Alverno Productions.

Locke, E. A., & Latham, G. P. (1990). *A theory of goal setting and task performance.* Englewood Cliffs, NJ: Prentice Hall.

lopez, g., & Chism, N. (1993). Classroom concerns of gay and lesbian students. *College Teaching, 41*(3), 97–103.

Lowther, M. A., Stark, J. S., & Martens, G. G. (1989). *Preparing course syllabi for improved communication*. Ann Arbor: NCRIPTAL, University of Michigan.

MacGregor, J. (1993). Learning self-evaluation: Challenges for students. In J. MacGregor (Ed.), Student self-evaluation: Fostering reflective learning. *New Directions for Teaching and Learning, 56* (pp. 35–46). San Francisco: Jossey-Bass.

Macomber, F. G., & Siegel, L. (1957a). A study of large-group teaching procedures. *Educational Research, 38,* 220–229.

———. (1957b). Experimental study in instructional procedures. *Progress Report No. 2.* Oxford, OH: Miami University.

———. (1960). Experimental study in instructional procedures. *Final Report.* Oxford, OH: Miami University.

Maier, N. R. F. (1952). *Principles of human relations*. New York: Wiley.

———. (1971). Innovation in education. *American Psychologist, 26*(8), 722–725.

Maier, N. R. F., & Maier, L. A. (1957). An experimental test of the effects of "developmental" vs. "free" discussion on the quality of group decisions. *Journal of Applied Psychology, 41,* 320–323.

Mann, R. D., et al. (1970). *The college classroom: Conflict, change, and learning*. New York: Wiley.

Marcinkiewicz, H. R., & Clariana, R. B. (1997). The performance effects of headings within multiple-choice tests. *British Journal of Educational Psychology, 67,* 111–117.

Markies, G. B., Howard, J., & King, D. C. (1993). Integrating community service and classroom instruction enhanced learning: Results from an experiment. *Educational Evaluation and Policy Analysis, 15,* 410–419.

Marsh, H. W., & Dunkin, M. J. (1997). Students' evaluations of university teaching: A multidimensional perspective. In R. P. Perry & J. C. Smart (Eds.), *Effective teaching in higher education: Research and practice* (pp. 241–320). New York: Agathon.

Marsh, H. W., & Roche, L. (1993). The use of students' evaluations and an individually structured intervention to enhance university teaching effectiveness. *American Educational Research Journal, 30,* 217–251.

Marton, F., & Säljö, R. (1976a). On qualitative differences in learning: I—Outcome and process. *British Journal of Educational Psychology, 46,* 4–11.

———. (1976b). On qualitative differences in learning: II—Outcome as a function of the learner's conception of the task. *British Journal of Educational Psychology, 46,* 115–127.

Matthews, J. (1991). The teaching of ethics and the ethics of teaching. *Teaching of Psychology, 18*(2), 80–85.

McCluskey, H. Y. (1934). An experimental comparison of two methods of correcting the outcomes of examination. *School and Society, 40,* 566–568.

McCombs, B. L., & Marzano, R. J. (1990). Putting the self in self-regulated learning: The self as agent in integrating will and skill. *Educational Psychologist, 25*(1), 51–69.

McKeachie, W. J. (1990). Learning, thinking, and Thorndike. *Educational Psychologist, 25*(2), 127–141.

McKeachie, W. J., et al. (1980). Using student ratings and consultation to improve instruction. *British Journal of Educational Psychology, 50,* 285–291.

McKeachie, W. J., Lin, Y-G., Forrin, B., & Teevan, R. (1960). Individualized teaching in elementary psychology. *Journal of Educational Psychology, 51,* 285–291.

McKeachie, W. J., Pintrich, P. R., & Lin, Y-G. (1985). Teaching learning strategies. *Educational Psychologist, 20*(3), 153–160.

McKeachie, W. J., Pintrich, P. R., Lin, Y-G., Smith, D. A. F., & Sharma, R. (1990). *Teaching and learning in the college classroom: A review of the research literature* (2nd ed.). Ann Arbor: NCRIPTAL, University of Michigan.

McKeachie, W. J., Pollie, D., & Speisman, J. (1955). Relieving anxiety in classroom examinations. *Journal of Abnormal and Social Psychology, 50,* 93–98.

McMillan, J. H., & Forsyth, D. F. (1991). What theories of motivation say about why learners learn. *New directions for teaching and learning, 45,* (39–52). San Francisco: Jossey-Bass.

Means, G., & Means, R. (1971). Achievement as a function of the presence of prior information concerning aptitudes. *Journal of Educational Psychology, 62,* 185–187.

Menges, R. J. (1990). Teaching: Beliefs and behaviors. *Teaching Excellence, 2*(6), 1–2.

Menges, R. J., & Austin, A. E. (in press). Teaching in higher education. In V. Richardson (Ed.), *Handbook of research on teaching.* Washington, DC: American Educational Research Association.

Menges, R. J., & Brinko, K. T. (1986, April). *Effects of student evaluation feedback: A meta-analysis of higher education research.* Paper presented at the American Educational Research Association, San Francisco. (ERIC Document Reproduction Service No. ED/270/408)

Menges, R. J., & Mathis, B. C. (1988). *Key resources on teaching, learning, curriculum, and faculty development.* San Francisco: Jossey-Bass.

Mentkowski, M., & Loacker, G. (1985). Assessing and validating the outcomes of college. In P. Eutell (Ed.), *Assessing Educational Outcomes:*

New Directions for Institutional Research (pp. 47–64). San Francisco: Jossey-Bass.

Metzger, R. L., Boschee, P. F., Haugen, T., & Schnobrich, B. L. (1979). The classroom as learning context: Changing rooms affects performance. *Journal of Educational Psychology, 71*(4), 440–442.

Miller, J. E., & Groccia, J. E. (1997). Are four heads better than one? A comparison of cooperative and traditional teaching formats in an introductory biology course. *Innovative Higher Education, 21,* 253–273.

Moffat, M. (1989). *Coming of age in New Jersey: College and American culture.* New Brunswick, NJ: Rutgers University Press.

Monaco, G. E. (1977). *Inferences as a function of test-expectancy in the classroom.* Kansas State University Psychology Series, KSU-HIPI Report 73–3.

Mueller, D. J., & Wasser, V. (1977). Implications of changing answers on objective test items. *Journal of Educational Measurement, 14*(1), 9–13.

Murray, H. G. (1983). Low-inference classroom teaching behaviors and student ratings of college teaching effectiveness. *Journal of Educational Psychology, 75,* 138–149.

———. (1997). Effective teaching behaviors in the college classroom. In R. P. Perry & J. C. Smart (Eds.), *Effective Teaching in Higher Education: Research and Practice.* New York: Agathon.

Murray, H., Gillese, W., Lennon, M., Mercer, P. & Robinson, M. (1996). Ethical principles for college and university teaching. In L. Fisch (Ed.), *Ethical dimensions of college and university teaching: Understanding and honoring the special relationship between teachers and students. New Directions for Teaching and Learning, 66* (pp. 57–64). San Francisco: Jossey-Bass.

Myers-Lipton, S. (1994). The effects of service-learning on students' attitudes toward civic responsibility, international understanding, and racial prejudice. Doctoral dissertation, University of Colorado.

———. (1996). Effect of a comprehensive service-learning program on college students' level of modern racism. *Michigan Journal of Community Service Learning, 3,* 44–54.

Naveh-Benjamin, M., & Lin, Y-G. (1991). *Assessing students' organization of concepts: A manual of measuring course-specific knowledge structures.* Ann Arbor: NCRIPTAL, University of Michigan.

Naveh-Benjamin, M., Lin, Y-G., & McKeachie, W. J. (1989). Development of cognitive structures in three academic disciplines and their relations to students' study skills, anxiety and motivation. Further use of the ordered-tree technique. *Journal of Higher Education Studies, 4,* 10–15.

Naveh-Benjamin, M., McKeachie, W. J., Lin, Y-G., & Tucker, D. G. (1986). Inferring students' cognitive structures and their development using the "ordered tree" technique. *Journal of Educational Psychology, 78,* 130–140.

New Jersey Institute for Collegiate Teaching and Learning. (1990). *The challenges of the college classroom.* South Orange, NJ: Seton Hall University.

Nisbett, R. E., Fong, G. T., Lehman, D., & Cheng, P. W. (1987). Teaching reasoning. *Science, 238,* 625–631.

Novak, J. D. (1958). An experimental comparison of a conventional and a project centered method of teaching a college general botany course. *Journal of Experimental Education, 26,* 217–230.

Paris, S. G., Lipson, M. Y., & Wixson, K. K. (1983). Becoming a strategic reader. *Contemporary Educational Psychology, 8,* 293–316.

Parsons, T. S. (1957). A comparison of instruction by kinescope, correspondence study, and customary classroom procedures. *Journal of Educational Psychology, 48,* 27–40.

Parsons, T. S., Ketcham, W. A., & Beach, L. R. (1958, August). Effects of varying degrees of student interaction and student-teacher contact in college courses. Paper read at American Sociological Society, Seattle, WA.

Pascarella, F. T., & Terenzini, E. (1991). *How college affects students.* San Francisco: Jossey-Bass.

Paul, J. B. (1932). The length of class periods. *Educational Research, 13,* 58–75.

Pea, R., & Kurland, D. (1987). Cognitive technologies in writing. In E. Rothkopf (Ed.). *Review of Research in Education No. 14* (277–326). Washington, DC: American Educational Research Association.

Peper, R. J., & Mayer, R. E. (1978). Note taking as a generative activity. *Journal of Educational Psychology, 70*(4), 514–522.

Perry, R. P., & Smart, J. C. (Eds.). (1997). *Effective teaching in higher education: Research and practice.* New York: Agathon.

Perry, W. G., Jr. (1970). *Forms of intellectual and ethical development in the college years: A scheme.* New York: Holt, Rinehart, and Winston.

———. (1981). Cognitive and ethical growth: the making of meaning. In A. W. Chickering (Ed.), *The modern American college* (pp. 76–116). San Francisco: Jossey-Bass.

Pintrich, P. R., & De Groot, E. V. (1990). Motivational and self-regulated learning components of classroom academic performance. *Journal of Educational Psychology, 82,* 33–40.

Pintrich, P. R., & Schunk, D. H. (1996). *Motivation in education.* Englewood Cliffs, NJ: Prentice-Hall.

Pintrich, P. R., Smith, D. A. F., Garcia, T., & McKeachie, W. J. (1991). *A manual for the use of the Motivated Strategies for Learning Questionnaire (MSLQ)*. Ann Arbor: National Center for Research to Improve Postsecondary Teaching and Learning, University of Michigan.

Pintrich, P. R., Wolters, C. A., & Baxter, G. P. (in press). Assessing metacognition and self-regulated learning. In C. E. Weinstein & B. L. McCombs (Eds.), *Strategic learning: The merging of skill, will and self-regulation*. Hillsdale, NJ: Erlbaum.

Pressley, M., & McCormick, C. B. (1995). Cognition, teaching and assessment. New York: HarperCollins.

Pressley, M., et al. (1992). Encouraging mindful use of prior knowledge: Attempting to construct explanatory answers facilitates learning. *Educational Psychologist, 27*(1), 91–109.

Quinn, J. (1993). *University professors read about teaching*. Evanston, IL: Northwestern University, National Center for Postsecondary Teaching, Learning, and Assessment.

Ramsden, P., & Entwistle, N. J. (1981). Effects of academic departments on students' approaches to studying. *British Journal of Educational Psychology, 51*, 368–383.

Rando, W. C., & Lenze, L. F. (1994). *Learning from students: Early-term student feedback in higher education*. State College: Penn State University, National Center for Postsecondary Teaching, Learning, and Assessment.

Ray, T. (1996). Differentiating the related topics of ethics, morality, law and justice. In L. Fisch (Ed.), Ethical dimensions of college and university teaching: Understanding and honoring the special relationship between teachers and students. *New Directions for Teaching and Learning, 66* (pp. 47–54). San Francisco: Jossey-Bass.

Reder, L. M., & Anderson, J. R. (1982). Effects of spacing and embellishment on memory for the main points of a text. *Memory and Cognition, 10*(2), 97–102.

Remmers, H. H. (1933). Learning, effort, and attitudes as affected by three methods of instruction in elementary psychology. *Purdue University Studies in Higher Education, 21*.

Riordan, R. J., & Wilson, L. S. (1989). Bibliotherapy: Does it work? *Journal of Counseling and Development, 67*, 506–508.

Roberts, M. S., & Semb, G. B. (1990). Analysis of the number of student-set deadlines in a personalized psychology course. *Teaching of Psychology, 17*, 170–173.

Rodabaugh, R. (1996). Institutional commitment to fairness in teaching. In L. Fisch (Ed.), Ethical dimensions of college and university teaching: Understanding and honoring the special relationship between teachers and students. *New Directions for Teaching and Learning, 66* (pp. 37–46). San Francisco: Jossey-Bass.

Rojewski, J. W., & Schell, J. W. (1994). Instructional considerations for college students with disabilities. In K. W. Prichard & R. M. Sawyer (Eds.), *Handbook of college teaching* (pp. 387–400). Westport, CT: Greenwood Press.

Romig, J. L. (1972). An evaluation of instruction by student-led discussion in the college classroom. *Dissertation Abstracts International, 32,* 6816.

Ross, I. C. (1957). Role specialization in supervision. Ph. D. diss., Columbia University. *Dissertation Abstracts, 17,* 2701–2702.

Rothkopf, E. Z. (1970). The concept of mathemagenic activities. *Review of Educational Research, 40,* 325–336.

Royer, P. N. (1977). Effects of specificity and position of written instructional objectives on learning from a lecture. *Journal of Educational Psychology, 69,* 40–45.

Ruhl, K. L., Hughes, C. A., & Schloss, P. J. (1987). Using the pause procedure to enhance lecture recall. *Teacher Education and Special Education, 10,* 14–18.

Russell, T. L. (1997). The "No significant difference" phenomenon. New Brunswick, Canada: Home page of ND TeleEducation. http://temb.mta.ca

Sadker, M., & Sadker, D. (1992). Ensuring equitable participation in college classes. In L. Border & N. Chism (Eds.), Teaching for diversity (pp. 49–56). *New Directions in Teaching and Learning, 49,* San Francisco: Jossey-Bass.

Sadler, D. R. (1987). Specifying and promulgating achievement standards. *Oxford Review of Education, 13*(2), 191–209.

Scheidermann, N. V. (1929). An experiment in teaching psychology. *Journal of Applied Psychology, 13,* 188–191.

Schoem, D. , Frankel, L., Zúñiga, X., & Lewis, E. A., (Eds.), (1993). *Multicultural teaching in the university.* Westport, CT: Praeger.

Schomberg, S. F. (1986, April). Involving high ability students in learning groups. Paper presented at AERA in San Francisco.

Schultz, P. A., & Weinstein, C. E. (1990). Using test feedback to facilitate the learning process. *Innovation Abstracts, 12*(22).

Schunk, D. H. (1989). Social cognitive theory and self-regulated learning. In B. J. Zimmerman & D. H. Schunk (Eds.), *Self-regulated learning and academic achievement* (pp. 83–110). New York: Springer-Verlag.

Seashore, C. E. (1928). Elementary psychology: An outline of a course by the project method. *Aims and Progress Research,* No. 153. Iowa City: University of Iowa Studies.

Seldin, P. (1993). *Successful use of teaching portfolios.* Bolton, MA: Anker.

Siegel, L., Adams, J. F., & Macomber, F. G. (1960). Retention of subject matter as a function of large-group instructional procedures. *Journal of Educational Psychology,* 51, 9–13.

Siegel, L., & Siegel, L. C. (1964). The instructional gestalt: A conceptual framework and design for educational research. *Audio-Visual Communication Review, 12,* 16–45.

Silverman, R., Welty, W. M., & Lyon, S. (1994). *Educational psychology cases for teacher problem solving.* New York: McGraw-Hill.

Sleeter, C. E. (1991). *Empowerment through multicultural education.* Albany, N.Y.: State University of New York Press.

Smith, D. (1996). The ethics of teaching. In L. Fisch (Ed.), Ethical dimensions of college and university teaching: Understanding and honoring the special relationship between teachers and students. *New Directions for Teaching and Learning, 66* (pp. 5–14). San Francisco: Jossey-Bass.

Smith, W. F., & Rockett, F. C. (1958). Test performance as a function of anxiety, instructor and instructions. *Journal of Educational Research, 52,* 138–141.

Snow, R. E., & Peterson, P. L. (1980). Recognizing differences in student attitudes. In W. J. McKeachie (Ed.), Learning, cognition, and college teaching. *New directions for teaching and learning, 2.* San Francisco: Jossey-Bass.

Snyder, B. R. (1970). *The hidden curriculum.* Cambridge, MA: MIT Press.

Solomon, D., Rosenberg, L., & Bezdek, W. E. (1964). Teacher behavior and student learning. *Journal of Educational Psychology, 55,* 23–30.

Stanton, H. (1992). *The University Teacher,* 13(1).

Stark, J. S., & Lattuca, L. R. (1997). *Shaping the college curriculum: Academic plans in action.* Boston: Allyn and Bacon.

Stern, G. G. (1962). Environments for learning. In N. Sanford (Ed.), *The American college.* New York: Wiley.

Stern, G. G., & Cope, A. H. (1956, September). *Differences in educability between steropaths, non-steropaths and rationals.* Paper presented at the American Psychological Association meeting in Chicago.

Steyn, S. C., Marais, J. L., & Rens, J. A. (1996). Die kreatiewe gebruik van cribnotes as leerstrategie. *South African Journal of Higher Education, 10,* 218–221.

Strike, K. (1988). The ethics of teaching. *Phi Delta Kappan, 70(2),* 156–158.

Sturgis, H. W. (1959). The relationship of the teacher's knowledge of the student's background to the effectiveness of teaching: A study of the extent to which the effectiveness of teaching is related to the teacher's knowledge of the student's background. Ph.D. diss., New York University. *Dissertation Abstracts, 19*(11).

Sumner, R., & Buckingham Shum, S. (1998). From documents to discourse: Shifting conceptions of scholarly publishing. Processing of CHI 98: Human factors in computing systems. Los Angeles (18–23 April). New York: ACM Press.

Sutton, S. E. (1993). Seeing the whole of the moon. In D. Schoem, L. Frankel, X. Zúñiga, & E. A. Lewis (Eds.), *Multicultural teaching in the university* (pp. 161–171). Westport, CT: Praeger.

Svensson, L. (1976). *Study skill and learning.* Göteborg, Sweden: Acta Universitates Gothoburgensis.

Svinicki, M. D., Hagen, A. S., & Meyer, D. K. (1995). Research on learning: A means to enhance instructional methods. In R. Menges & M. Weimer (Eds.), *Better teaching and learning in college: Toward more scholarly practice* (pp. 257–296). San Francisco: Jossey-Bass.

Tabachnick, B., Keith-Spiegel, P., & Pope, K. (1991). Ethics of teaching: Beliefs and behaviors of psychologists as educators. *American Psychologist, 46*(5), 506–515.

Thistlethwaite, D. L. (1960). *College press and changes in study plans of talented students.* Evanston, IL: National Merit Scholarship Corporation.

Thomas, E. J., & Fink, C. F. (1963). The effects of group size. *Psychological Bulletin, 60,* 371–385.

Toombs, W., & Tierney, W. (1992). *Meeting the mandate: Renewing the college and department curriculum.* ASHE-ERIC Higher Education Report No. 91–6. Washington, DC: Association for the Study of Higher Education.

Travers, R. M. W. (1950a). Appraisal of the teaching of the college faculty. *Journal of Higher Education, 21,* 41–42.

———. (1950b). *How to make achievement tests.* New York: Odyssey Press.

Trawick, L., & Corno, L. (1995). Expanding the volitional resources of urban community college students. In P. Pintrich, (Ed.) *New directions for teaching and learning: Vol. 63. Understanding self-regulated learning* (pp. 57–70). San Francisco: Jossey-Bass.

Trujillo, C. M. (1986). A comparative examination of classroom interactions between professors and minority and non-minority college students. *American Educational Research Journal, 23,* 629–642.

Upcraft, M. L. (1996). Teaching and today's college students. In R. Menges, M. Weimer, & Associates (Eds.), *Teaching on solid ground: Using scholarship to improve practice* (pp. 21–41). San Francisco: Jossey-Bass.

Van Etten, S., Pressley, M., Freebern, G., & Echevarria, M. (in press). An interview study of college freshmen's beliefs about academic motivation. *European Journal of Psychology in Education.*

Van Overwalle, F., Segebarth, K., & Goldchstein, M. (1989). Improving performance of freshmen through attributional testimonies from fellow students. *British Journal of Educational Psychology, 59,* 75–85.

Veenstra, M. V. J., & Elshout, J. J. (1995). Differential effects of instructional support on learning in simulation environments. *Instructional Science, 22,* 363–383.

Vos, P. (1991). Curriculum control of learning processes in higher education. Paper presented at 13th International Forum on Higher Education of the European Association for Institutional Research, Edinburgh.

Wakely, J. H., Marr, J. N., Plath, D. W., & Wilkins, D. M. (1960, March). Lecturing and test performance in introductory psychology. Paper read at Michigan Academy, Ann Arbor.

Wales, C. E., & Nardi, A. (1982, November). *Teaching decisionmaking with guided design.* Idea paper no. 9. Kansas State University, Center for Faculty Evaluation and Development.

Walton, J. M. (1989). Self-reinforcing behavior change. *Personnel Journal, 68*(10), 64–68.

Walvoord, B. E., & Breihan, J. R. (1997). Helping faculty design assignment-centred courses. In D. DeZure (Ed.), *To improve the academy* Vol. 16, pp. 349–372). Stillwater, OK: New Forum Press and the Professional and Organisational Development Network in Higher Education.

Ward, J. (1956). Group-study vs. lecture-demonstration method in physical science instruction for general education college students. *Journal of Experimental Education, 24,* 197–210.

Warren, R. (1954). A comparison of two plans of study in engineering physics. Ph.D. diss., Purdue University. *Dissertation Abstracts, 14,* 1648–1649.

Waterhouse, I. L., & Child, I. L. (1953). Frustration and the quality of performance. *Journal of Personality, 21,* 298–311.

Weaver, R. L., II, & Cotrell, H. W. (1985). Mental aerobics: The half-sheet response. *Innovative Higher Education, 10,* 23–31.

Webb, N. J., & Grib, T. F. (1967, October). *Teaching process as a learning experience: The experimental use of student-led groups.* Final Report, HE-000–882. Washington, D.C.: Department of Health, Education and Welfare.

Weiland, A., & Kingsbury, S. J. (1979). Immediate and delayed recall of lecture material as a function of note taking. *Journal of Educational Research, 72*(4), 228–230.

Weimer, M. (1993). The discipline journals on pedagogy. *Change, 25*(6), 44–51.

Weinstein, C. E. (1988). Executive control processes in learning: Why knowing about how to learn is not enough. *Journal of College Reading and Learning, 21,* 48–56.

Weinstein, C. E., & Mayer, R. E. (1986). The teaching of learning strategies. In M. Wittrock (Ed.), *Handbook of research on teaching.* (pp. 315–327). New York: Macmillan.

Weinstein, C. E., Palmer, D. R., & Schutte, A. C. (1987). *Learning and study strategies inventory.* Clearwater, FL: H&H Publishing.

Weinstein, G., & Obear, K. (1992). Bias issues in the classroom: Encounters with the teaching self. In M. Adams (Ed.), *Promoting diversity in college classrooms: Innovative responses for the curriculum, faculty, and institutions* (pp. 39–50). *New Directions for Teaching and Learning, 52.* San Francisco: Jossey-Bass.

Wilhite, S. C. (1983). Prepassage questions: The influence of structural importance. *Journal of Educational Psychology, 75*(2), 234–244.

Williams, G. C., & Deci, E. L. (1996). Internalization of biopsychosocial values by medical students: A test of self-determination theory. *Journal of Personality and Social Psychology, 70,* 767–779.

Williams, W. M., & Ceci, S. J. (1997). How'm I doing? Problems with student ratings of instructors and courses. *Change, 29*(5), 13–23.

Wilson, R. C. (1986). Improving faculty teaching: Effective use of student evaluations and consultation. *Journal of Higher Education, 57,* 196–211.

Wilson, R. C., et al. (1975). *College professors and their impact on students.* New York: Wiley.

Wilson, T. D., & Linville, P. W. (1982). Improving the academic performance of college freshmen: Attribution therapy revisited. *Journal of Personality and Social Psychology, 42,* 367–376.

Witkin, H. A, & Moore, C. A. (1975). *Field-dependent and field-independent cognitive styles and their educational implications* Princeton, NJ: Educational Testing Service.

Wlodkowski, R., & Ginsberg, M. (1995). *Diversity and motivation: Culturally responsive teaching.* San Francisco: Jossey-Bass.

Wulff, D. H., Nyquist, J. D., & Abbott, R. D. (1987). Students' perceptions of large classes. In M. G. Weimer (Ed.), Teaching large classes well. *New directions for teaching and learning, 32,* (pp. 17–30). San Francisco: Jossey-Bass.

Zimbardo, P. G., & Newton, J. W. (1975). *Instructor's resource book to accompany psychology and life.* Glenview, IL: Scott, Foresman.

Zimmerman, B. J. (1989). Models of self-regulated learning and academic achievement. In B. J. Zimmerman and D. H. Schunk (Eds.), *Self-regulated learning and academic achievement: Theory, research, and practice.* New York: Springer-Verlag.

————. (Ed.) (1990). Self-regulated learning and academic achievement [special issue]. *Educational Psychologist, 25*(1).

————. (1994). Dimensions of academic self-regulation: A conceptual framework for education. In D. H. Schunk & B. J. Zimmerman (Eds.), *Self-regulation of learning and performance: issues and educational applications.* Hillsdale, NJ: Erlbaum.

————. (1995). Self-regulation involves more than metacognition: A social cognitive perspective. *Educational Psychologist, 30*(4), 217–222.

Zimmerman, B. J., & Paulson, A. S. (1995). Self-monitoring during collegiate studying: An invaluable tool for academic self-regulation. In P. Pintrich (Ed.), Understanding self-regulated learning. *New Directions for Teaching and Learning, 63* (pp. 13–28). San Francisco: Jossey-Bass.